AF600452

THE *DECAMERON* FOURTH DAY IN PERSPECTIVE

The *Decameron* Fourth Day in Perspective

Volume Four of the Lectura Boccaccii

EDITED BY MICHAEL SHERBERG

UNIVERSITY OF TORONTO PRESS
Toronto Buffalo London

Toronto Buffalo London
utorontopress.com

ISBN 978-1-4875-0747-3 (cloth)
ISBN 978-1-4875-3632-9 (ePUB)
ISBN 978-1-4875-3631-2 (PDF)

Library and Archives Canada Cataloguing in Publication

Title: The Decameron fourth day in perspective / edited by Michael Sherberg.
Names: Sherberg, Michael, editor.
Series: Toronto Italian studies. | Toronto Italian studies. Lectura Boccaccii ; v. 4.
Description: Series statement: Toronto Italian studies | Lectura Boccacci ; volume 4 | Includes bibliographical references and index.
Identifiers: Canadiana (print) 2020023143X | Canadiana (ebook) 20200231626 | ISBN 9781487507473 (cloth) | ISBN 9781487536329 (EPUB) | ISBN 9781487536312 (PDF)
Subjects: LCSH: Boccaccio, Giovanni, 1313–1375. Decamerone.
Classification: LCC PQ4287 .D4257 2020 | DDC 853/.1–dc23

University of Toronto Press acknowledges the financial assistance to its publishing program of the Canada Council for the Arts and the Ontario Arts Council, an agency of the Government of Ontario.

Canada Council for the Arts
Conseil des Arts du Canada

Funded by the Government of Canada
Financé par le gouvernement du Canada
Canada

Contents

Preface

This latest volume in the *Lectura Boccaccii* series advances a project begun some two decades ago under the aegis of the American Boccaccio Association: to provide readings of the one hundred tales and other signal passages of the *Decameron*, by leading North American scholars of Boccaccio. To be sure, the qualification of "North American" was loosely conceived and has come to include Italians teaching in North America or, as in the present volume, a scholar working elsewhere who studied in Canada. The first volume in the series, published in 2004, offered readings by a group of luminaries akin to the *bella scola* of poets Dante meets in *Inferno* 4. Some of those great critical voices have already fallen silent, but they leave in their wake another generation of Boccaccio scholars, well represented here, whose energy and insight demonstrate yet again that the *Decameron* is an infinitely renewable cultural resource.

Some thanks are in order. First and foremost, my gratitude to the eleven contributors whose essays fill this volume, and who crafted thoughtful and stimulating readings destined to become part of the critical conversation. I thank as well our editor at the University of Toronto Press, Suzanne Rancourt, for her warm spirit and forebearance as this volume moved, sometimes even lumbered, into print. The anonymous readers for Toronto offered generous and helpful suggestions for how to improve the volume. Finally, my thanks to Barbara Schaal, Dean of the Faculty of Arts & Sciences at Washington University, and Andrew Brown, Chair of the Department of Romance Languages and Literatures, for their financial support of this endeavour.

While this volume was in process we lost the co-editor of the Day Three volume, Pier Massimo Forni, who also happened to be a revered classmate of mine at UCLA. Like too many he is gone too soon, and we miss him not only for his insightful readings of the *Decameron* but for his advocacy of courtesy, a practice evanescent these days. It seems only fitting that volume of the *Lectura Boccaccii* be dedicated to his memory.

Note on *Decameron* Citations

All citations from the *Decameron* in Italian refer to Branca's edition in *Tutte le opere di Giovanni Boccaccio*, volume 4 (Milan: Mondadori, 1976). Unless otherwise specified, English translations are by G.H. McWilliam.

THE *DECAMERON* FOURTH DAY IN PERSPECTIVE

Introduction

MICHAEL SHERBERG

Throughout his literary career Giovanni Boccaccio remained an eager experimenter in both Latin and the vernacular, writing in a variety of genres and testing the limits of each. His approach to the novella is no exception, as he himself affirms in the Proem to the *Decameron*. Stating that the tales consist of "novelle, o favole o parabole o istorie che dir le vogliamo" [Proem. §13: stories or fables or parables or histories or whatever you choose to call them], he acknowledges the range of possibility of the short narrative form that he has inherited and transformed, whose varied nomenclature reflects its adaptability to mythic, moral, or historical purpose. Boccaccio's interest in the plasticity of the novella, however, is not limited to theme. As the *Decameron* itself demonstrates, the novella offers a strikingly elastic form, ranging from a narrative of little more than a page to one that runs for dozens of pages, and from a narrative that focuses on a single moment in a single place to one that pursues years of action over a vast geography. Tonally, too, it can run from the silliest to the most serious, the comic to the tragic, and there are no limits to the linguistic registers it can deploy. Through the one hundred stories of the *Decameron*, Boccaccio explores these many possibilities, demonstrating not only his own mastery of the genre but the genre's own seemingly infinite capacities.

By the time the reader reaches Day Four of the *Decameron*, Boccaccio has already been busy testing the formal limits of the novella. If he structured the stories of Day One around a dispositive incident, Days Two and Three frequently dabbled in the adaptability of romance forms to the novella. Thus we have stories that cross vast spaces and times and that often involve a quest. The stories of the first three days also all generally end happily, either through reconciliation of conflict (Day One), or through luck or industry (Days Two and Three respectively). Day Four, however, marks a significant tonal break with the pattern

Boccaccio has established up to this point, in apparent violation of the rule promulgated by Pampinea in the Introduction to Day One, that "dove che egli vada, onde che egli torni, che che egli oda o vegga, niuna novella altra che lieta ci rechi di fuori" [I.Intro. §101: every one ... should take good care, no matter what they should hear or observe in their comings and goings, to bring us no tidings of the world outside these walls unless they are tidings of happiness]. This is an apparent reference to the bad news swirling about the *brigata*, and from which Pampinea seeks to insulate it, but in her use of the word *novella* she appears to bar any type of news or story that is "altra che lieta," other than happy. Abandoning the comic mode for the tragic, Boccaccio also finds a way not only to plumb new formal angles of the novella but also to demonstrate his virtuosity with regard to tone and linguistic register. On top of all this, Day Four witnesses the dramatic return of the authorial voice, last heard from in the Introduction to Day One, to report on and respond to reviews of his efforts so far.

It is perhaps no coincidence that these changes coincide with the appointment of the *Decameron*'s first king, Filostrato, whose leadership will also have significant consequences for a text that plumbs gender politics. As is the group's practice, Filostrato is crowned at the end of Day Three, and he announces his theme for storytelling at that time: "coloro li cui amori ebbero infelice fine" [III.Concl. §6: those whose love ended unhappily]. Characterizations of the theme sometimes elide the particulars of Filostrato's phrasing, making Day Four one that features stories of unhappy or tragic love, but in fact such a reductive reading overlooks the importance that Boccaccio affords to the protagonists of the stories themselves. That importance, first underlined in the theme of Day Two, redoubles here, because the new king's theme explicitly reflects his own situation:

> E per ciò non d'altra materia domane mi piace che si ragioni se non di quello che a' miei fatti è più conforme, cioè di coloro li cui amori ebbero infelice fine, per ciò che io a lungo andar l'aspetto infelicissimo, né per altro il nome, per lo quale voi mi chiamate, da tale che seppe ben che si dire mi fu imposto ... (III.Concl. §6)
>
> [I therefore decree that the subject of our discussions for the morrow should be none other than the one which applies most closely to myself, namely, *those whose love ended unhappily*. For my part, I expect my own love to have a thoroughly unhappy ending, nor was it for any other reason that I was given (by one who knew what he was talking about) the name by which you address me.]

This passage compels our attention for a variety of reasons. Formulated as a litotes (*non ... non ... né*), the command suggests that Filostrato reflexively thinks in negative terms; indeed, he expects his own love story to end *infelicissimo*. Its self-referentiality is unique among the themes thus far promulgated, conveying a subtle change in the nature of his monarchy with respect to those that have preceded it. Then the statement takes a strange turn. Filostrato explains that his very name, Filostrato, was appropriately given to him by one who already knew how his story would end. In a Pirandellian twist *ante litteram*, Boccaccio installs a character who is capable of explaining why his author assigned his name to him.

With this manoeuvre, Filostrato effectively invites his companions to write the ending to his own story, presenting himself as narrative fodder. The emphasis on the stories' protagonists finds reinforcement in the king's own sense of being himself a protagonist. In a book that offers "piacevoli e aspri casi d'amore e altri fortunati avvenimenti" [Proem. §14: a variety of love adventures, bitter as well as pleasing, and other exciting incidents], the capacity of the human actor to respond to challenges beyond her control becomes a singular lesson. And like Filostrato, who already knows how his story will end, the theme renders his protagonists passive to their fate. The specific construction, "coloro li cui amori ebbero infelice fine," makes the "coloro" at once subjects of their love (through the echo of the objective genitive in Boccaccio's relative "li cui") and objects of it, as their loves become the subject of the verb "ebbero." The syntactic specificity of his command puts the onus on his narrators to construct characters who are at once agents in their pursuit of love and victims of love's betrayal.

The inability of the characters to defeat fate, which Filostrato highlights here, connects to yet another protagonist to which his statement alludes: the author. By offering himself as a fiction created by a *tale*, an unnamed somebody, the new king establishes a second level of discourse, beyond that of the narrative content: the meta-discourse of storytelling. By his account, characters exist both within stories and in the speech act that is storytelling itself. To the extent that they are alive, they live by the grace of those who narrate them. Small wonder, then, that before his companions get a chance to tell their tales, the author of the *Decameron* steps in to tell one of his own, prefaced with the phrase "dico che," I say that (IV. Intro. §§11–12). He thus turns the entire tale of Filippo Balducci into one long objective clause and signals that, for Day Four at least, the stories are as much about the telling as they are about their content.

The "non una novella intera" [IV.Intro.11: not a complete story] of Filippo Balducci and his son partakes, as readers of the *Decameron* know, of a lengthy authorial self-defence that opens Day Four. In his essay, which opens this volume, Timothy Kircher highlights the meta-narrative arguments that fill out the Introduction to Day Four, particularly the tension between nature and art in storytelling. He explores both Boccaccio's replies to his critics' accusations and the meta-novella of Filippo Balducci and his son as comprising a *sed contra* in which Boccaccio offers a parody of scholastic reasoning. In his desire to control his son, Filippo impersonates the *Decameron*'s author himself, who claims ultimate control over his protagonist; he holds the power of art. The son, on the other hand, is the protagonist who eludes capture, driven by a nature that art can endeavour to control but never really master.

Taken together, these elements portend a unique narrative experience. Filostrato's self-awareness as a fiction, his suggestion that his companions are likewise aware that they are fictions, his paradoxical affirmation of a negative, the simultaneous agency and passivity of the protagonists he asks his companions to feature, combine to create singular challenges for his companion narrators.

The tales of Day Four feature characters who, like Filippo Balducci and his son, leap from the page, though for different reasons. While love, variously understood to refer to something ranging from carnal desire to something rooted in the philosophical lyrics of the *stilnovisti*, impels the characters to action, what makes them memorable is not so much the love that drives them as the way they respond to the crisis of love into which their stories plunge them. Many of these stories, as the essays in this volume highlight, contrast a loquacious character with a taciturn one, calling into question the role and power of the word in a moment of crisis. Sometimes the essays shine light on an unanticipated protagonist, as is the case in the first tale, read by Tobias Gittes. For all the attraction of Ghismonda, Gittes focuses instead on the figure of her father, Tancredi, reopening the much-debated question as to what motivates the king to take mortal action against his daughter and her lover. Reading the story through the lens of both the *Filocolo* and Dante's encounter with Ulysses in *Inferno* 26, Gittes concludes that this is not a story about incest but rather one about old age and its dangers, and about how an old king tries to stave off his own death by visiting it on others.

Despite its deliberate atonality with respect to the other stories of the day, the second tale of Day Four offers yet another striking protagonist: the city of Venice, locus of Frate Alberto's seduction of a vain woman who foolishly believes her lover to be the Archangel Gabriel. As Alison Cornish demonstrates in her reading, the Annunciation, here parodied, is a particularly Venetian theme, and it serves as a vehicle for the meticulous subversion of the courtly love ethos that Frate Alberto exploits in effectuating his seduction. Cornish also identifies important connections between the rhetoric of this story and Filostrato's own language, describing an important moment of tension between the king and his friends. If this story can provoke derisive laughter – it is the most overt example of the *brigata*'s objection to Filostrato's harsh theme – the next tale returns the day to the more serious purpose that Filostrato had demanded. In his essay, Michael Papio discusses the role that jealousy plays as a driver of plot, and the philosophical basis of both anger and the desire for vengeance. These are central concerns of the tale of the daughters of N'Arnald Civada and their lovers, all of whom flee Marseille for a new, independent, wealthy life. As Papio shows, Ninetta's response to the unhappy end of her own love – her betrayal by Restagnone – engenders a chain of actions and reactions that will come to affect everyone. Papio's reading highlights the contagious toxicity of anger, a lesson well learned.

The fourth story features another striking protagonist: the young lover Gerbino, who defies his grandfather's edict in order to claim his beloved, only to end up decapitated after she too is killed. In his reading, Gur Zak focuses on how the novella explores the relationship between heroism and notions of masculinity. He also describes a trajectory of the question in Boccaccio's writing, running from the *Filocolo* through *Decameron* V.1 (the tale of Cimone), showing how the questions treated here are not unique to the story but rather reflect an ongoing concern. By Zak's reckoning, the story exemplifies how Boccaccio does "ethical work" in his writing, posing the same question in diverse settings and considering it from a variety of perspectives.

Day Four reaches a new milestone in the fifth tale, that of Lisabetta da Messina and her lover Lorenzo. In her reading Kristina Olson first reflects on the importance of geography to the story – not just Messina, but its relationship to San Gimignano and Pisa as well – and how it functions as a determinant of relationships, before turning to the two lovers. Like Cornish, she identifies another protagonist of the tale: the *fondaco*, a locus that in Boccaccio lies at the intersection of historical realism and fictions of erotic adventure. Lisabetta is one of the more taciturn characters in the *Decameron*, and by Olson's reading it is precisely her reluctance to speak that enables others to write the ending of her story, up to and including Steven James in his 2009 novel, *The Knight*.

As readers of the *Decameron* recognize, with the story of Lisabetta the day changes course. If the first half of the day included tales set in the royal court of Salerno and in such watery venues as the Mediterranean and the canals of Venice, the turn to the quotidian world of the Messinese *fondaco* signals a shift to tales with more intimate settings in which happy lovers suffer terrible fates. Such is the case of the sixth story, in which Gabriotto suddenly dies after dismissing a cautionary dream of his own death that his beloved, Andreuola, recounts to him. For Regina Psaki this story exemplifies Boccaccio's ability to write variants of the same basic story, here in contrast to the three "scaffolding tales" of the day, the first, the fifth, and the ninth, which offer a darker vision of the love story. Like Panfilo, the tale's narrator, who prefaces his story with some dream theory, Psaki too centres her analysis on Andreuola's dream and its impact. In her essay on the seventh story, that of Simona and Pasquino, Suzanne Magnanini picks up on the notion of the variant to demonstrate how this tale stands apart from others that feature women who speak in their own defence. She finds in the protagonist Simona, whose work as a spinner associates her metaphorically with storytelling, a contrastive model to the loquacity of other protagonists, inasmuch as she is utterly at a loss to narrate what has happened to her dead lover. Magnanini finds a key to Simona's inarticulateness in other tales that Emilia narrates, and that together constitute a polemic against an institutional deafness to women's voices that compels women to show, rather than tell, their experience.

In several of the tales of Day Four, the different social status of the protagonists plays a significant role in the development of the plot. The eighth story is no exception, as it finds two lovers separated from one another because the mother of young Girolamo cannot abide that her son has fallen in love with a girl, Salvestra, of a lower class than his own. In her essay Annelise Brody shows how the rule of the mother conflicts with the laws of love, and how the latter, which inevitably draw Girolamo back to Salvestra, lead to tragic consequences. Brody retraces this conflict of authority in several of Boccaccio's works and in Ovid's tale of Pyramus and Thisbe. The tale, she argues, exemplifies the *Decameron*'s lesson for women, that they should reject an authority that manifests itself as a form of repression.

In a day that emphasizes both the order of storytelling and the identity of the storyteller, the ninth story emerges as a critical point of arrival, as it is the tale that Filostrato himself tells. This has been the monarch's place in the order of telling since Day Two, but it is especially important here, as we finally get to hear Filostrato's ideal ending to his own story. Not surprisingly, perhaps, given Filostrato's own meta-narrative self-awareness, Julie Singer finds in the tale significant meta-narrative threads. By her account, the preparation, presentation, and digestion of the eaten heart, which echo for example Petrarch's use of digestion as a metaphor for reading, serve here to foreground the transformation of source material into new literary texts: in the present case, the transformation of the Provençal sources into an Italian novella. She offers a thorough demonstration of how Boccaccio performs this operation on his source material. In effect, the tale becomes a lesson about medieval cultural transmission, and fittingly so as a reflection on Boccaccio's own experimentation with form.

The last story of the day, narrated as usual by Dioneo, recapitulates many of the themes set forth by the other narrators. In his essay Fabian Alfie focuses on Dioneo's self-appointed task, to provide a "happy ending" for the day by veering off topic, and the story's specific implications for a day that mines unhappiness as thoroughly as it does. The tale, by his account, provides a comic antidote to the tragic tones of Day Four by employing comic tropes and even plumbing earlier comic poetry in the vernacular. Alfie also shows how Dioneo weaves elements from the day's other stories into his own, effectively satirizing the medieval notion of the ennobling power of love that informs so many of these tales.

And so a day in which the *brigata* must navigate both the challenges of male leadership and a lugubrious theme comes to an end. As is true throughout the *Decameron*, the storytellers' most effective tool turns out to be language itself. They use it here to share their grief, to polemicize with their leader, and ultimately to do what he had narcissistically asked them to do: write his own story over and over again. Their purpose, unique to this day, involves not just storytelling but the gratification of their leader's need for recognition. Given all that we learn as this dynamic unfolds, it seems unlikely that Filostrato, so occupied with his own feelings, could possibly succeed at love. As our narrators repeatedly demonstrate, love is rooted in a mutual desire, in a disposition to altruism and a willingness to take risks that potentiates the fulfilment of desire even as it exposes lovers to danger. By putting himself at the centre and disregarding the painful consequences for his companions, Filostrato exposes the limits of his own capacity for altruism and emotional risk-taking. While he may not emerge from the day with a more refined sense of self, his readers most certainly understand him better. They also understand the potent elixir that love and pain create, and how it informs storytelling.

Love, Latinity, and Aging in the Introduction to Day Four

TIMOTHY KIRCHER

"Carissime donne" [dearest ladies]. Boccaccio writes these opening words to the Introduction to Day Four, the author recalling his address to the "graziosissime donne" [fairest ladies] of the Introduction to Day One (I.Intro. §2); in his Conclusion to the entire work, he will speak again directly to his audience, proclaiming them "nobilissime giovani" [Concl. §1: most noble young women].[1] His words in IV.Intro. are suspended between these other two interventions, hearkening to both, as he weaves, it would seem, an imaginary defence of his work.

The author speaks to these ladies about various critics who have castigated him for devoting so much time to the needs of women instead of writing about matters belonging to a higher literary register. In his opening Proem, the author had announced his intention to console the closeted, lovelorn ladies through a series of stories that might divert them from their cares. Now, after thirty *novelle*, he returns to voice his own cares to them, being buffeted by "lo 'mpetuoso vento e ardente della 'nvidia" [§2: the furious and fiery wind of spite].

Scholars have been struck by this apparently sudden intervention. Joy Potter has written about how the Introduction has resonance as another frame for the work, through which Boccaccio reveals his narrative craft. Roberto Fedi has also analysed this section's extradiegetic quality, looking back to the Conclusion to Day Three, when Filostrato, as the newly crowned king, refers to an external author who has given him his name. Michael Sherberg has discussed the ways Boccaccio employs gender distinctions in this Introduction in order to separate his feminine readership from the masculine critics.[2]

1 Here as throughout this essay the translations from the *Decameron* are mine.

2 Potter, *Five Frames*, 120–32; Fedi, "Il 'regno' di Filostrato," 42–4; Sherberg, *Governance*, 22–5; see also Psaki, "The One and the Many," 222–7. Picone has examined what he

Apart from the narratological dimension, other readers have attended to the form and content of the Introduction. Guido di Pino, Aldo Scaglione, Raffaele Ramat, and Millicent Marcus, among others, have understood this Introduction to declare the rights of naturalism, or, in Janet Smarr's view, to rebel against contemporary social restrictions. Lucia Battaglia Ricci and Michelangelo Picone see Boccaccio advocating a worldly, hedonistic, even philogynistic culture, while Giuseppe Mazzotta interprets the section as a defence against the critics' charge that the book is debased erotica: since Boccaccio here equates women and Muses, he asserts a "unity of life and literature."[3]

My present inquiry follows upon these commentaries by exploring the ways the intervention asks about the relation between "nature" and "art." The author's remarks suggest new ideas about each of these concepts as they define one another in the course of the storytelling. In his universe, "nature" refers to time-bound contingency and circumstance, expressing individual talent, inclination, and local linguistic idiom; "art" connotes something learned and acquired, including grammar, logic, and rhetoric, the topics of the trivium. My point of departure is that Boccaccio works here at being an artist of nature. In order to illuminate this paradox, which alludes to his figure of Giotto in *Decameron* VI.5, I would have us look at the larger construct of the author's apology and also at the specific tale that serves as its fulcrum, the story of Filippo Balducci and his son. The author not only discourses on *amore* as a force of nature or natural instinct, but also associates erotic love with the force of time. This phenomenon of love, in its powerful transience, is recorded in language. The author's appreciation of love and his desire to console his ladies therefore shape his narrative art. To cite the term of Barthes, the "carissime donne" pose a "hermeneutic code": they present an enigma that requires an ongoing effort at interpretation.[4] The intervention of IV.Intro. offers a moment to disclose their meaning, even as this moment of meaning pushes the reader on in the work towards the *donne* of the final Conclusion. But more than that: may we ask to what degree have the author himself – and his readers – changed in their continued dialogue? I will remark, at the close, on this intersubjectivity that the work entertains, as the author marks changes

calls a "cornice dialogica," in which the author discusses his work with his audience: *Boccaccio e la codificazione*, 179.

3 Di Pino, *La polemica di Boccaccio*, 209–20; Scaglione, *Nature and Love*, 101–6; Ramat, *Saggi*, 50–69; Marcus, *Allegory*, 50–1; Smarr, *Boccaccio and Fiammetta*, 177, 280; Mazzotta, *World at Play*, 69–70. See also Baratto, *Realtà e stile*, 56–9; Battaglia Ricci, *Ragionare*, 85–94; and Picone, *Boccaccio e la codificazione*, 183.

4 Barthes, *S/Z*, 19, 75–6.

over time in life, love, and language. The question shaping his artistic endeavour at this moment appears to be: how can the author also be an authority, when he with his readers is changing throughout and through the narratives?

His focus on change is indicated by the Introduction's opening lines, which explain his efforts to flee the critics' spiteful gaze by composing his *novellette* in vernacular prose, "in fiorentin volgare e in prosa scritte" [§3: written in Florentine vernacular and in prose].[5] In the Trecento, the vernacular was considered a *lingua naturalis*, as distinct from the *lingua artificialis* of Latin. Even while Dante seeks to ennoble the vernacular with literary status, he asserts in both the *Convivio* and the *De vulgari eloquentia* that Latin belongs to a higher linguistic register than the vernacular. Latin is "artificial" and constructed. On account of this crafted quality, Latin withstands changes in time; it perdures across ranges of time and space, unlike the vernacular, which is lowly and local. "[L]o latino è perpetuo e non corruttibile, e lo volgare è non stabile e corruttibile" [Latin is perpetual and incorruptible, while the vernacular is unstable and corruptible], he writes in the *Convivio*, for "lo volgare seguita uso, e lo latino arte" [the vernacular follows usage, while Latin follows art].[6] In the later fifteenth century, Cristoforo Landino accents, in a critical way, the *Decameron* author's choice of linguistic dialect. Explaining to his students in the Florentine *studium* the proper models of vernacular prose, he asserts that Boccaccio "tanto nel dono della natura confidato che nell'arte" [tended to rely on his natural gifts rather than art].[7] Yet to the author of the Introduction, it is crucial that the vernacular is culturally coded as "natural," as unstable, *mobile*, indeed female, and tailored by the circumstances of a given place and moment.[8] For then Tuscan is suited to the *donne*, and to his broader purpose: it

---

5 See Marchesi's commentary on Boccaccio's apologetic adaptations of Dante, *Epistle to Can Grande* and more distantly of Horace in *Stratigrafie*, 42–3.

6 Dante, *Convivio* I.5.7 and I.5.14, cited by Zygmunt G. Barański in "Dante Alighieri," 561–82; 570. Cf. Mazzocco, *Linguistic Theories*, 24–30; Celenza, "Petrarch, Latin, and Italian Renaissance Latinity." The source texts are *De vulgari eloquentia* I.9.6–10 and *Convivio* I.5.

7 Cristoforo Landino, "Prolusione petrarchescha," 35.

8 For a point of comparison with Dante and Petrarch, cf. *Vita Nuova* 25.6 and Rizzo, *Ricerche sul latino umanesimo* 1:31–7, especially 37: "Possiamo dunque concludere che il Petrarca condivideva le idee del suo tempo sul rapporto latino-volgare: da un lato i volgari, lingue naturali apprese dalla nutrice, dall'altro il latino, lingua artificiale creata dagli antichi Romani, soggetta a regole grammaticali, che è necessario apprendere a scuola con libri e maestri, lingua di cultura, che ha permesso non solo il propagarsi, ma il sorgere stesso delle arti e delle scienze, *radix artium nostrarum e omnis scientie fundamentum* [Sen. 9.1]."

highlights the force of time; it lays open the phases of day, setting, story, and mood; and it showcases the way love itself moves in time.

But if the author forgoes writing in the artful Latin language, Latin and Latinity remain foils for his parody. The entire apology in fact has a Latinate construct or model. We do not know whether his critics recognized the parody, but it is possible that Petrarch and other humanist friends of Boccaccio perceived it. Trecento humanists pursued Latin for its *vetustas*, its classical flavour, to cite Ronald Witt's phrase. Boccaccio in this introduction is mocking not simply Latin *vetustas* but more directly – for the humanists – its antithesis: medieval scholastic argument, introduced into Italy in the thirteenth century from French studies in grammar and logic.[9] Petrarch had criticized scholastic Latin at almost every turn. Boccaccio for his part exposes the pretence of scholasticism, since it contradicts the force of nature: it would deduce atemporal conclusions about morality by using a dialectic that failed to account for the lived experience of author and reader.

By the latter part of the twelfth century, scholastics had embraced as part of their intellectual apparatus newly translated works of Aristotle, the so-called *logica nova*. Writing his *Metalogicon* in 1159, John of Salisbury stated that "natural and moral philosophers can construct their principles only by proofs derived from logic. Not one of them defines or divides correctly unless logic favours him with its art. Otherwise he will succeed not by science but by accident or circumstance [non scientia sed casus promovet]."[10] Scholastics codified their method of academic debate through a written form of argument known as the *quaestio disputata*, the question subject to disputation. Thomas Aquinas, to cite one influential example, investigates a given *quaestio* initially by advancing the *videtur quod*, "it appears or it seems that." These are a series of arguments in support of one side, and the wrong side, of the question. He then refutes these arguments in the next section, which begins with the *sed contra*, an "on the other hand" statement, most often an isolated quote from a recognized authority like Augustine or Aristotle (whom Thomas simply calls The Philosopher). Thomas concludes the *sed contra* with a number of counter-assertions, using logic or authorities, in response to the claims put forward in the opening *videtur quod* section.[11]

9 On this development, see Witt, *Two Latin Cultures*.

10 *Metalogicon* 2.5: "Physicus enim et ethicus in suis assertionibus non procedunt nisi probationibus a logico mutuatis. Nemo eorum recte diffinit aut dividit [*sic*] nisi eis artis sue logicus gratiam faciat; alioquin successus eorum non scientia sed casus [*sic*] promovet"; cited by Lawn, *Rise and Decline*, 21–2.

11 On the scholastic method, see Marenbon, *Later Medieval Philosophy*, 27–9; see also Kenny and Pinborg, "Medieval Philosophical Literature," 25–7.

In the Introduction to Day Four, the author plays with the Thomistic *quaestio* form. While Simone Marchesi, among others, has recognized this adaptation, my analysis emphasizes the way Boccaccio places the largely deductive scholastic method under an inductive lens, with an eye that attends to the shifting phases of life experience.

The claims of the author's critics in the intervention's opening *videtur quod* section are five: 1) he is too devoted to women, a devotion "disonesta"; 2) he is too old to be chatting about them or seeking to please them; 3) he should be residing among the Muses rather than mixing with women "con queste ciance" [by these trifles]; 4) he should earn his bread by other means; and 5) the stories he reports may not mesh with the facts (IV.Intro. §§5–7).

The author answers each of these claims in turn, writing his own concluding section of the *sed contra*. Contra 1) he has striven to love women, their beauty and their "onestà," "dalla mia puerizia" [§32: since my boyhood]; contra 2) he will continue this striving "infino nello stremo della mia vita" [§33: until my life's final breath], just as Cavalcanti, Dante, and Cino did; contra 3) we cannot reside among the Muses, but we may among those they resemble – namely women – for women inspire his verses; contra 4) poets find their bread through their stories, certainly "assai già ... fecero la loro età fiorire, dove in contrario molti nel cercar d'aver più pane, che bisogno non era loro, perirono acerbi" [§38: enough to live to a flourishing old age, whereas many others, chasing more bread than they need, die green and bitter]; and contra 5) if he has falsely reported anything, may others provide "gli originali," a veridical record of events.

Therefore, we may phrase the question under dispute as: should the author be writing the *Decameron*? He answers by citing a number of counter-assertions. Donning the mask of a Certaldan San Tomaso, he expresses his reply more with rhetorical than logical argument, by persuasion rather than demonstration.[12] As he parades and parodies the scholastic form, the author uses inference and induction to allude to aging and the passing of time, to boyhood and senectitude, to youthful sighs and dying breaths. This sense of transience allows us to articulate the Introduction's underlying existential question, in variation with that posed by the opening Proem. If Boccaccio asked, at the outset of the work: what is the power of love among the young?, he now asks: what does it mean to be in love as one grows older? The answer is

12 On the *quaestio* form, see Kircher, *Poet's Wisdom*, 259–63; cf. the comment by Marchesi, *Stratigrafie*, 55. On Boccaccio's use of rhetoric in this intervention, see Tronci, *La novella*, 55–104.

founded on the crucial moment of the *quaestio*, when a scholastic would cite a timeless, ahistorical authority. The intervention instead chooses the authority of "raccontare non una novella intera" (IV.Intro. §11), telling an incomplete story.

The story recounts the actions of Filippo Balducci, who brings his son to Mount Asinaio to live in isolation, only to see how the boy later becomes entranced by the women of Florence. Scholars have examined the way the story shows Boccaccio's praise of naturalism, his sense of morality, and his linguistic skill. In light of the guiding question of this intervention, I would investigate the story's phenomenological quality, the way it expresses Boccaccio's views on the temporal triad of life, love, and language.[13]

The phenomenological aspect of the novella is indicated by it being "non intera," less than whole. It unveils its meaning in time and over time, as it encounters its various readers. Similar to Petrarch's autobiographical letter *Ad posteritatem*, it displays its unfinished nature, which suggests that the tale, along with its meaning, escapes authoritative, conclusive interpretation. Carlo Delcorno among other scholars has traced antecedents to the story in religious exempla, in the *Novellino*, and in the lives of the desert fathers.[14] Filippo Balducci might have read these *vite* to his son as he "sempre della gloria della vita eterna e di Dio e de' santi gli ragionava" [§15: continually spoke to him about the glory of eternal life, and of God and his saints]. Several of these tales recount how a pious hermit fasts and prays in the desert, and then quickly succumbs to temptation when he ventures to a city.

Two other analogues are often cited as precedents to the novella, the fourteenth story of the *Novellino* and an exemplum from the English preacher Odo of Cheriton. They deserve our attention, as they reveal

13 Among the many commentators: Di Pino, *La polemica di Boccaccio*, 209–20; Scaglione, *Nature and Love*, 101–6; Ramat, *Saggi*, 50–69; Neuschäfer, *Boccaccio*, 56–8; Marcus, *Allegory*, 50–1; Sanguineti, "La novella delle papere nel *Decameron*"; Goldin, "Il Boccaccio e la poesia latina francese del xii secolo," 345–7; Degani, "Riflessi quasi sconosciuti di *exempla* nel *Decameron*"; Mazzotta, *World at Play*, 133–7; D'Andrea, *Strutture inquiete*, 95–108; Mazzacurati, "Rappresentazione, " 296–9; Battaglia Ricci, *Ragionare*, 85–94; Marchesi, *Stratigrafie*, 49–64; Best, "*La peste e le papere*"; Gittes, *Boccaccio's Naked Muse*, 50–1, 234–6; Sherberg, *Governance*, 24–30; Psaki, "The One and the Many," 222–5.

14 Delcorno, "Modelli agiografici," in addition to the writings by Scaglione, Goldin, and others mentioned above. Fourteenth-century mendicants, such as the Dominicans Domenico Cavalca and Jacopo Passavanti, transcribed and translated these lives. See Kircher, *Poet's Wisdom*, 105–9, and Battaglia Ricci, *Ragionare*, 89. Battaglia Ricci (86–93) and Picone (*Boccaccio e la codificazione*, 174–80) discuss a primal source in the *Storia di Barlaam e Josaphat*.

Boccaccio's innovative treatments of aging, love, and linguistic artifice. The *Novellino* recounts:

> A uno re nacque uno figliuolo. I savi strolagi providero che s'elli non stesse anni diece che non vedesse il sole, che perderebbe lo vedere. Allora il re il fece notricare e guardare in tenebrose spelonche. Dopo il tempio detto lo fece trarre fuori, e innanzi lui fece mettere molte belle gioie e di molto belle donzelle, tutte cose nominando per nome. E dettoli le donzelle essere dimonî, poi li domandaro qual d'esse li fosse più graziosa; rispuose: "I domonî." Allora lo re di ciò si maravigliò molto, dicendo: "Che cosa tirànnia è bellore di donna!"
>
> [A boy was born to a king. His wise astrologers advised him that the boy must remain in darkness for ten years, or otherwise he would lose his sight. Therefore the king had the boy raised and watched in dark caverns. After the time was up, he had him brought out and placed before him many beautiful jewels and many beautiful maidens, identifying everything by its name. Having told his son that the maidens were said to be demons, he then asked him which of these things was most attractive; and he replied, "The demons." The king was greatly amazed at his answer, and said, "What a tyranny is the beauty of women!"][15]

The story emphasizes the boy's seclusion and the passage of time, as well as the king's attempt at moral suasion by labelling the young women with a fiendish name. In Odo's exemplum, it is the abbot who strives through language to have the young monk shy away from erotic enticement:

> Quidam iuvenis Heremita cum Abbate suo ad unam civitatem ivit, ubi mulieres in corea conspexit. Et, cuiusmodi res esset, ab Abbate sollicite quesivit. Cui Abbas asserens esse anseres respondit. Reversus puer in claustrum flere cepit. Cui Abbas: Quid vis, fili mi? Et ille: Volo de illis anseribus, quos vidi in civitate. Tunc Abbas, convocatis fratribus, dixit: Fratres, considerate mente sollicite, quam periculosa sunt mulierum spectacula. Nam hic puer innocens, qui prius mulierum non viderat, in hermo nutritus, solo visu sic est temptatus, sic est igne concupiscientie succensus.
>
> [Once a young monk went with his abbot to a town, where he saw women dancing. He repeatedly asked his abbot what this was. The abbot answered him, declaring that that they were geese. After he returned to the cloister,

---

15 *Il novellino*, 33–4.

> the boy began to weep. The abbot asked, "What ails you, my son?" And he said, "I want some of those geese that I saw in town." Then the abbot convened all the monks and said: "Brothers, consider unceasingly how dangerous is the sight of women. For this innocent boy, who had never seen a woman, having been raised in the monastery, was sorely tempted only by seeing them, so quickly was he set aflame by the fire of desire."][16]

In contrast to the *Novellino* story, the cloister replaces the royal cave; and the city, in its secular ways, allures the young man's sensual feelings. The dancing women are no longer called "demons" but the Latin "anseres," geese, adding another measure and clue to Boccaccio's adaptation.

Like Odo's abbot, Filippo Balducci imagines his son spiritually fortified for his exposure to the beauties of Florence. Yet in ways the two analogues do not address, the author's novella not only offers a distinct geographical locale, but also conveys a greater sensibility to the passing of time and to life's ineluctable finitude. The story, like that of the *Novellino,* is about father and son, two generations. But the novella also emphasizes how they grow older together and respond to life's changes over a period of sixteen years. Filippo loses the love of his life, his wife, to death, which, the author remarks, "sì come di tutti avviene" [§13: happens to us all]. Yet for Filippo, her death catalyses an existential and spiritual crisis. Completely disconsolate ("sconsolato"), he withdraws with his son from the secular world ("mondo") and abstains from temporal things ("temporal cosa").[17] The child is two years old at this time. Years later, the boy travels to Florence with his father, "essendo già il garzone d'età di diciotto anni e Filippo vecchio" [§16: being now a youth of eighteen years and Filippo an old man]. In asking to travel with him, the boy tells Filippo, "Padre mio, voi siete oggimai vecchio e potete male durare fatica" [§17: Father, you are old now and can bear the strain only with difficulty], whereas "io che son giovane e posso meglio faticar di voi" [I, who am young, can more easily bear the effort]. The story thus accentuates the existential process of aging.

But aging, mortality, and the facticity of existence are aspects of life from which Filippo would escape in his hermitage. His mistake is to overlook

16 Hervieux, *Études de Cheriton*, 4.409; cited by Sanguineti, "La novella delle papere," 143. Branca (*Decameron*, 1199n13) recounts a number of antecedents. The middle High German analogue *Das genselîn* has a diminutive for its title, but the abbot calls the women "gense," "geese." Cf. *Decameron*, ed. Segre, 1271. Boccaccio distinguishes "oca" from "papero" in *Dec.* VIII.3.9.

17 Battaglia Ricci discusses Balducci's "encounter with death" as a typological moment in spiritual awakening, without addressing its implications for aging and the temporality of existence (*Scrivere un libro*, 193–4).

his son's maturation into manhood. The raw youth becomes enchanted with the appearance, the phenomenon, of the "belle giovani donne e ornate" [§20: beautiful, elegant young ladies]: "a me non è ancora paruta vedere alcuna così bella né così piacevole come queste sono. Elle son più belle che gli agnoli dipinti che voi m'avete più volte mostrati" [§28: there has never appeared to me anything so beautiful and pleasing. They are more beautiful than the painted angels that you have so often shown me].

With the aid of his artful angels, Filippo has sought to withstand time and, in a sense, to infantilize his son by closing off to him the natural world, the world of time and change. His undertaking is in vain. The author writes that Filippo "sentì incontanente più aver di forza la natura che il suo ingegno" [§29: realized, all of a sudden, that nature had more power than his efforts]. The contrast between artifice and nature comes to the fore: painted angels and linguistic industry are no match for physical, personal experience. This explicit contrast is missing in the two analogues, which end with a moral aphorism or sermon. That the author's tale is "incomplete" points also to Boccaccio's playful portrayal of "natura." "Natura" means more than amorous desire or, in the medieval lexicon, concupiscence. It also conveys temporality and time's passing. Filippo's lesson therefore reflects and comments on the efforts of the familial authorities in the book's Proem: they would deny their daughters and sisters their time in the sun of the larger world, outside the "piccole cellette," the little rooms, in which they are cloistered.

The author's critics, like these overseers of domestic decorum, contend against eros and more fundamentally against time, striving to master both life's ripeness and its transience. They build moral strictures in not only the physical but also the linguistic domains. The *sed contra* novella of Filippo Balducci therefore also shows up the pretensions of scholastic Latinity: it reveals how language arts would conceal reality, the phenomena of love and life. Similar to the two thirteenth-century analogues we examined, father and son discuss the names of things, now as they walk through Florence: they employ language to bring to light the phenomena they come across. When they meet the young ladies, however, Filippo asks his son to avert his gaze, and declares the women "mala cosa." Yet after the son – no doubt with rapt attention – asks repeatedly what they are called, Filippo names them "papere," baby geese. In line with other commentators, Mazzotta stresses the father's *equivocatio* as he tries by way of language "to control and mask what to Boccaccio is the irreducibility of the reality of desire."[18] We

18 Mazzotta, *World at Play*, 137.

may add, too, that Filippo's apodictic moral lessons founder on the phenomenal, on the reality of the moment.

For why does Filippo call the Florentine maidens "papere"? We have seen that the abbot in Odo's exemplum designates women "anseres," "geese." Myra Best has written about "papere" as a misogynistic pejorative, and as a word that also emphasizes sexuality while it tries to repress it.[19] My reading brings this fear of "donne," of women and sexuality, into Filippo's larger anxiety over life's stages and transience. He calls the women goslings, *young* or baby geese, adding, "non sai donde elle s'imbeccano" [§29: You don't know how they feed/how they fill their bills]. This reply both masks and discloses his trepidation of not only women but also the young, on account of their unpredictability. They change with time; they are pushed out into the variable world by eros. The little geese the son encounters, the elegant, pretty young women, are just returning from two weddings, flush with experiencing youth's rite of passage in love. Like the authorial censors, Filippo seeks to command life – not merely eros – through the use of language; they would rule the phases of life according to a sense of propriety, their notion of *onestà*, and govern the existential, temporal flow of life, love, and language. These efforts contrast with those of Boccaccio and other vernacular poets who use the humble idiom in order to reveal phenomena in their passing splendour.

The author's opening words to the Introduction to Day Four, "carissime donne," call into memory the "graziosissime donne" of the Introduction to Day One. The "graziosissime donne" are now "carissime" as the author reminds them how, he says, critics claim that "io tanto diletto prenda di piacervi e di consolarvi" [§5: I take so much delight in pleasing and consoling you]. But how does he do this, and on what authority? Presenting a puzzle, the Introduction opens with alternate critiques and praises of past authority. In his first line (§2), the author calls into question the "savi," the wise men who would know the nature of things: they were wrong about envy striking only the summits of accomplishment. For even his humble, Tuscan prose has been subject to remorseless criticism. And yet he now knows, he says in line 4, as "sogliono i savi dire, che sola la miseria è senza invidia nelle cose presenti" [the wise often say, that only misery is free from envy in the things of this world].

19 Best, "*La peste e le papere*," 158–61; see also Ramat, *Saggi*, 56; Marchesi, *Stratigrafie*, 55. Marcus (*Allegory*, 51) states that it demonstrates Filippo's verbal dexterity.

The wise men are recalled as authorities, speaking truths the author now understands through his bitter experience. He found the earlier wise counsel mistaken, however, even though he thought his prior experience ("le cose da me molte volte e vedute e lette" [§2: the things that many times I have both seen and read]) confirmed its validity. With changing experience, he suggests, we may find different wisdoms, with the result that we continually resort to *a posteriori* maxims, like the *Novellino*'s king, Odo's abbot, and in particular Filippo Balducci: we may come to realize, all of a sudden, that nature – the elusive turns of life's way – has more power than our conscious efforts (*ingegno*). The author uses the verb *ingegnare* twice in the second sentence, describing how he strove, in vain, to avoid the fiery blasts of spite (§3: "essendomi di fuggire ingegnato ... mi sono ingegnato d'andare" [thinking out ways to flee ... I thought out ways to go]).

And yet his message becomes, in large measure, precisely this portrayal of change, affirming, unlike Balducci and the Latinate critics, that youth will mature, that time must pass, and that a language that shows fragility and transience may be best suited to disclose the true nature of the "cose presenti," the things before us. This brings me to a closing thought on the narrative's sense of time through its appeal to the "donne." The author states that he "non essendo ... al terzo della [sua] fatica venuto" [§10: is not yet come to the third of his undertaking] at this juncture. His narrative thus recalls at this instant what has been said while anticipating what will be written; in this way it understands time to convey a dimension beyond past, present, and future. For the past lies in wait and reaches out to the present through the modality of its absence, through the author and reader's awareness of what has been, just as they wait upon what is to come. Past and future attend the present, are present at any given moment through memory or anticipation.[20] And the "carissime donne," by recalling the "graziossime donne" of the Proem, also mark how the author too has changed in the course of his undertaking, as he confronts the headwinds of criticism; his dialogue with his "donne" undergoes intersubjective shifts from the outset of the work to the final Conclusion. We may ask about similar intersubjective changes among the *brigata*, over the course of their two weeks together. While many scholars have explored intratextual resonances and references among different sections of the *Decameron*, I think this basic point is often overlooked: that the resonances echo with the passing of time and the re-visions of author and audience.

20 On this thematic, see Heidegger's "Zeit und Sein," 13–16.

Time in the *Decameron* thus has a meaning different from being linear or cyclical, from tracing spiritual or secular pathways.[21] There is a crossing of past, present, and future akin to Dante's progress in the *Commedia* or Petrarch's composing of the *Canzoniere.* Boccaccio would show his readers the way his devotion to his "donne," his erotic loyalty, makes the music by which he keeps time. In keeping time, he records its sway over his life and work.[*]

21 Branca, *Boccaccio medievale,* 521–38. See also Gagliardi, *L'esperienza del tempo.*

* I am indebted to the anonymous reviewers for their comments on the draft of this article.

"A questa tanto picciola vigilia de' vostri sensi": Senile Recidivism, Incest, and Egotism in *Decameron* IV.1

TOBIAS FOSTER GITTES

Confronted with the mangled corpse of a young woman shoved up a chimney flue, the decapitated body of an old woman, bloodied grey tresses torn from a human scalp, evidence of a violent struggle, and thousands of golden francs scattered about the floor, the Parisian police detectives of Poe's brilliant tale "The Murders in the Rue Morgue" are at a loss to identify the murderer or to account for a motive. Billed as "The Tragedy in the Rue Morgue" in the next morning's paper, the murder, with its bizarre and seemingly unconnected trail of evidence, catches the attention of Monsieur C. Auguste Dupin, who, having read the description of the crime, reviewed the various depositions, and briefly visited the crime scene, is able, by dint of his gift for imaginative analysis, to identify the murderer: an orangutan of the East Indian Islands. The tragic events of the Rue Morgue that had utterly confounded the Prefect of Police – a man, in Dupin's words, "too cunning to be profound" – are easily revealed to Dupin's more abstract, far-reaching intellect, and with the identification of the murderer, the apparently arbitrary bits and pieces of evidence suddenly fall neatly into place, forming a coherent narrative.

Like the "Tragedy in the Rue Morgue," the events described in *Decameron* IV.1, Boccaccio's novella of Tancredi and Ghismonda, have long struck critics as being at once tragic and fundamentally incoherent. How, indeed, does one account for Tancredi's behaviour? Why would a doting father with a history of benevolence choose to bloody his hands in his old age without just cause? What motive could possibly underlie and lend coherence to the erratic behaviour and incongruous violence of the actions described in Boccaccio's novella? Ghismonda's punishment, to put it simply, does not – at least by any familiar standard – fit her alleged crime. The history of the criticism of *Decameron* IV.1 is, to a certain degree, the history of the critical response to this essential problem.

The simplest, if least satisfactory, solution to this problem was proposed by De Sanctis, who, in his excellent and enormously influential essay on Boccaccio's *Decameron* in *Storia della letteratura Italiana,* asserts: "Il motivo della tragedia è il punto d'onore" [The motive of the tragedy is the point of honour].[1] Tancredi's draconian response is motivated, De Sanctis argues, by the dishonour brought upon him by his daughter's illicit relationship with a social inferior. If De Sanctis's explanation has a familiar ring, it is probably because he is simply reproducing Tancredi's own justification for his anger. Had he not seen it, he tells Ghismonda, with his own eyes, he could never have imagined her capable of sleeping with a man who was not her husband, let alone a young man of "vilissima condizione" who had been raised in his household "quasi come per Dio da piccol fanciullo" [§27: exceedingly base condition ... from early childhood mainly out of charity].

Since, as we know, critics tend to read texts in the key of their own cultural experience, values, and assumptions, it is possible that De Sanctis's readiness to take Tancredi at his word reflects a greater sympathy between Tancredi's social prejudices and autocratic approach to parenthood and those of De Sanctis's own historical period than we feel in our own. However this may be, it is, as Pier Massimo Forni observes in his masterful retracing of the critical responses to *Decameron* IV.1 in the appendix to *Forme complesse nel "Decameron,"* a solution that has failed to satisfy critics at least since the time of Attilio Momigliano. Struck by the incongruity between Tancredi's violent actions and the scarce evidence of psychological motive or emotional depth, Momigliano concludes that the novella is logically coherent but aesthetically flawed.[2] Tancredi's drastic response to his daughter's illicit love is, to cast this aesthetic flaw in Aristotelian terms, not only unnecessary but, given his long history of benevolence and pronounced affection for his daughter, highly improbable.

This suggestion that IV.1 is aesthetically flawed – and that the artistic weakness lies principally in the characterization of Tancredi – was, as Forni points out, readily taken up and refined by Luigi Russo, who, emboldened by Momigliano's critique, famously declares Tancredi a "personaggio-schema" [scheme-character] or "personaggio mancato" [missing character].[3] Tancredi's disconcerting changeability derives, Russo declares, from his function as a sort of "espediente della narrazione" [narrative expedient]; the heroism of the two young lovers demands

1 De Sanctis, *Storia*, 309.

2 Momigliano in Boccaccio, *Il Decameron: 49 novelle.*

3 See Russo's essay in *Letture critiche.*

a variety of "heavy." Like De Sanctis's, Russo's solution to the enigmatic incoherence of the tale has the virtue of simplicity; however, it has the less welcome effect of casting Tancredi as a caricature in lieu of a fully realized character – something like the Pantalone of *commedia dell'arte*.

Just as Poe's Prefect of Police, stymied by the apparent incoherence of the evidence, concludes that the crime that took place at the Rue Morgue is irrational and therefore defies rational analysis (thus absolving the police of responsibility and deferring blame to the criminal, who, it is assumed, has an obligation to behave rationally!), these critics have, it seems, preferred to see the apparent incoherence of certain elements of Boccaccio's tale as evidence of an aesthetic weakness, evidence of flawed artistry on Boccaccio's part, sooner than consider the possibility that their weakness as critics is at fault.

Giovanni Getto, more generous in his assessment of Boccaccio's narrative skills, and unwilling to view Tancredi either as an aesthetic failure or as a literary expedient, comes up with an ingenious and often cited solution. Critics, he claims, have made the mistake of conflating the categories of the aesthetic and the psychological; it is, he maintains, Boccaccio's aesthetic aim to portray a character whose defining trait is lack of character: "Tancredi's character consists, really, in his lack of character."[4] While this may sound like a bit of casuistry on Getto's part – the equivalent of saying that someone's brilliance lies in stupidity or honesty in deceit – it has the virtue of rescuing Tancredi from the limbo of bad art, where he had been consigned by Momigliano and Russo, and making him once again an object worthy of critical study.

In the wake of Getto's study, it was no longer possible to assign blame for the perceived incoherence of Boccaccio's novella to some sort of intrinsic, artistic fault. The time had come to uncover the "orangutan" at the centre of IV.1: the elusive entity, object, or fact whose discovery would, with the force of a revealed truth or the rigour of a scientific proof, unmask an order underlying the superficial incongruities.

For many critics, 1964 represents the year of this unmasking, for it is in his essay on Boccaccio in *L'uomo come fine e altri saggi* that Alberto Moravia first makes explicit a feature of the novella that had previously received only oblique, and embarrassed, glances. Tancredi's tender love for Ghismonda has, Moravia declares, "un sapore incestuoso," an incestuous taste.[5] Incest, it would seem, is the "orangutan"; Tancredi's erratic behaviour betrays the tortured psyche of a man buffeted by illicit passion, an unconscious, irrepressible desire for his own daughter.

4 Getto, *Vita di forme*, 98.

5 Moravia, "Boccaccio," 156.

In 1965, Carlo Muscetta elaborates on this idea, reminding us that the blood with which Tancredi sullies his hands is not just any blood, but "sangue amoroso," amorous blood; this, Muscetta insists, is a crime of passion, a father's erotic (albeit unconscious) passion for his daughter.[6] The incest theme reaches a sort of culmination in Guido Almansi's treatment of *Decameron* IV.1 in *The Writer as Liar*, where Almansi not only recovers Tancredi's psychological integrity by proposing that the "continuous unspoken current of incestuous sentiments" restores him to "a fully-rounded character, unlocking him from a series of irreconcilable gestures,"[7] but reveals a hidden metaphorical integrity uniting the various physical elements of the drama's backdrop – the bramble-choked shaft, subterranean cavern, and well-barred bedchamber – which, he argues, may be viewed as "objective correlatives"[8] for Ghismonda's body, thereby allowing us to view Guiscardo's descent into the cave and Tancredi's penetration of the bedchamber as elaborate metaphors for erotic engagement.[9] Every important critical study of IV.1 written after the publication of Almansi's analysis has not only accepted but premised its own arguments on the assumption that Tancredi's passion for Ghismonda has a distinctly incestuous cast.[10]

We have, as Forni makes clear in his compelling account of this critical discovery – or invention, as the case may be – of the incest motive, come full circle: a resolution to the aesthetic integrity of the tale that was once unthinkable has become normative and eclipsed any other social or psychological factors that might have helped determine the tragic denouement.[11] Forni's important observation that the incest theory has gradually moved from the margins of the critical response to

6 Muscetta, *Giovanni Boccaccio*, 221–5.

7 Almansi, *Writer as Liar*, 136.

8 Ibid., 142.

9 With reference to the incest thesis, Baratto notes: "All that is important not only in order to ascertain, as others have done successfully, the characters' psychological coherence, but for its implications for the *novella*'s exemplary structure, with disturbing implications" (*Realtà e stile*, 188).

10 See for instance Baratto, *Realtà e stile*, 184–5; Marcus, *Allegory*, 48; Mazzotta, *World at Play*, 134.

11 In "Boccaccio pornoscopo," M. David argues that the incest motif is more complex, less "unilaterale," than has been suggested by critics. In his stratified view of Tancredi's incestuous longing, David sees beneath Tancredi's erotic feeling for his daughter a more primitive and essential longing for his mother. According to David, this Oedipal desire accounts for Boccaccio's emphasis on Tancredi's infantile qualities. Twentieth-century critics, longtime travellers through a Freudian architecture of the unconscious, cannot resist the temptation of putting Tancredi on the couch in the interest of reconstructing his repressed fantasies and desires.

IV.1 into its very centre, where it threatens to pre-empt any alternative approaches, is at once a challenge and a call to reconsider what we have come to take for granted.

This paper is, in a sense, a response to Forni's challenge, an attempt to scrutinize and re-evaluate a critical approach that has become canonical. Like Ptolemy's model of the universe, the incest theory creates a false, if highly functional, centre which has the advantage of accounting – if not fully, at least to a great degree – for the observed evidence. However, like all rigidly constructed theoretical frameworks, its imposition of order comes at a cost. Having accepted the shaping role of incest in IV.1 as self-evident, we have, as Forni illustrates in his appendix with a few convincing examples, blinkered ourselves to other possible motives, and raised invisible barricades to other possible readings.

Might it be that in identifying incest as the "orangutan" of the tale of Ghismonda, the elusive first cause of the chain of events that culminates in the tragic death of the two young lovers, we have mistaken an effect for a cause?

Boccaccio's habit of recycling and reconfiguring narrative plots, themes, and motifs has long provided critics with privileged access to what is most essential in his works, that resilient latticework of ideas that remains more or less constant and that each work merely reclothes in a new robe of circumstantial detail. This compositional principle is well represented in the *Decameron*, where numerous tales appear to reflect each other, often with a through-the-looking-glass variety of inversion brought about by a change of gender, class, or other circumstance that dramatically alters the outcome of the tale without, however, altering the underlying principles.[12]

Among the most studied examples of this procedure is Boccaccio's "rewriting" of the Ghismonda story in the tale of Caterina and Ricciardo (V.4). That the situation of V.4 appears to deliberately echo that of IV.1 but is nonetheless resolved in a comedic denouement – marriage in lieu of death – has prompted numerous critics to read the two *novelle* in parallel, as glosses to one another (Filostrato himself endorses this comparative approach by proposing that his tale is a sort of

12 Almansi observes that while tales of fathers "faced by discovery of their daughter's fornication" are quite common in the *Decameron* and have widely varying outcomes, there is in all these tales "one constant element; fornication and adultery are only apparently condemned as they relate to the inflexible canons of religious morality. In actual fact, the degree of guilt is simply measured in accordance with the socio-economic standing of the woman in question" (*Writer as Liar*, 147). Almansi argues that the denouement of IV.1 is not guided by this principle, but by the *force majeure* of incestuous passion.

compensation for subjecting the *brigata* members to the tragic tales of Day Four). Where one critic sees the comedic resolution as hinging on socio-economic factors and, therefore, stresses the very different "social configuration" presented in the two stories,[13] another will focus on the psychosexual factors, the critical presence of a wife in V.4, whose presence "defuses the incestuous possibilities which govern Ghismonda's fate."[14] The numerous parallels between the Filippo Balducci story interpolated in Boccaccio's Introduction to Day Four and the tale of Ghismonda have encouraged critics to apply a similar procedure with equally rewarding results.

This method of using Boccaccio's fictions to gloss one another is by no means limited to tales of the *Decameron* but can be profitably extended to his entire literary corpus. As Teodolinda Barolini has pointed out, the whole of the *Fiammetta* is, in a sense, a rewriting of the *Filostrato* in which the numerous inversions (most conspicuously the substitution of a female for a male protagonist) attest to the purely literary character of Boccaccio's poetics; it is the motif that is essential, and the production of fiction is, for Boccaccio, a procedure akin to writing variations on a series of such abstract motifs in order, by casting them in the concrete form of widely varying social realities, to reveal their hidden contours.[15]

Among the works that have proven most useful as a key for understanding both the formal and thematic elements of the *Decameron* is the *Filocolo*, one of Boccaccio's earliest publications, a text, as critics have long noted, that presents us not only with a sort of prototype for the *Decameron*'s framing device – the Neapolitan interlude with its "Questions of Love" in Book IV – and earlier versions of two stories that will be retold in the *Decameron* (X.4 and X.5), but also with various other elements destined to be recycled in the *Decameron*. Of particular relevance to the interpretation of IV.1 is Forni's view that *Decameron* V.6, the tale of Gian di Procida, is actually a reworking of the *Filocolo* episode where the covetous and sadistic Amiraglio, having discovered Florio and Biancifiore asleep in each other's arms, attempts to have

13 Migiel observes: "Ricciardo can fall in love with Caterina, even fiercely (*fieramente* [V.4.6]), and is not necessarily destined for a tragic end because the social configuration of the characters is different from the social configurations we see both in the tragic stories of *Decameron* 4 and the French and Provençal sources and analogues" (*Rhetoric*, 129).

14 See Marcus, *Allegory*, 56. Muscetta also identifies the absent wife (and mother) as an aggravating circumstance: "Tancredi's tragedy lies in his very tenderness, and he will lose himself in crime because life's events have determined that he and his only daughter are prematurely widowed" ("Giovanni Boccaccio," 412).

15 Barolini, "Giovanni Boccaccio."

them summarily burnt at the stake; the Amiraglio's behaviour, Forni observes, appears to prefigure that of Tancredi in IV.1.[16]

In the pages that follow, I will try to show that the *Filocolo* may have a more central, and sustained, bearing on IV.1 than has been imagined, supplying not only the emotional colour to Tancredi's wayward character but also the main contours of the peculiar father-child dynamic that is such a prominent feature of IV.1. This interpretative approach is susceptible to the same temptations and pitfalls as those encountered by the family historian who, constrained to use the present as a template for the past, will invariably find a familiar profile, curl, or kink of character where none exists. However, the risks of this approach are far outweighed by its potential reward: that of encouraging readers to re-evaluate the primacy of incest as a motivating factor.

With remarkable efficiency, the first line of IV.1 establishes not only the tale's genre, tragedy, and structuring pattern, paradox, but the specific socio-economic, geographic, psychological, and somatic coordinates that define its context and influence its outcome: "Tancredi, prencipe di Salerno, fu signore assai umano e di benigno ingegno, se egli nell'amoroso sangue nella sua vecchiezza non s'avesse le mani bruttate" [§3: Tancredi, Prince of Salerno, was a most benevolent ruler, and kindly of disposition, except for the fact that in his old age he sullied his hands with the blood of passion]. Like the biographical vignettes of *De casibus*, but with far greater concision, this single line traces a prince's fall: Tancredi's precipitous trajectory from enlightened humanity ("umano e di benigno ingegno") to sheer bestiality ("le mani bruttate") – a state of animalistic degradation underscored by the phonetic similarity of *bruttare* to *bruto*. The jarring juxtaposition of these antithetical traits succinctly captures the paradoxical nature both of Tancredi and of this tale which begins with his name. How, indeed, can one reconcile Tancredi's violent behaviour with his history of benevolent, humane governance? An earlier dramatization of the particular circumstance of a monarch who, in the autumn of his years, betrays his former equanimity and humanity by engaging in irrational behaviour destructive both to himself and to those closest to him is found in the first book of the *Filocolo*, where the Pagan king of Spain, Felice, stops at nothing – perjury, conspiracy, and the trafficking of humans – in his campaign to prevent his son, Florio, from forming a union with Biancifiore, a Roman orphan of patrician descent.[17]

16 Forni, *Forme complesse*, 38–9.

17 Kirkham explores the possible autobiographical stimulus in Boccaccio's use of this motif: "In the father's rigidity and the son's rebellion we can recognize an actual

Once allowances are made for differences stemming from the simple fact that in one case – that of Ghismonda and Guiscardo – the union is already consummated whereas in the other it is not, the similarities between the two fathers' responses are noteworthy. Both fathers begin by addressing the propriety of falling in love. While conceding that Florio's submission to passion is, by popular standards at least, forgivable, it ill suits a man of Florio's condition and character (*Filocolo* II.14). Tancredi, having caught his daughter *in flagrante delicto,* is more severe: "E or volesse Idio che, *poi che a tanta disonestà conducer ti dovevi* ..." [§27: And now may God grant that, since you had to behave so dishonorably ... (emphasis added)]. Both fathers deplore, in particular, their children's poor judgment in choosing lovers whose social station is so inferior to their own:

> Felice: "E certo io non mi dolgo che egli ami, ma duolmi di colei cui egli ama, perché alla sua nobiltà è dispari. Se una giovane di real sangue fosse da lui amata, certo tosto per matrimonio gliele giugneremmo" [*Filocolo* II.7: And certainly I do not grieve that he should love; but I do regret that he should love someone inferior to himself in nobility. If a young lady of royal blood were loved by him, surely we would quickly unite them in matrimony]; "Deh! or ti fossi tu d'una valorosa e gran donna simile alla tua nobiltà innamorato! assai mi dorrebbe, ma ancora mi sarebbe alcuna consolazione" [*Filocolo* II.14: Alas, if only you were enamored of a worthy and noble lady of your own class! That would be painful enough to me, but there would be some consolation (trans. Cheney)].
>
> Tancredi: "avessi preso uomo che alla tua nobiltà decevole fosse stato; ma tra tanti che nella mia corte n'usano eleggesti Guiscardo, giovane di vilissima condizione" [§27: you might at least have chosen someone whose rank was suited to your own. But of all the people who frequent my court, you have to choose Guiscardo, a youth of exceedingly base condition].

And finally both fathers emphasize the wardlike status of their children's lovers, both of whom are presented as dispossessed and utterly

conflict reproportioned to the measure of a time-honoured fictional motif. How much of a story could there have been in the *Filocolo* if the king of Spain had not been so determined to keep his son, the prince, from loving Biancifiore? What sad conflict would have developed in Filostrato if the priest Calcas had not wanted to reclaim his daughter? In the *Decameron,* where a younger generation over and again presses its natural demands, Cimone of Cyprus and Filippo Balducci are only two among many fathers and sons caught in family tugs-of-war. To deny Nature invites trouble, if not tragedy, as Prince Tancredi of Salerno bitterly learned when he refused his daughter Ghismonda's needs" (*Fabulous Vernacular,* 138).

dependent on the generosity of the princes in whose households they have been raised:

> Felice: "... una romana popolaresca femina, non conosciuta e nutricata nelle nostre case come una serva" [*Filocolo* II.7: a common Roman woman, someone of no name who has been brought up like a servant in our household]; "ma non consideri tu di cui tu ti sei innamorato, e per cui tu così faticosa passione sostieni? *e ciò è d'una serva nata nelle nostre case*, la quale a comparazione di te non ti si confarebbe in niuno atto" [*Filocolo* II.14: but don't you realize whom you have fallen in love with, and for whom you are experiencing so troublesome a passion? Namely, a maidservant born in our household, someone who could not be compared to you in any respect? (emphasis added)]
>
> Tancredi: "nella nostra corte quasi come per Dio da piccol fanciullo infino a questo dì allevato ..." [27: whom we took into our court and raised from early childhood mainly out of charity ...]

The behaviours that define the main lines of Tancredi's character – the senile conversion to violent, irrational behaviour; the obsessive interference in the erotic affairs of an only child; the apparent immunity to reasoned argument – are fully represented in the figure of Felice, whom his son, Florio, describes in terms that closely resemble those in which Ghismonda describes Tancredi. Just as Ghismonda suspects Tancredi of yielding, in his extreme old age, to a sadistic impulse completely foreign to his youthful self and urges him to make her, rather than Guiscardo, the target of his cruelty – "se tu nella tua estrema vecchiezza a far quello che giovane non usasti, cioè a incrudelir, se' disposto, usa in me la tua crudeltà" [§44: If you are intent, in your extreme old age, upon behaving as you never behaved in your youth, and resorting to cruelty, then let your cruelty be aimed at me] – Florio describes his father, Felice, as a wicked old man who, in the twilight of his years, at a time when even miscreants are moved to virtue in hope of reconciling themselves to the gods, has started to become cruel and engage in iniquitous acts: "vecchio iniquissimo ch'egli è che nell'ultima parte de' suoi giorni, alla quale quando gli altri, che sono stati malvagi pervengono, si sogliono col bene operare riconciliare agl'iddii, incomincia a divenire crudele e a fare opere ingiuste" [*Filocolo* II.44: Wicked old man that he is, in the last part of his life (when others who have spent their youth in wickedness are wont to reconcile themselves to the gods by doing good), he now begins to become cruel and commit injustices].

In both cases, the young accusers emphasize the fundamental perversity of their fathers' senile susceptibility to violence. While the specific circumstance that precipitates these eleventh-hour conversions to violence is in both cases the father's discovery of his child's illicit love, the condition that makes this vehement response possible in these formerly even-tempered governors appears to be somehow related to a somatic factor: their "vecchiezza."

In her study of IV.1, Millicent Marcus observes that Tancredi "violates the distinctions between successive generations by failing to pass on to his juniors the privilege of marriage and procreation that he enjoyed in his own time."[18] Marcus attributes this behaviour to Tancredi's inability to "differentiate between the demeanor proper to old age and youth," noting that instead of exhibiting the positive attributes of old age enumerated by Dante in *Convivio* IV, he has been reduced to a sort of "senile infantilism."

Certainly, the three most prominent characteristics of Tancredi's character, and those which account for the changeability which has been so variously interpreted – his infantilization, his feminization, and his irascibility – may all be chalked up to his "estrema vecchiezza" (§44). A quick review of the treatises on old age circulating in Boccaccio's time (among them, Cicero's *De senectute,* Boncompagno da Signa's *De malo senectutis et senii,* and Petrarch's *De senectute* in *De remedies utriusque fortune*) confirms that this sort of behaviour was commonly – if not always correctly – associated with old age. Consequently, it could be argued that it is not Tancredi's behaviour *per se* that is aesthetically incoherent or psychologically improbable, but the last stage of life, *senilitas,* which, according to popular belief at least, is both of these things.[19]

Changeability may be a universal symptom of old age, but its destructive capacity is in direct proportion to the social importance and political influence of the afflicted individual. Whereas the capricious behaviour of a senile herdsman may disrupt his family life and disgruntle

---

18 Marcus, *Allegory,* 53.

19 Old age – particularly extreme old age – is a time of contradiction. Physical frailty, Cicero writes, is a universal complaint of the old. Some old men, Petrarch tells us, desperate to "hold back their fleeting youth," engage in activities so puerile and dissolute that even the young would not deign to act in similar fashion (*Sine nomine* XVIII, 5). In book 2, par. 69 of his *Invective contra medicum,* Petrarch cites Aristotle and Horace in support of his characterization of old age. David Marsh's I Tatti edition of the *Invectives* points to *Rhetoric* 2.12–14, 1388b–1390b and *Ars poetica,* 158–79 as the passages Petrarch has in mind. For old age as return to childhood, see also *Invectives* bk. 3, par. 145. The association of irascibility with old age is ancient and epitomized by the stock character of Roman comedy: the *senex iratus,* described by Northrop Frye as a "heavy father, who with his rages and threats, his obsessions and his gullibility, seems closely related to some of the demonic characters of romance, such as Polyphemus" (*Anatomy of Criticism,* 172).

a few cows, similar conduct in a governor of people can easily lead to the collapse of a whole principality or nation. In his treatise *On Kingship*, Saint Thomas notes that as kings are mortal, they are subject to changes of character or professional competence that can compromise their suitability to govern: "the life of a man is subject to many changes, and thus a man is not equally suited to the performance of the same duties through the whole span of his life."[20] Addressing this same concern in *Li livres dou tresor*, Brunetto Latini observes that "there are two types of children, for one can easily be old in age and childish in behaviour, and one can be a child in age and old in one's honest life; therefore, the science of governing cities is for a man who is not a child in his behaviour and who does not pursue his inclinations, except when it is appropriate, and to the extent it is appropriate, and in an appropriate manner."[21]

While it is certainly possible to see Felice's and Tancredi's behaviour as a vivid dramatization of the dangerous excesses, arbitrary actions, and irrational desires of old age – dangers exponentially enhanced by the coupling of this "senile infantilism" with political influence – this is to minimize the underlying consistency of their actions, which are not, like the childish caprices of the clerical *senes pueros* described in Petrarch's *Liber sine nomine*[22] or the tantrums of the *senex iratus* of Roman comedy, incidentally destructive, but appear to be guided by the specific goal of self-destruction – both on the corporate and on the personal level.[23] Though passion may be the gale that fuels Felice's and Tancredi's fierce responses, reason is quite clearly the chart: far from submitting to paroxysms of grief or fits of violence, they each proceed to mount a meticulous attack against their children's lovers which, pursued in a conspiratorial atmosphere of carefully staged deceptions, midnight ambushes, and trumped-up accusations, has all the earmarks of a military campaign. Felice's and Tancredi's histrionics, a counterpoint of stern admonishments and blubbering plaints, may appear to be spontaneous displays of affect, but they are actually carefully scripted *intermezzi* in the drama that each has devised to reassert control over his child's social and erotic life; premeditation, not passion, is the hallmark of both princes' method.

---

20 Aquinas, *On Kingship*, chap. IV [I, 15].

21 Latini, *The Book of the Treasure*, II 3, "The Government of a City." Though Goneril's damning characterization of Lear as one whose age is "full of changes" (1.1.290), and therefore unsuited to govern himself, let alone others, may be punitive and nourished by personal ambition, it is fully consistent with these views.

22 Petrarch, *Sine nomine*, XVIII, 5.

23 It is interesting to note that in Robert D'Orbigny's twelfth-century *Conte de Floire et Blanchefleur*, Felix's (Felice's) age is not similarly stressed.

The poignancy of Florio's threatened, and Ghismonda's real, death is clearly enhanced by their status as only children upon whom the future of their respective bloodlines hinges. Florio is a much prayed for child of Felice's old age: "niuna allegrezza fu mai maggiore a noi, che quella quando il nostro unico figliuolo dagl'iddii lungamente pregati ricevemmo" [*Filocolo* II.7: We have never had any joy greater than that when we received our only son from the gods after lengthy prayers] and the only hope for the survival of Felice's dynasty:

> "Con ciò sia cosa che niuna speranza rimasa fosse alla mia lunga età di gloria, agl'iddii piacque di donarmi te, in cui la mia speme, sanza fallo già secca, ritornò verde, e dissi: 'Omai la fama del nostro antico sangue non perirà, poi che gl'iddii ci hanno conceduto degna erede'; e sopra te tutto il mio intendimento fermai, sì come sopra unico bastone della mia vecchiezza." (*Filocolo* II.10)
>
> ["Inasmuch as there was no hope of further glory remaining at my advanced age, it pleased the gods to give me you, in whom my hope became green again, where it would otherwise inevitably have withered; and I said, 'Now the fame of our ancient line will not perish, since the gods have granted us a worthy heir.' And I fixed all my hope on you, as the only staff of my old age."]

Ghismonda, similarly, is the passionately loved child of Tancredi's old age and an only child: "in tutto lo spazio della vita non ebbe che una figliuola" [§3: In all his life he had but a single child, a daughter]. Consequently, the aggressive and sustained interference of both fathers in this process of succession is an act of violence not merely against their children, but against their political and genetic legacy: a form of corporate suicide. The strange tenacity with which both Felice and Tancredi interfere with the action that Marcus has described as a passing of the "privilege of marriage and procreation"[24] must, under the circumstances, be viewed as a reckless flight towards self-destruction.

The Western literary canon is filled with examples of unconventional, at times even unlawful, acts fuelled by the conscious or unconscious urge to secure a political or genetic succession at all costs. The stories of Lot and his daughters, Tamar and Judah, and the rape of the Sabine women all attest to the urgency of this imperative, one that transcends conventional ethics. What, then, are we to make of the manifestly self-destructive and fundamentally perverse nature of Felice's

24 Marcus, *Allegory*, 53.

and Tancredi's actions? Where are the literary prototypes of this sort of behaviour?

Giuseppe Mazzotta has noted that the formula "con doloroso avvenimento la letizia de' due amanti rivolse in tristo pianto" [§15: a calamity, turning the joy of the two lovers into tears and sorrow] used to signal the tragic pattern of IV.1 is "filtered through the language of *Inferno* XXVI," the canto of Ulysses, where the phrase "'noi ci allegrammo, e tosto tornò in pianto' sanctions the hero's quest as a tragic transgression." Mazzotta views this allusion to "Ulysses' tragic knowledge for the lover's experience" as a "retrieval of the grandeur of tragic discourse" and a hint that the "story's concern is the probing of how desire may be related to knowledge."[25] While Mazzotta only addresses this single allusion to *Inferno* 26, a second allusion to the canto of Ulysses is found at the beginning of Tancredi's indictment of Ghismonda, where he laments her fallen virtue and claims, "io, in questo poco di rimanente di vita che la mia vecchiezza mi serba, sempre sarò dolente di ciò ricordandomi" [§26: the memory of it will always torment me during what little remains of my old age], words, as Vittore Branca confirms in his notes, clearly inspired by the first verses of Ulysses' "orazion picciola":[26]

"O frati," dissi, "che per cento milia
perigli siete giunti a l'occidente,
a questa tanto picciola vigilia
d'i nostri sensi ch'è del rimanente
non vogliate negar l'esperïenza,
di retro al sol, del mondo sanza gente ..." (*Inf.* 26.112–17)

["Brothers," I said, "o you, who having crossed
a hundred thousand dangers, reach the west,
to this brief waking-time that still is left
unto your senses, you must not deny
experience of that which lies beyond
the sun, and of the world that is unpeopled ..." (trans. Mandelbaum)]

By calquing Tancredi's words on those of Ulysses, Boccaccio has effectively affiliated Tancredi with Dante's Ulysses, introducing the

25 Mazzotta, *World at Play*, 139.

26 A similar passage is found in the *Filostrato*, where Calchas is accused of senile iniquity: "iniquo vecchio, che negli ultimi anni della tua vita, hai fatto tali inganni!" [93: iniquitous old man, who in the last years of your life have been so deceitful!].

possibility that the presence of *Inferno* 26 in *Decameron* IV.1 not only confirms Boccaccio's wish to inscribe the tale within an established tradition of high "tragic discourse" and draw attention to the relation of desire to knowledge, but also supports a more direct relation between the actions and objectives of Ulysses and Tancredi.[27]

A similar elegiac reflection on old age and the fast-closing horizon of life is found in Felice's appeal to Florio in *Filocolo* III.69: "Statti meco quelli pochi giorni che rimasi mi sono della presente vita" [Stay with me for those few days that remain to me in this present life]. Though the verbal congruity with *Inferno* 26 is perhaps less striking, the similarity of sentiment and circumstance is nonetheless unmistakable.[28] Another, earlier, echo of this same cluster of ideas is found in Florio's bitter characterization of Felice as a "vecchio iniquissimo," an iniquitous old man, who, "nell'ultima parte de' suoi giorni, alla quale quando gli altri, che sono stati malvagi pervengono, si sogliono col bene operare riconciliare agl'iddii, incomincia a divenire crudele e a fare opere ingiuste" [*Filocolo* II.44: in the last part of his life (when others who have spent their youth in wickedness are wont to reconcile themselves to the gods by doing good), he now begins to become cruel and commit injustices]. Those familiar with Dante's *Inferno* will recognize in these words not only a resonance with his Ulysses, but strong affinities with the case of Guido da Montefeltro, that other great representative of sinners guilty of "mal consiglio" (the term used by Boccaccio in his poetic paraphrase of the *Commedia*).[29] Upon entering the final stage of life, a time when "ciascun dovrebbe / calar le vele e raccoglier le sarte" [*Inf.* 27.79–81: it is fitting for all men / to lower sails and gather in their ropes], Guido, Dante tells us, having duly

---

27 These two allusions bracket the "orazion picciola," thereby cementing the connection of Tancredi not only with Ulysses in the abstract, but more precisely with Ulysses in his oratorical mode.

28 A plea uttered by Florio's mother strengthens this association with Dante's Ulysses: "Deh, or non ti muove a rimanere la pietà del tuo vecchio padre, il quale vedi che del dolore che sente di questa partita si consuma tutto? Non ti muove la pietà di me, tua misera madre, la quale ho de' miei occhi per te fatte due fontane d'amare lagrime? Oimè, caro figliuolo, rimani" [*Filocolo* III.72: Ah, are you not moved to remain by any pity for your aged father, whom you see all undone by the sorrow he feels at this departure? Are you not moved by pity for me, your wretched mother, who have made two fountains of bitter tears out of my eyes, because of you?].

29 Boccaccio writes: "e poi chi mal consiglio como- / da, como Ulisse, in fiamme acceso andando, / vede riprender dattero per pomo" (*Argomenti*, lines 175–7, in *Tutte le opere*, vol. 5, part 1, 161–2). Though Guido accuses himself of having offered "consiglio frodolente" (*Inf.* 27.116), Dante does not actually identify the flame-swathed occupants of the eighth bolgia as "fraudulent counsellors."

repented, confessed, and donned the Franciscan *capestro*, tragically undoes all this good by reverting to his political plotting and scheming.[30] Dante's discussion of old age in the fourth book of the *Convivio* identifies Cicero's treatise on old age, *De senectute*, as the source for this nautical metaphor: "E qui è da sapere, che, sì come dice Tullio in quello *De Senectute*, la naturale morte è quasi a noi porto di lunga navigazione e riposo"' [*Conv.* IV.28.3: Here it should be observed that a natural death, as Tully says in his book *On Old Age*, is, as it were, a port and site of repose after our long journey].[31] Those, Dante tells us, who approach death like a sailor entering port, by "furling the sails" of their "mondane operazioni," their earthly activities (*Conv.* IV.28.3), and turning to God, will find no bitterness or pain in death, for their souls will part from their bodies without violence, just as an apple, when fully ripe, drops from a branch.

Felice and Tancredi are, by this definition, senile recidivists, old men whose "unripe" – that is, unseasonable – passion for knowledge, political action, and control suggests a reversion to "mondane operazioni" better suited to an earlier stage of life.[32] Their dynamic ambivalence, marked by ceaseless fluctuations between such antithetical traits as tyranny and benign governorship, love and hate, repentance and recidivism, heroism and villainy, is one of the defining qualities of their literary precursors, Dante's Ulysses and Guido da Montefeltro. As Aldo Rossi has noted, it is precisely this oxymoronic quality that accounts for Boccaccio's particular attraction to the figure of Dante's Ulysses: "è la figura dell'ossimoro che tanto attrae i medievali e il Boccaccio in particolare, così diffuso e compiaciuto nel fermare una condizione umana nata, per una subitanea inversione del destino o della volontà, dal suo opposto (prosperità/miseria, amore/tradimento, difficoltà/superamento, e ad ogni binomio il suo corrispettivo."[33]

The fortunes of these senile recidivists revolve about a single point, one which – like Francesca's fatal kiss or Buonconte's salvific tear – forever fixes their destiny, determining, in a temporal context, whether the outcome will be comedic or tragic, and, in an eternal context, whether they will be saved or damned. Since, as Augustine reminds

30 It is amusing that while the verb *calare* does occur in IV.1, it is in the context of Tancredi's lowering himself out of Ghismonda's bedroom window!

31 "This ripeness is so delightful to me that, as I approach nearer to death, I seem, as it were, to be sighting land, and to be coming to port at last after a long voyage" (*On Old Age* II, 19).

32 Baratto alludes to Tancredi's recidivism in *Realtà e stile*: "A father who is at once a habitual offender, who monotonously copies his own stance" (186).

33 Rossi, "Dante nella prospettiva del Boccaccio," 81.

us, this point of conversion is scribed neither in time nor space, but in the human will, senility – a season of the human life characterized by a heightened volatility of the will – represents a time of particular danger. Just as the newly minted soul, according to Dante's Marco Lombardo, is innocent as a "fanciulla / che piangendo e ridendo pargoleggia" [*Purg*. 16.86–7: like a child who weeps and laughs in sport] and demands guidance, the senile soul, at least in the case of these aging princes and patriarchs, is in constant jeopardy of wandering from the path of virtue. However, whereas the "fanciulla" in Marco Lombardo's exquisite simile has ample time to repent of her wandering and find her way back to the "vera cittade," the senile recidivist teeters at the brink of death, where every single choice is potentially definitive and carries the weight of eternal judgment. The particular susceptibility of Ulysses, Guido, Felice, and Tancredi suggests that the same greatness of spirit reflected in the imperious actions, intellectual convictions, and temporal passions that served them so well in their youth has become a liability in their old age.

That Dante's Ulysses epitomizes the volatility of character, radical ambivalence, and tragic grandeur of the senile recidivist is made clear by the history of his reception: his oratorical skill, charisma, and destructive egotism resurface in characters as varied as Milton's Satan, Conrad's Kurtz, Melville's Ahab, and Nabokov's Humbert Humbert; his appeal to human dignity and heroic plunge into the unknown to expand the horizons of human knowledge have enshrined him as a proto-humanist and pure scientist – a powerful reminder of human worth and the redemptive value of knowledge, even, as Primo Levi tells us, in the dehumanizing depths of Auschwitz.[34] It is too easy to forget that Ulysses' "humanistic" agenda is pursued at the cost of social obligations and sympathy – qualities that, for many, are the defining traits of humanity.

This tendency to refract Dante's Ulysses into a full complement of contradictory "Ulysseses" is already evident in the many evocations of the "orazion picciola" of *Inferno* 26 strewn throughout Boccaccio's works, allusions which can be roughly grouped under three rubrics: the "elegiac" (the poignant shortness of life and imminence of death); the "tragic" (the dark charisma of the egotist who, a master of oratory, embroils others in a deadly mission); and the "heroic" (the call to distinguish ourselves from the "bruti" by launching out in search of knowledge, with the promise of fame to preserve the memory of our

34 Levi, *Se questo è un uomo*, "Il canto di Ulisse."

names).[35] More often than not, however, Boccaccio links these different facets of Ulysses together in elegiac/tragic or elegiac/heroic couplings. For instance, Florio's valedictory speech in *Filocolo* III.67 and Panfilo's address to the *brigata* members in *Decameron* IX.Concl. §5 both fall under the rubric of the elegiac/heroic (with the melancholic insistence on the shortness of life underscoring the rousing call to fulfil our potential and seek temporal fame), whereas Tancredi's and Felice's various evocations of the "orazion picciola" fall under the rubric of the elegiac/tragic (drawing together the melancholic motif of old age with Ulysses's oratorical guile and deadly egotism).

Tempting as it is to see Tancredi's regular excursions between the door jambs of his daughter's bedchamber as a parody of the Ulyssean journey between the columns of Hercules (with a virtual "Non plus ultra" posted above the bedroom door), Tancredi's real transgression, like that of Felice, consists, I would argue, in his use of specious arguments to embroil others in his egotistic, and ultimately self-destructive, bid to stave off the threat of death and dissolution through a radical, eleventh-hour exercise of autocracy. Just as Ulysses epitomizes the glib rhetorician's dangerous charisma – a destructive capacity dramatized by the "orazion picciola" and eternalized by the searing tongues of flame that enswathe the individual sinners – Felice and Tancredi are cast as "fraudulent counsellors," retailers of fictions that prove to be as dangerous to those they love as Ulysses' oration was to his faithful shipmates. As the Renaissance critic Castelvetro (1570) snidely notes of Ulysses' proposed excursion to a "mondo sanza gente": "if Ulysses knew that there were no people on the other side of the earth, then why go there?"[36]

As we shall see, Felice and Tancredi invite similar accusations, for both enlist arguments that prove to have no foundation and are revealed to be a feeble pretext for a deeper emotional, perhaps unconscious, desire. What is apparent is a procedure of rationalization – of marshalling arguments which, though unreasonable, have been ratified by convention and consequently have the outward appearance of reason – to satisfy a purely passional need.

In the *Filocolo*, Felice's allegation that Biancifiore is a "romana popolaresca femina, non conosciuta e nutricata nelle nostre case come una

35 Felice's and Tancredi's mournful laments about the imminence of death fall into this first category, the "elegiac," as does Boccacio's reference to "questa brieve vita che posta n'è" [the brief life that we are given] in the Introduction to IV.42. The heroic Ulysses is best represented by Boccaccio's glowing portrait in *De casibus* III.13.

36 Dartmouth Dante Project, *Inferno* 26.114–15. https://dante.dartmouth.edu/.

serva" is in complete contradiction of fact. Biancifiore's patrician pedigree is not only explicitly acknowledged by both the queen (*Filocolo* I.34) and Florio's tutor, Ascalion (*Filocolo* II.44), but is also quite literally graven in stone. The epitaph engraved on the tomb of Biancifiore's mother, Giulia, reads: "Qui d'Antropòs il colpo ricevuto, / giace di Roma Giulia Topazia, / dell'alto sangue di Cesare arguto / discesa" [*Filocolo* I.43: Here, by a blow received from Atropos, / There lies Giulia Topazia of Rome, / From the mighty line of proud Caesar / Descended].[37]

Puzzled by this glaring inconsistency, readers may well be inspired to conclude, with Antonio Enzo Quaglio, that it is futile to seek a *vita interiore* let alone a *coerenza psicologica* in such figures as Ascalion, the king and queen, and so forth: they are, Quaglio claims, best understood as "secondary characters, just means to sustain the action."[38] This rather dismissive assessment of Boccaccio's skill for characterization bears an uncanny resemblance to Russo's definition of Tancredi as a "personaggio-schema" or "personaggio mancato," a mere "espediente della narrazione" or narrative expedient. Once again, we are faced with a critical resistance to the possibility – indeed likelihood – that this apparent lack of *coerenza psicologica* does not reflect an aesthetic weakness, but attests, rather, to Boccaccio's far keener understanding of human psychology.

Like Tancredi, Felice is a character whose changeability is driven by a powerful, undeclared – and perhaps unconscious – desire. Felice's sudden and unaccountable amnesia concerning Biancifiore's noble pedigree is not, like Sancho's disappearing donkey in the *Quijote*, an accidental oversight on the part of the author, nor is it a case of the author's subordinating character to plot for the sake of expedience; indeed, it is an inconsistency for which Florio himself takes his father to task, noting, in his impassioned response to his father's false allegations, that while Biancifiore's nobility cannot be ascertained with any certainty, "noi pure avemo udito che la madre di costei, la quale voi non serva prendeste, discese dell'alto sangue del vittorioso Cesare, già consquistatore de' nostri regni per adietro" [*Filocolo* II.15.5: yet we have heard that her mother, whom you did not take as a servant, descended from the mighty line of victorious Caesar, who once conquered our

37 Though there is much confusion regarding Boccaccio's sources for the *Filocolo*, it is, perhaps, significant that in Robert D'Orbigny's twelfth-century version, Blanchefleur's epitaph simply reads: "Ci gist la bele Blanceflor, / a cui Flores ot grant amor" (ll. 659–60 of *Le conte de Floire et Blanchefleur*). Given this precedent, Boccaccio's insistence on Biancifiore's patrician pedigree is striking.

38 Boccaccio, *Filocolo*, ed. Quaglio, 50.

realms in an earlier time].[39] Whereas the Pagan king of Boccaccio's sources bases his objection to the young couple's union on religious (Muslim/Christian) or ethnic (Spanish [of African descent]/Roman) differences whose reality is borne out by the narrative, Boccaccio's Felice gratuitously invents obstacles based on a class distinction that does not exist.

While Felice stresses his particular distress at Florio's choice of a woman whose social standing was so distinctly inferior to his own, it is notable that he goes on to say that though he would have been somewhat consoled had Florio fallen for a social equal, he would nonetheless have found this painful: "assai mi dorrebbe" [*Filocolo* II.14: That would be painful enough to me]. This raises the question of what, precisely, he has in mind for his son's future. Had this over-zealous protection of an only child concerned a daughter, critics might perhaps have been moved – and with some reason – to suspect Felice of an incestuous interest. However, unless one is willing to make the argument that Felice's overly solicitous attitude towards his son derives from an erotic interest that is both homosexual and incestuous, it is perhaps better to look for another motive. Why, indeed, would Felice have objected to his son's liaison with a woman of equal nobility?[40] There is something in the manic, obsessive, and purely conventional quality of the arguments used in the campaign Felice mounts against Biancifiore that suggests they are disingenuous and most likely mask a deeper, perhaps unconscious, motivation. As we have seen, the clear-headed Florio is utterly flummoxed by his father's unfounded arguments and erratic behaviour.

Much the same can be said about Tancredi's principal objection to Ghismonda's union with Guiscardo: Guiscardo's social inferiority. Indeed, Guido Almansi has observed that when Tancredi "criticizes Ghismonda for having chosen as her lover a 'youth of exceedingly base condition,' this reproof bears all the appearance of a flimsy

---

39 A comparison with the Cantare and the Old French sources confirms the suspicion that Boccaccio has actually gone out of his way to emphasize Biancifiore's great nobility and the plebeian origin imputed to her by Felice as though he wished to underscore the irrational, even bizarre, nature of Felice's allegations.

40 See Forni, *Forme complesse*, 84n19: "In prospettiva psicologistica o psicoanalitica si potrebbe anche dire che re Felice è geloso della conquista (Biancifiore) del figlio (ciò che spiegherebbe il successivo allontanamento del giovane, etc.)." We cannot simply discount the possibility that Felice's distress is related not only to Florio's choice of partner but also to the fact that he was not consulted, etc. In *Dec.* IV.6 Messer Negro tells his daughter that he would have preferred it had she taken a husband chosen by him, and, indeed, that he would even have accepted a husband of her choice; what truly disturbs him is the lack of faith implied by her decision to pursue a clandestine relationship (see Forni, *Forme complesse*, 109–10).

pretext devised by Tancredi to justify his subsequent cruelty both in his own eyes and those of others. The insincerity of his criticism on this count is borne out by the contradictions in his behaviour."[41] Certainly, Ghismonda is not oblivious to these contradictions but calls her father to task, alleging that his decision to follow "la volgare oppinione" [§38: a common fallacy] and "contraria usanza" [§40: contrary practice] to characterize Guiscardo as a young man of "vilissima condizione" [§27: exceedingly base condition] contradicts – in spirit, if not in the letter – his earlier assessment of Guiscardo, whom, she observes, he had praised above all others: "Chi il commendò mai tanto quanto tu commendavi in tutte quelle cose laudevoli che valoroso uomo dee essere commendato?" [§42: For was it not you yourself who sang his praises more loudly than any, claiming for him all the qualities by which one measures a man's excellence?]. Though, she boasts, Guiscardo not only met but exceeded the expectations created by Tancredi's praise, had he fallen short of these expectations, the fault would have lain not with Guiscardo, but Tancredi: "e se pure in ciò alcuno inganno ricevuto avessi, da te sarei stata ingannata" [§42: So that if I was deceived in my estimate of Guiscardo, it was you alone who deceived me]. By praising Guiscardo to his daughter, Tancredi has effectively mediated the liaison. From Ghismonda's perspective, it is not she who has betrayed Tancredi but he who has betrayed her by responding with such violence to a circumstance which he has aided and abetted. Her incredulous observation "Chi vide mai alcuno altro che te piagnere di quello che egli ha voluto?" [§60: Who ever heard of anyone, other than yourself, who wept on achieving his wishes?], uttered just moments before dying, is the most incisive expression of this paradoxical pattern that informs all of Tancredi's actions and clearly attests to the puzzling dissonance between his declared and his hidden desire. For Baratto, Tancredi's decision to honour Ghismonda's request that she be buried with Guiscardo merely confirms the suspicion that Tancredi's obsession with honour is pure pretext: "l'onore sembra dunque ridursi a ragione del tutto pretestuosa."[42]

---

41 Almansi, *Writer as Liar*, 148. Almansi also observes: "Even in the second half of the novella we shall see that these class prejudices are presented in highly ambiguous form and are actually contradicted by other elements in the narrative" (139). Forni sees Almansi's characterization of Tancredi's socio-economic objection to the union as a pretext to justify the cruelty of his subsequent behaviour as far too categorical: "But why limit the meaning in this way? It seems to me that Guiscardo's 'exceedingly base condition' can be taken at least as an aggravating circumstance, given the rigid conception of hierarchies in that society" (*Forme complesse*, 130).

42 Baratto, *Realtà e stile*, 188.

Like Geryon, Dante's personification of Fraud, whose benign "faccia d'uom giusto" [*Inf.* 17.10: face ... of a just man] and body embellished with an Arachne-like web of arabesques mask the poisonous guile of a scorpion's sting, Felice and Tancredi have the outward appearance of equanimity and benevolence, but the weblike arabesques of their discourse obscure the truth: in short, their rationalizations are potentially deadly lies which have the appearance of truth.[43] Each of their children, by contrast, produces a sincere, heartfelt discourse that, tragically, has the outward appearance of a lie, a "ver c'ha faccia di menzogna" [*Inf.* 16.124: that truth which seems a lie]. Florio sues for his father's compassion, declaring that to separate him from Biancifiore would be to separate him from life: "Onde io caramente vi priego che voi della mia vita aggiate pietà sì come padre di figliuolo, la quale sanza fallo, dividendomi io da Biancifiore, si dividerà da me" [*Filocolo* II.13: And so I lovingly pray you to have the pity on my life that a father should have for his son; for without fail that life, if I am separated from Biancifiore, will be separated from me]. Ghismonda, having resolved not to compromise her integrity by pleading, provides Tancredi with a formal ultimatum: "io t'acerto che quello che di Guiscardo fatto avrai o farai, se di me non fai il simigliante, le mie mani medesime il faranno" [§44: I swear that unless you do the same to me as you have already done, or intend to do, to Guiscardo, these hands of mine will do it for you]. In both cases the fathers assume that their children's rhetoric is as false as their own and consequently fail to take them at their word. Unable to articulate the depth of their feelings except in the formulaic language of Ovidian elegy (Florio and Biancifiore are, Boccaccio tells us, weaned on the "santo libro d'Ovidio" [*Filocolo* I.45]) or the stylized discourse of courtly love, Florio and Ghismonda inadvertently give the impression of insincerity. Felice's false promise to allow Biancifiore to join Florio in Montoro – a Guido-like variety of "lunga promessa con l'attender corto" [*Inf.* 27.110: long promises and very brief fulfillments] – confirms his belief that his son's high-spirited words reflect more rhetorical posturing than true resolution. Tancredi similarly acknowledges the noble spirit that animates Ghismonda's words but discounts their sincerity: "Conobbe il prenze la grandezza dell'animo della sua figliuola ma non credette per ciò in tutto lei sì fortemente disposta a quello che le parole sue sonavano" [§46: Although Tancredi knew that his daughter had a will of iron, he doubted her resolve to translate her words into action].

It is not, of course, the screen of conventional rhetoric alone that blinds Felice and Tancredi to the truth of their children's words, but their radical

43 In the *Filocolo* we find the phrases "maladetto consiglio" (II.30) and "iniquo consiglio" (II.31) used with regard to the conspiracy to frame Biancifiore.

egotism – like Dante's Ugolino, they see themselves mirrored in their children, and therefore assume that their children's words are as empty as their own. Egotism and the inability to sufficiently distinguish between themselves and their children create a pathological, and ultimately fatal, attachment. Tancredi, as Marcus incisively notes, "persists in considering his daughter as an extension of himself ('non sappiendola da sé partire') and disbelieves any evidence of her autonomy."[44] Tancredi's "incest" is not motivated by a prurient love for his daughter – for this would assume a greater degree of separation between the two – but a morbid love of self. Tancredi's words to Ghismonda in the wake of his discovery of her affair clearly indicate that he views her secret liaison with Guiscardo as a form of *lese-majesté*, a treacherous attack on his person.

In both stories, this condition of inadequate differentiation is brought into higher relief through the programmatic exaggeration of the differences – sexual, socio-economic, cultural, and religious – that distinguish the young lovers. These are relationships that openly acknowledge and productively bridge difference rather than relationships based on a furtive, destructive, and perhaps unconscious effacement of social difference. Whereas Dante uses Ugolino and the theme of cannibalism as a sort of metaphor for this radical form of egotism that, like Saturn devouring his children, absorbs its offspring, Boccaccio exchanges a digestive metaphor for a sexual one: incest.[45]

This metaphoric incest, however, does not point to erotic passion so much as a lust for authority, Tancredi's desperate bid to retain control as he confronts the absolute loss of temporal power implied by death. As in the case of Shakespeare's Lear or Molière's Orgon, this fear of losing authority takes the form of an obsessive, apparently erotic passion. Lear's rash decision to disown Cordelia, his "best object" and "balm" of his old age (1.1.214–15), is precipitated by the discovery of her difference, her candid declaration that she intends to function as a separate social and sexual entity. Orgon falls beneath Tartuffe's infatuating spell and treats him with more tenderness than any mistress not because he actually wants to sleep with him, but because Tartuffe plays to his ego and facilitates his illusion of control.[46] Like Tancredi, Lear and Orgon are domestic despots, senile absolutists ready to sacrifice their own daughters if necessary to nourish their illusion of control.

---

44 Marcus, *Allegory*, 54.

45 Nabokov's Humbert Humbert, having assumed the social functions and legal status of a father, exploits the opportunities afforded by this role to "safely solipsize" his "daughter."

46 *Tartuffe*, Act 1, scene 2: "Il le choie, il l'embrasse, et pour une maîtresse / On ne saurait, je pense, avoir plus de tendresse."

The association of incest with egotism is ancient and powerfully represented in the figures of Ovid's Narcissus and Pygmalion. The tale of Narcissus is a striking dramatization of the tragic consequence of the most perfect form of incest: an eroticized love of self. In Ovid's tale of Pygmalion, artistic creation is conflated with biological creation, and the artist's excessive attachment to his creation ("eburnea," the ivory girl) gradually acquires the form of an unmistakable, albeit highly aestheticized, father-daughter incest. Perhaps the most vivid example of this unholy trinity of egotism, incest, and death is found in Gower's gruesome genealogy of Satan in the fourteenth-century *Miroir d'omme* (the source of Milton's more famous allegory in *Paradise Lost*), where we read that Satan fathered Death on his daughter, Sin.

Perhaps the time has come to reevaluate the orangutan. Perhaps, as I suggested above, we have mistaken effect for cause, and morbid egotism, of which incest is merely an expression, is the thread that binds IV.1 together. Saturn does not eat his children because he is hungry, and Tancredi does not dote on his daughter because he would like to sleep with her; where authority is synonymous with identity, the loss of the former has fatal implications for the persistence of the latter, and both Saturn and Tancredi are responding to an existential anxiety, an overwhelming fear of losing their social identities and, therefore, ceasing to be. Perhaps the time has come to scrape Tancredi's name from the grim roster of sex offenders and inscribe it in a different catalogue, one where it appears alongside those of his literary precursors – Narcissus, Pygmalion, Ulysses, Guido, and Felice – and his literary progeny: Shakespeare's Lear and Moliere's Orgon.

Incarnation in Venice (IV.2)

ALISON CORNISH

The tale of Frate Alberto has been admired for its realism, more specifically its comic realism, with its exposure of a vulgar reality beneath exalted pretence, localized in the city of Venice, erstwhile ally to Florence, the city of our narrators. Erich Auerbach extolled this tale in particular for bestowing on literature "a world of reality and the present."[1] Its explicit theme is the power of appearance over reality: how belief in the good enables the wiles of the wicked. Pampinea's sarcasm brings angels and angelicized ladies, as well as presumptuous and deceitful friars, down to earth. Yet the significance of the Annunciation scene, central parody of the tale, where unseen divinity became flesh within the body of a mortal woman, which is to say, when the really real finally appeared, suggests that the target of her ferocious satire is not the sacred, but its desecrators.

Pampinea tells the second tale of Day Four as a form of protest against the king's law. Filostrato, who dictated the sad theme because of his own unhappy love for one of the ladies of the *brigata*, comments on Fiammetta's macabre story, which made all the girls cry, declaring that he would have given his life for only half the pleasure Guiscardo took from Ghismonda. He thus takes a morose satisfaction in ill-starred romances and eagerly expects Pampinea to continue in the same vein, claiming that such tearful tales might dampen, that is, relieve, his amorous fire. Yet Pampinea, who is something of a natural leader, has another idea. Sensitive to the ladies' weepy reception of the first tragic story, her solution is to lighten their spirits by making them laugh, with a story that is not technically a comedy and follows the king's rule because it ends badly, but only for the scoundrel who

1 Auerbach, *Mimesis*, 219.

is its protagonist. Frate Alberto is, like Don Giovanni, an *empio punito* (a wicked man justly punished), and like that *dramma giocoso* this novella similarly cuts across generic lines. Pampinea uses comic realism as comfort to the company on their sad day, but also as a brisk reminder of the selfishness and vanity that might in fact underlie tragic and romantic sentimentalism.

An evil man, Berto della Massa had to leave his native town of Imola, near Bologna, because his vices had become so well known that no one trusted him anymore. He goes to Venice, which Pampinea cheerfully describes as "d'ogni bruttura ricevitrice" [IV.2.8: the receptacle of all such trash], and, as if converted from his former life, becomes known as a pious and abstemious friar: Brother Alberto da Imola. Frate Alberto is all about appearances. He seems to have reformed his life; once a thief, pimp, counterfeiter, and assassin, he becomes a great preacher. This apparent transformation from one moral extreme to the other makes him resemble the protagonist of the *Decameron*'s first tale, Cepperello/Ciappelletto. Unlike Ciappelletto, Alberto is not on his deathbed when he makes the change, or appearance of change; in fact, he is rather robust and good looking, with handsome legs. He abstained from meat and wine, Pampinea comments, that is, when he did not have any he liked. The reform of his reputation rather than his life enables him to continue in perfidious activities without being suspected. He has a particular gift of tears, able to bring them on in great lamentations for the Lord's Passion when enough people are watching. His performance of an authentically penitent friar is so convincing that his sanctity becomes more celebrated than that of Saint Francis of Assisi himself, and he becomes a trusted messenger, guardian and trustee of many people's money, as well as confessor and counsellor of the majority of men and women in the city. Thus, Pampinea says, "di lupo era divenuto pastore" [§11: transformed from a wolf into a shepherd]. This remark takes us outside the frame of the novella, since at the moment of crowning Filostrato, the present day's king, at the end of Day Three, Neifile had suggested that the men of the *brigata* are wolves and the women, sheep. With the first male leader of the group, she notes, the wolves will in fact be guiding the sheep: "Tosto ci avedremo se i' lupo saprà meglio guidar le pecore che le pecore abbiano i lupi guidati" [III.Concl. §1: Now we shall discover whether the wolf can fare any better at heading the sheep than the sheep have fared in leading the wolves].

In Venice, Friar Alberto has the good fortune to encounter a particularly vain and idiotic woman in confession, Madonna Lisetta from Ca' Quirino, whom he recognizes as fertile ground for his plough: "parendogli terreno da' ferri suoi" (§14). Making a house call, he throws himself at her feet, recounting how the Angel Gabriel came to beat him up with a big stick for failing to acknowledge the "celestiali bellezze" [§18: celestial charms] of this lady with whom the angel claims to be in love. As penance for this failure, the friar asks that his own body be the vehicle for the incorporeal angel to visit the lady. The angel thus requires a borrowed body, a human appearance, to do "queste cose" [§42: that sort of thing] that, as Lisetta later confides in her girlfriend, they also do "colassù" [§43: up there]. Coming in human form will require that the woman's door be left open (Frate Alberto does not omit to remind her), which presumably it would not if he came as the angel did to Mary. Yet the angel does not come simply in the form of a man. He brings his wings with him, dressing up for the occasion in the house of a friendly woman who lives nearby; and this same feathery equipment he leaves behind when the unexpected arrival of Lisetta's suspicious in-laws at the door forces him to dive into the Grand Canal.

A good swimmer, naked and dripping he begs mercy from "un buono uomo" [§46: an honest-looking fellow] whose house he finds open on the other side of the canal, recounting some "favole" [§46: yarn] that convinces him to shelter the poor unfortunate in his own bed while he goes out about his business in town. It is only when this Venetian fellow hears about the flight of the angel Gabriel in the public chatter at the busy Rialto bridge that he realizes who it is he must have in his house. He first demands payment of fifty ducats and then proposes a plan of escape involving an undignified and uncomfortable disguise, with the excuse of a public festival involving a hunt and a wild man. Without much alternative, Alberto submits to the plan and finds himself covered in honey and feathers with a stick in his hand – oddly resembling the angel with the stick that he described in the tall tale he first told to Lisetta. Led by a chain and tied to one of the pillars in the Piazzetta, bitten by flies, he is then exposed by the "buon uomo" [good man] as that Angel Gabriel "il quale di cielo in terra discende la notte a consolare le donne viniziane" [§55: who descends by night from Heaven to earth to amuse the women of Venice]. As Pampinea acidly remarks, "fu lealtà viniziana questa" [§52: it goes to show how far you can trust a Venetian]. The crowd the man has deliberately gathered there hurls insults at the miserable sticky-feathered freak and pummels him with garbage. Alberto's fellow friars arrive to claim him and he passes the rest of his wretched life in jail where, presumably, he dies. Unlike Ciappelletto, Alberto brings disrepute on the people with whom he lives. Filostrato will in fact acknowledge that the ending was moderately pleasing to him even as he rebukes Pampinea for the laughter the rest of the tale provoked.

The tale is comedic first of all in its popular register, evident from the start as it begins and ends with a proverb that is explicitly of the common people. Also vulgar are the semi-obscene *doubles entendres* about ploughing a field and horseback riding and a very unladylike "non le toccava il cul la camiscia," her undershirt didn't touch her ass (§29, translated more delicately by McWilliam as "her smock rose clear of her bottom"). The talk of common people is a thread running through the whole narrative. Lisetta cannot resist bragging about her superhuman lover to her "comare," or gossip, a neighbour woman to whom it seems like "mille anni" [§44: a thousand years], before she can get away and tell everyone else. She waits, however, until she has the ideal platform – a party that gathers together a great company of ladies, a *brigata* like the one presently listening to Pampinea's tale and proceeds to tell the novella carefully and in order.

As with Virgil's *Fama*, or Rumour, another feathered monster that flies between heaven and earth spreading news of Aeneas's affair with Dido through great Libyan cities, we see how quickly news travels: these women tell their husbands and other women, and those women others, until Venice is full of it. Eventually word reaches the ears of interested parties – not Lisetta's husband, who is away on business in Flanders, but his brothers. Unlike the garrulous females, these brothers say nothing about it, but take the news to heart, ominously keeping guard at night, waiting and watching "di trovar questo agnolo e di sapere se egli sapesse volare" [§44: to run this angel to earth and discover whether he could fly]. The gossip's novella becomes a *novelluzza*, a rumour that reaches the ears of Frate Alberto himself, who incautiously goes to his mistress once again, ostensibly to reproach her for her lack of circumspection. The "honest man" who took in the naked Alberto learns who he is through the word on the street, and arranges his punishment by spreading news of his staged humiliation so that the people come from Rialto to the Piazzetta in order to take their mob vengeance upon him.

The great twentieth-century German philologist Erich Auerbach chose the story of Frate Alberto from among all the tales of the *Decameron* as a key example of a new European realism in his landmark book of literary criticism, *Mimesis*. It is in Boccaccio, Auerbach declares, that "the world of sensory phenomena is first mastered." He contrasts the elegant style of the narrative with the "sensory vividness" of an Old French *fabliau* that gives "a graphic picture of the situation through the most unpretentious means and the most everyday words." Whereas the French narrator's tone is "not essentially different from that of his characters," Boccaccio deftly shows how the vernacular can "accommodate itself to the requirements of a discriminating social life of refined sensuality." Auerbach's conclusion regarding Boccaccio's accomplishment is epochal: "The literature of society acquired what it had not previously possessed: a world of reality and of the present."[2]

Auerbach particularly admired the conversation between Lisetta and her gossip (*comare*) for its convincing naturalism: "it is not at all literary; the tone is not that of written language but of oral narrative." In this cozy chat, as in most of what seems real in the tale, there is falsehood: one is telling a fantastic tale, "lo 'ntendimento mio è l'agnolo Gabriello" [§41: my admirer is the Angel Gabriel], and the other one "pur si tenne" [§42: continued to keep a straight face]. Auerbach finds the detail of Alberto returning to reproach ("riprendere") Lisetta after having got wind of the rumour somewhat unrealistic, since he too easily falls into the trap of the brothers-in-law. Others have suggested that the passage should be read as meaning that since no ("alcuna") word of it had reached the ears of the friar, he went back to re-take ("riprendere"), that is, enjoy his mistress as usual.

What has been seen as the most vernacular, or localized, aspect of the tale, and an important component of its realism, is its collocation in Venice. Unlike the Old French *fabliau* with which Auerbach contrasts it, which could have happened "anywhere in France," Pampinea's tale is emphatically Venetian, so much so that some critics have declared Venice to be its true protagonist. This local texture and colour is in names (Lisetta "da ca' Quirino," §12) and place-names (Rialto, San Marco, the Grand Canal), but also in snippets of recognizable dialect ("Che s'è quel? che s'è quel?" [§53: Whoever is it?] and "mo vedì vu?" [§43: Now do you see?]). To these we can add "cassesi," a term of Arabic origin for Christian priests, apparently in use in Venice at the time, the Venetian coin called a "mattapan" (§24), also of Arabic origin, the form "amadore" for "amante" [§12: lover], "marido" for "marito" [§43: husband], the term "galloria" [§29: happiness], and the colourful expletive "per le plaghe di Dio" [§43: by God's wounds], which is the first line of a popular Venetian song cited by Dante in his tour of the unpalatable dialects of the Italian peninsula in his treatise on vernacular eloquence (*De vulgari eloquentia* I.14.6).

Giorgio Padoàn argued that the specificity of Venetian markers in the novella indicated not just realism, but something real: evidence of Boccaccio's presence in the city before writing the *Decameron*, before his documented visits to see Petrarch there in the 1360s. In a gloss to the Tuscan version of Valerius Maximus's *Facts and Deeds* attributed to Boccaccio, dated to around 1346–7 when Boccaccio was in the Romagna region,

2 Ibid., 216–19.

there is a comment about a public festival in Venice called "il giuoco de le Marie." The uniquely Venetian "Festa delle Marie" was associated with the feast of the purification of the Virgin on 2 February. It involved a procession of boats carrying wooden statues of Mary and concluded, according to at least one account, with a priest dressed up as the Angel Gabriel speaking the words of the Annunciation to the Virgin. Over the course of the fourteenth century, it became a carnivalesque celebration that provoked sumptuary legislation to tone down its pomp and luxury.[3] The Feast of the Annunciation, 25 March, is also the traditional date of the founding of Venice, a connection that would be repeatedly represented in civic art in the city throughout the Renaissance.[4] The universal event of Mary's first Joyful Mystery is thus also especially and specifically Venetian. Apparently historical is the masquerade of the wild man, in which the local "honest man" convinces the friar from Imola to take part. Evidently carnival festivities closely following the feast of the three Marys really did involve men dressed up as bears or wild men (hairy like bears) and a hunt of pigs or bulls on the city square, concluding between the columns of the Piazzetta, where the larger Piazza di San Marco opens onto the water.

While Pampinea's tale is funny, it is also vicious in its sarcasm. It may be comic, but it is not light-hearted. Pampinea's sarcasm, which the critics describe as ferocious, has three main targets: hypocritical friars, stupid women, and Venice. Frate Alberto is not just a bad apple; he is representative of a class, and his portrayal is part of the anti-clericalism that is a constant theme of the *Decameron*. Pampinea's opening shot is that the friars comport themselves as if they were lords of paradise and controlled access to it – as if, she says, they did not have to work at getting there like everyone else. Women are at particular risk of becoming victims of the hypocrisy of the friars (although perhaps, just as often, we see them colluding with them and sometimes duping them). The novella's narrator has no compassion at all for Lisetta, who is crowned with a string of mocking nicknames involving pumpkins, a lot of wind, and little salt.[5] Her vacuousness is connected with her city: "sì come colei che viniziana era" [§12: being a Venetian]. Boccaccio's animus against the city of Venice may not be just a general municipal rivalry, since events that led up to Venice's acquisition of Treviso in 1339 involved what the Florentines considered a profound Venetian betrayal of their previous alliance. That is the animus behind Pampinea's remark about

3 Padoàn, "Sulla novella veneziana."

4 Rosand, *Myths of Venice*, 16.

5 Psaki calls Lisetta a "lovely moron" in "The One and the Many," 238.

Venetian "loyalty." Francesca Pennisi has suggested that it is the false appearance or "myth" of Venice as "most serene republic," that is really under attack here.[6]

The question of the "real" haunts this novella. Certainly part of its realistic feel stems from its comic register. Roman comedy was always set in the streets of the city, rather than in the halls of great lords, and involved everyday sorts of "real" people, such as servants and their masters, rather than kings or heroes. Yet the unheroic ethos of merchants, cheating wives, and self-serving friars is common to many of the tales of the *Decameron*. What is key to this one is the central parody around which the plot and many of the jokes turn: the scene of the Annunciation, one of the most frequent subjects of representative art of the time, in which a spectacular angel kneels before a beautiful and modest young girl. This is the event of the Incarnation, the moment in which God becomes man in history, when what is divine and unseen becomes human and tangible. What is at stake is the relationship between the visible appearance of everyday life and the immanent reality of a world unseen.

Boccaccio's story is surely influenced by at least two late antique tales about mortal women tricked into adulterous encounters under the impression that they would be sleeping with a god. In one, Decius Mundus persuades a pious and chaste married Roman woman named Paulina into sleeping with him in the temple, where she was told she would encounter the god Anubis, who was in love with her. In his *Zibaldone Magliabechiano* Boccaccio transcribed the story as he found it in a fourth-century Latin adaptation of Josephus's *Jewish Antiquities*. He retells it in Chapter 91 of *On Famous Women*, remarking that this Paulina became a topic of common gossip at Rome, famous for her naïvety. In the other story, widely available in the many "Alexander romances" circulating in the Middle Ages, Nectanebus, exiled king of Egypt as well as magician and astrologer, convinces Olympias, wife of Philip of Macedon, that the god Amon will visit her in a dream and conceive a son. Nectanebus himself visits her in the form of a dragon, becoming the father of Alexander (Olympias, Queen of Macedonia, is the subject of *On Famous Women* 61).[7] Against this background, the sacred mystery of the Incarnation as recounted in the Gospel of Luke becomes just one more legend of a divine being consorting with a mortal woman to engender the hero or protagonist of a tradition.

---

6 Pennisi, "Un-Masking Venice."

7 For these sources, see Branca's note in his edition of the *Decameron*, 487–8.

Michelangelo Picone argued that an even closer source for *Decameron* IV.2 is one of the *lais* of Marie de France, *Yonec*, where a young unhappily married woman acquires a love who enters by the window of her room in the shape of a bird, a "gran oisel." This story is no comedy; when their liaison is found out, the bird-knight is fatally wounded, leaving great trails of blood behind him as he flees. Marie's conclusion is to emphasize the sadness of the lay, the "sorrow and grief that they suffered for love."[8] This is just the sort of story Filostrato would have liked to have heard told on his day, which Pampinea has mischievously transformed into a comic parody.

By dressing up as the Angel Gabriel and fornicating with a vain and silly woman who imagines she could be preferred to the Virgin Mary, Frate Alberto reduces ubiquitous sacred iconography to pornographic purpose. The *Yonec* intertext underlines the fact that this is also a parody of courtly love, in which noble lovers revere and worship their beloved ladies. Such "honest" or "refined" but nonetheless adulterous love, the stuff of troubadour poetry and medieval French romances that were popular reading particularly among women, is the lens through which Lisetta understands the scenes of the Annunciation that she frequently encounters in her Venetian environment. Gabriel must be a lover of Mary since he is always depicted as kneeling before her, in the idolatrous stance of a Lancelot before a Guinevere. Lisetta's capacity to miss the point is clear in her claim to have lit numerous candles before the image of Gabriel instead of the Virgin. In the more specifically Italian iteration of courtly love, the idealized lady was not only beautiful and exalted in terms of noble rank, but was also good and virtuous, beautiful in her soul to the point of being expected and awaited in heaven, the so-called *donna angelicata* of stilnovist lyric that we see in Guido Guinizelli and then in Dante, both in the poems of the *Vita nuova* ("Oltre la spera") and ultimately in Beatrice's role in the *Divine Comedy*. Guinizelli's most influential poem, "Al cor gentil rempaira sempre amore," declares that his lady is "desired in heaven" ("Madonna è disiata in sommo cielo").[9] Frate Alberto makes this literal: he flatters Lisetta that she is desired in heaven by no less than the Angel Gabriel. Courtly love and the cult of Mary are of course connected, as they were contemporaneous phenomena of the twelfth century, particularly in France. One is a secular or profane aristocratic counterpart to the other, a sensual interpretation or literalization of the mystical love of the Virgin. In that sense the friar is

8 Picone, "Alle fonti del *Decameron*"; Marie de France, *Lais*, 93.

9 Clubb, "Boccaccio and the Boundaries of Love."

assisted in his blasphemous incarnation of the Annunciation scene by expectations inculcated by romantic literature.

Millicent Marcus argues that the ultimate sin of Frate Alberto is a kind of vulgar literalism, a crime against allegory. In his *Genealogia deorum gentilium* [Genealogy of the Gentile Gods], Boccaccio explains that the surface meaning of poetry is a veil over and a vehicle of underlying truth that always, regardless of the individual poet's intentions, points towards virtue.[10] This defence of poetry as cognate with theology, which he elaborated also in his biography of Dante, draws heavily on a similar argument that Petrarch makes in a letter to his brother Gherardo, the monk. On this view, it is the noble, virtuous purpose of poetry that Frate Alberto violates in his rendering literal what should be read allegorically, bringing down to earth, into base sensuality, what should instead lead always towards a higher significance. Patrizio Alberto Andreaux makes much of the iconographic aspects of the tale; not just the Annunciation, but also the wild man, or *uomo salvatico,* whose adjective in Italian puns on the word for salvation. The historical Festa delle tre Marie, which may have inspired the tale, is also a display of images. As Andreaux points out, the whole problem of icons is how to read them, how to use them, without taking them literally.[11]

At the same time, it is worth pointing out that the Annunciation itself is not supposed to be an allegory, like representational art, or inspired poetry. It is actually to be taken literally. The truth that the subject of painted Annunciation scenes is pointing to is the truth of Christ concealed in Mary's womb. It is not just another legend of divinity consorting with a mortal woman, but God entering history as man. The Incarnation is the ultimate intersection of appearance with reality; it is the moment where the real appears.

Because of its focus on the Annunciation scene, the relation between invisible and visible reality is the crux of this tale that Auerbach chose as an epitome of a new sensory realism. The proverb with which it opens and closes has to do with the contradiction possible between appearances and reality – the evil it is possible to do under the guise of goodness, a possibility facilitated by belief, especially by false belief: "Chi è reo e buono è tenuto, può fare il male e non è creduto" [§5: He who is wicked and held to be good, can cheat because no one imagines he would]. Forced to leave Imola, where he was too well known, Alberto manages to give a convincing show of religiosity and asceticism in

10 Marcus, "The Accommodating Frate Alberto."

11 Andreaux, "Cosa resta degli angeli?"

Venice that enables him to carry on as he likes. Lisetta is a great believer in appearances. She rebukes her confessor for his failure to appreciate her superior beauty, which would gain her any number of lovers if she wanted them: does he not have any eyes in his head ("non avete voi occhi in capo," §13)? Do her charms seem to be those of other women ("paionvi le mie bellezze fatte come quelle di queste altre")? It is a beauty that is literally out of this world, since she asserts confidently that she would be beautiful even in paradise ("sarei bella nel Paradiso"). A large hickey she left under the friar's left breast is evidence of the reality of her intercourse with the angel, a long-lasting sign that should cancel any disbelief: "e se voi non mi credete, guateretevi sotto la poppa manca, là dove io diedi un grandissimo bascio all'agnolo, tale che egli vi si parrà il segnale parecchi dì" [§36: and if you don't believe me, take a look under your left breast, where I gave the Angel such an enormous kiss that it will leave its mark there for the best part of a week]. The devious friar is himself deceived by the apparently "good" man who first harbours him and then betrays him to the violence of the Venetian mob. Finally, there is an uncertainty about reality injected into the conclusion of the tale, since Pampinea does not confirm that the friar died in prison, but only suggests that prison is the place where it is believed [si crede] he must have died: "dove, incarceratolo, dopo misera vita si crede che egli morisse" [§57: and there he is believed to have eked out the rest of his days in wretchedness and misery]. Thus the doubt about appearances – what people say and believe – and their relation to reality persists to the end.

The disconnect between appearance and reality is the essential characteristic of fraud, and the most sinister form of fraud is treachery. The fraudulent but fairly amusing escapades of the friar lead finally to their punishment in the treacherous behaviour, leading to violence, of the sarcastically named "honest man," whom Pampinea associates with the equally ironic label of "Venetian loyalty." Albert Ascoli finds a specifically infernal subtext to the tale in the figure of Frate Alberigo, whose soul Dante encounters in the region of treachery at the bottom of hell, even though this individual is not yet dead. Overstepping the bounds of orthodoxy, Dante here pretends that there are some acts that are so heinous that a soul can go straight to hell while his body stays on earth, inhabited by a devil. In a similar way, Frate Alberto claims that an angelic spirit can take over his body while his own soul has a temporary sojourn in paradise. While both Dante and Boccaccio use deep sarcasm to expose the deceptions of friars, Ascoli further suggests that the tale of Frate Alberto contains a subtle critique of the *Divine Comedy* itself, because in a certain sense it does what Pampinea attacks the friars for doing: deciding who gets to go to heaven.[12]

Heaven is a key motif in the novella. The friars pretend to be lords of paradise, Lisetta boasts that she would be beautiful even there, the angel promises to remove the friar's soul from his body and place it in paradise, whence the friar reports on its delights, and the angel spends the evening with his mistress recounting to her many things "della gloria di vita eterna" [§34: about the glories of the Life Eternal], including details about how the angels make love, which Lisetta stupidly repeats to her marvellously amused and gossipy girlfriend. The feathered wild man ("uomo salvatico") is announced in the public square as the Angel Gabriel, "il quale di cielo in terra discende la notte a consolare le donne viniziane" [§55: who descends by night from Heaven to earth" to amuse [consolare] the women of Venice]. Moreover, heaven has a particular relationship to appearances and reality. Because heaven is an unseen and unseeable place, it has no appearance. Paradise is precisely that which cannot be taken literally. Any description of it is, as Richard of St Victor explained, perforce metaphorical:

> None of the faithful who reads in holy Scripture about hell, the flames of Gehenna and the outer darkness believes that these things have been said figuratively, but he does not doubt that these things exist somewhere truly and bodily ... he does not doubt these things are said not figuratively but literally ... But when we read about a land flowing with milk and honey or heavenly Jerusalem having walls of precious stones, gates of pearl and streets of gold, what person of sane sense would wish to interpret these things according to the literal sense?[13]

Erotic love is one of its most powerful metaphors, as in the Song of Songs, which begins: "Let him kiss me with the kiss of his mouth: for thy breasts are better than wine, smelling sweet of the best ointments." Only a pumpkin-head like Lisetta da Ca' Quirino would take these things literally.

Pampinea's hostility to the dim-witted Lisetta is not just because of her ability to be duped by the friar, which makes her a victim among many. Her folly is not just to imagine that paradise is sex and that an immaterial angel naturally wants to copulate with the woman he admires; it is to miss the point of the Annunciation scene with which she is so familiar. The point of the Annunciation is not the angel, before

---

12 Ascoli, "Boccaccio's Auerbach."

13 Richard of St Victor, *Twelve Patriarchs*, 70.

whose image Lisetta claims to have lit so many candles, but Mary. And Mary *is* paradise. The enclosed garden (*hortus conclusus*) of the Song of Songs was identified with Mary, specifically Mary's womb, locus of the incarnation of Christ: "Hortus conclusus soror mea, sponsa, hortus conclusus, fons signatus" [My sister, my spouse, is a garden enclosed, a garden enclosed, a fountain sealed up].[14] Rupert of Deutz (1075–1129) identifies Mary specifically as the *celestial* paradise, the new paradise in counterpoint to the ancient, earthly paradise of Eden. Frate Alberto's report of how his soul fared while his body was copulating with Lisetta evokes a paradise full of flowers, specifically roses – the flower most associated with Mary, the "mystical rose," the "rose without thorns," to whom the series of prayers known as the "rosary" and numerous rose windows in Gothic cathedrals were dedicated. She is the rose, Dante says, in whom the divine Word made itself flesh.[15] Rachel Fulton, scholar of the medieval cult of Mary, has traced her association with flowers in general:

> As one twelfth-century preacher put it: "These are [the flowers] with whose sweet perfume you filled the house of God, O Mary: the violet of humility, the lily of chastity, and the rose of love." In their beauty and simplicity, the flowers signify Mary's virtues, her virginity, fertility, purity and piety. They may also, however, signify Mary herself. She is the mystic rose (*rosa mistica*) of the Loretan litany, the lily among thorns (*lilium inter spinas*) of the Song of Songs (Song 2:2). She is the rose "of swych vertu" because it was she – in the words of one of the most beautiful late medieval carols – "that bare Jesu."[16]

It is precisely Mary who renders unseen divinity not just literal, but concrete and carnal. The omnipresent scene of the Annunciation is a continual reminder that Mary, a mortal woman, incarnates the living God; she is the visible paradise.

The significance of this sacred mystery is precisely that it is real: that God's unseen reality is now going to be brought down to earth, made flesh. The Incarnation of Christ also problematizes Pampinea's

14 Canticum 4:12.

15 *Paradiso* 23.73–4: "Quivi è la rosa in che 'l verbo divino / carne si fece" [The Rose in which the Word of God became / flesh grows within that garden (trans. Mandelbaum)].

16 Fulton, "The Virgin in the Garden," 1, citing Ekbert of Schönau, Panegyricum ad B. Virginem Deiparam, in *Patrologia latina*, vol. 184, cols. 1009–14, at col. 1012, and "Ther is no rose of swych vertu," *English Medieval Religious Lyrics*, 12.

claim that friars pretend to make themselves lords of paradise, which must in reality be energetically pursued by each individual: "non come uomini che il Paradiso abbiano a procacciare come noi, ma quasi come possessori e signori di quello" [§6: excused, unlike the rest of us, from working their way to Heaven on their merits, for they behave as though they actually own and govern the place]. Yet even before Luther, no one was thought to achieve heaven solely on his own merits. To the question, "Whether anyone without grace can merit eternal life," Thomas Aquinas reponds by pointing to Paul's Letter to the Romans 6:23: "Gratia autem Dei, vita aeterna, in Christo Jesu Domino nostro" [But the grace of God, life everlasting, in Christ Jesus our Lord].[17] It is rather the humble acceptance of Christ, of which Mary is the supreme model, that opens the door to salvation. If there were a doorkeeper to paradise, such as the friars fashion themselves, it would be Mary.

Cormac Ó Cuilleanáin has articulated the corrosive power of Boccaccio's parody, whereby, because of the silliness of Lisetta, "the Blessed Virgin, officially accounted the wisest of women, might seem to the sceptic a remarkably gullible girl."[18] After all, he notes, after the angel's visit, Mary finds that she is pregnant. In other words, Lisetta makes the Madonna look silly. Yet we can also see it the other way around. Mary's wisdom, or rather, Mary's "somma umilità" [§9: sublime humility] (Pampinea uses this unmistakable Marian oxymoron sarcastically to describe Frate Alberto), is the crucial lesson lost on Lisetta.[19] More than her stupidity, it is the *veneziana*'s pride and vanity that give the friar such ample opportunity, what he instantly recognizes as "fertile ground for his plough." Mary is precisely what is missing in this Venice of the "tre Marie."

Whether Pampinea's tale is meant to scandalize her mostly female audience, in the sense of occasioning their spiritual ruin, speaks to the question of what is meant by the *Decameron*'s subtitle of *Galeotto*. Is this a warning that such a book is apt to seduce and corrupt women, to lead them into the damnation of Dante's Francesca, for which she cursed a French romance as the guilty go-between who made her do it? Or does it suggest that the scurrilous tales can themselves be read as a salubrious warning against the dangers of the real world, exposing the frank lust that underlies the aggrandized sufferings of self-styled tragic

17 Thomas Aquinas, *Summa*, IIa IIae 114. 2.

18 Ó Cuilleanáin, *Religion and the Clergy*, 212.

19 Clubb, "Boccaccio and the Boundaries of Love," refers to the phrase "somma umilità" as the "familiar Angelus bell which rings in religious poetry for Christ and his mother, in stilnovist lyrics for their agent, the angel-lady" (193).

lovers like Filostrato? Boccaccio's realism can be read as an exposé, a deflation of myths and pieties. The story of Frate Alberto seems to bring crashing down to earth (or into a sobering plunge into the Grand Canal) the elitist superstructure of *fin amor* and the *dolce stil novo,* with their refined sensibilities, tragic exaggerations, and quasi-religious veneration of women, or angelicized ladies. Both are keyed to the Marian cult, essentialized in the Annunciation scene, which is the fulcrum of this novella. Parody deflates the sacred, and reality without the sacred seems to be only farce. Yet the ferociousness of Pampinea's unforgiving sarcasm suggests that perhaps such parodies are really not all that funny. Friars who seduce women, women who forget who they are, and self-aggrandizing cities who betray their alliances: this is what the world looks like when nothing is sacred.

The Tale of the Three Ill-Starred Sisters (IV.3)

MICHAEL PAPIO

Little critical attention has been paid to the tale of Ninetta, Magdalena, and Bertella, the three sisters whose disastrous demise is set into motion by a single instance of insane fury. For the most part, scholars tend to mention it only briefly in support of some other argument or simply as a story that, in its poetic awkwardness, aesthetically missed the mark. Indeed, Giovanni Getto called it "forse la novella più debole dell'intero *Decameron*" [perhaps the weakest story in the whole *Decameron*].[1] Is Lauretta's tale really the least beautiful of the collection, or are we missing something?

Its immediate purpose in Day Four is to correct the storytellers' thematic course back towards sadness after Filostrato had expressed his displeasure at the overly amusing "tragedy" of Frate Alberto: "Un poco di buono e che mi piacque fu nella fine della vostra novella; ma troppo più vi fu innanzi a quella da ridere, il che avrei voluto che stato non vi fosse" [IV.3.2: The ending of your story was not without a modicum of merit, from which I drew a certain satisfaction. But there was far too much matter of a humorous kind in the part that preceded it, and this I would have preferred to do without]. Lauretta first playfully scolds him for taking pleasure only in heartbreak but then agrees to tell the story of a triple catastrophe: "Troppo siete contro agli amanti crudele, se pur malvagio fine desiderate di loro; e io, per ubidirvi, ne racconterò una [novella] di tre [amanti che] igualmente mal capitarono, poco de' loro amori essendo goduti" [§3: You are being much too unkind towards lovers ... if all you demand is an unhappy ending ... [F]or the sake of obedience I shall tell you a story about three lovers, all of whom met an unpleasant fate before they were able to enjoy their separate

1 Getto, *Vita di forme*, 122.

loves to the full]. Filostrato's desire to wallow in his suffering is, from several points of view, perfectly understandable. He wants to hear sad stories – just as the Fiammetta of the *Elegia* is compelled to write her own – because doleful self-indulgence can be a soothing balm for those who suffer. Lauretta provides here a tale of sorrowful betrayal but further embellishes it with murder, intrigue, sex, vendetta, and torture, all in about eight or nine pages. It is precisely this sense of inharmonious superfluity that has put off many modern readers. Mario Baratto complained:

> Passion (love-jealousy-anger) generates an unrestrained chain of events and crimes. The novella's defects derive not from an inferior style of romance, but instead from an overabundance of psychological elements and love story motifs that remain abstract, that break up and fritter away the rhythm of a story whose dark denouement unmasks more than a few moments of unevenness. After Restagnone is poisoned, the plot falls headlong into a hurried and almost disconcerting series of plot twists. It is there, in the very last pages of the unadorned and hasty story, that the whole novella could have been given greater harmony.[2]

Baratto's observation that the novella simply contains too much stuff should make us wonder why Boccaccio kept adding to it. Had it been composed for a different purpose, he certainly could have ended it in several places, any of which would have produced a significantly different result. He might have put an end to it, for instance, after the three couples arrive in Crete in order to give the reader a utopian fantasy (§19); after Ninetta poisons her husband for a tale of treachery and revenge (§23); after she is apprehended for a drama of rational justice (§24); after Magdalena offers herself to the duke for an inspiring anecdote of self-sacrifice (§28); or even after Folchetto cuts her down in revenge for a macabre moral lesson (§30), as in some of the best tales of Masuccio and Bandello.

Now, if our story really is reducible to the triad of "love-jealousy-anger," it is not hard to understand why Baratto was so disappointed by all its extraneous bits, especially since so many other tales in the *Decameron* deal with similar themes in ways that are as artistically economical as they are famous. Consider, by contrast, the story of Zinevra (II.9), whose husband, after falling for Ambruogiuolo's trick, flies into a jealous rage and orders her murder; or the justly celebrated novella of the eaten heart (IV.9); or the disturbing crimes of Rinieri, whose

---

2 Baratto, *Realtà e stile*, 100–1.

sensation of jilted love – just like Ninetta's – turns to hatred (VIII.7). In fact, the frustration of vengeful jealousy, one of the recurrent motifs of Boccaccio's prose fiction (from the early *Elegia di Madonna Fiammetta* to the late *Corbaccio*), is remarkably flexible. Beyond its role as a catalyst of calamity in the tale that concerns us here, it is fundamental to nearly all stories of betrayed love and therefore useful to his plots, no matter in which direction he wishes to take them. We see its heroic side in Troiolo's fatal rush into battle in the *Filostrato* and in the enduring emotional distress of the cousins Palemone and Arcita in the *Teseida*. We see the theme amusingly derided in the story of Ricciardo di Chinzica (II.10), highlighted in almost all of Day Seven wherever the *gelos* is "humorously" punished, brought to ridiculous extremes in the novella of Calandrino and Niccolosa (IX.5), and even played upon in the minimally vindictive scene of sex on a box (VIII.8). In short, love triangles are everywhere; they span the entire range of narratological outcomes in the *Decameron*, from our tale, in which the scorned Ninetta murders Restagnone and the betrayed Folco runs Magdalena through with his blade, to the remarkably chivalrous liberality of Dianora's husband (X.5) and, ultimately, to the immeasurable meekness of Griselda, who, though woefully aggrieved, resigns herself to accepting Gualtieri's new "bride" (X.10).

Many of the *Decameron*'s best-known stories are loved because their aesthetic representation is immediately intuitable from our modern point of view. In the face of what seems like an overabundance of plot elements or needless repetition, however, we feel restless. We no longer effortlessly recognize the beauty, for example, of a Homeric catalogue of ships or enjoy Lauretta's portrayal of the three sisters' cascading afflictions. If we are to understand and appreciate the story on its own terms, we should first recognize how our modern sensibilities colour our opinions about this tale and then try to filter out those that are historically irrelevant. Lauretta intends to abide by Filostrato's demand for stories regarding "coloro li cui amori ebbero infelice fine" [III.Concl. 6: those whose love ended unhappily]. Unhappiness, though, is not the same as tragedy, which modern readers have commonly (and somewhat anachronistically) assumed to be the underlying component of Day Four's most successful tales. Among such readers was Vittorio Russo, who claimed:

> Boccaccio's dramatic sensitivity is most easily recognized when the themes of pain and happiness are dialectically interwoven among the deeds and the psychology of his characters; that is, in the novellas in which tragedy, in its plainest state, springs forth from the depths of man's irrational

> instincts, from the sudden whirlwind of fate that befalls unprepared creatures and hounds men on the way to their violent and deadly end, where love, virtue and magnanimity are powerless against the blindness and malice of humankind, where tragedy reaches the very limits of violence and horror, and has no hope for a new dawn.[3]

Russo's studies on the subject do often provide convincing analyses of the *Decameron*'s Day Four, but we must be careful not to forget that sublime tragedy of the type described here is more characteristic of Desanctisian Romanticism (or even Frankenstein's monster) than of medieval Italy. Boccaccio never uses the words "tragico" or "tragedia" [tragic, tragedy] anywhere in this work, nor in any preceding work; it is not until first the *De casibus* and then the *Genealogie* and *Esposizioni* that he seems to understand these concepts in a way that would seem somewhat familiar to modern readers. Boccaccio knew Seneca's tragedies as early as the years of the *Fiammetta* but read them principally through the lens of Trevet's commentaries, and knew nothing (or, at best, almost nothing) about Aristotle's notions of fear and pity. The *Decameron* does foreshadow all of this and more, especially in Day Four, but we cannot assume that Filostrato's theme must necessarily be so lofty. Above all, he wants "infelicità" and "tristizia" [unhappiness and sadness], which certainly do appear in the *Decameron*.

We may dispense, then, with sublime self-sacrifice (e.g., Ghismonda's suicide), (proto?)-neo-Gothic ghastliness (e.g., Guiglielmo Rossiglione's wife, who throws herself from a castle window), and stories of great men and women who faced ruin (as in the *De casibus*). Instead, Boccaccio consciously has Lauretta introduce and relate what we could call a moral-philosophical tale. Represented by the short works of authors like Petrus Alphonsi, Jacques de Vitry, and Domenico Cavalca, this genre was once widely popular and figured in practically every educated person's readings. In accordance with a long-established aesthetic code, the narrator would frequently present a series of events, linked together with minimal ambiguity, that gave the reader the opportunity to reflect upon a specific subject, often one of the virtues or vices.

With this in mind, let us read what she says as she prepares to tell her tale (§4):

> Giovani donne, sì come voi apertamente potete conoscere, ogni vizio può in gravissima noia tornar di colui che l'usa e molte volte d'altrui. E tra gli

3 Russo, "Il senso tragico," 30.

altri che con più abandonate redine ne' nostri pericoli ne trasporta, mi pare che l'ira sia quello; la quale niuna altra cosa è che un movimento subito e inconsiderato, da sentita tristizia sospinto, il quale, ogni ragion cacciata e gli occhi della mente avendo di tenebre offuscati, in ferventissimo furore accende l'anima nostra. E come che questo sovente negli uomini avvenga, e più in uno che in un altro, nondimeno già con maggior danni s'è nelle donne veduto, per ciò che più leggiermente in quelle s'accende e ardevi con fiamma più chiara e con meno rattenimento le sospigne.

[Young ladies, as you are perfectly aware, all vices can bring enormous sorrow to those who practise them, and in many cases they also bring affliction to others. But it seems to me that the one that leads us into danger more swiftly than any other is the vice of anger. For anger is nothing more than a sudden, thoughtless impulse, which, set in motion by a feeling of sadness, expels all reason, plunges the mind's eye into darkness, and sets our mind ablaze with raging fury. And although men are not immune to this particular vice, and some men are more prone to it than others, nevertheless it has been observed to produce its most catastrophic effects among the ladies, for they catch fire more easily, their anger burns more fiercely, and they are carried away by it without offering more than a token resistance. (translation modified)]

The fact that Lauretta's story was told aloud to the other members of the *brigata* adds an oral, performative aspect to the tale that similarly links it to the homiletic tradition, complete with the practically obligatory *thema* and preliminary remarks that evoke the tone of a customary sermon. Naturally, Boccaccio's contemporaries would have easily recognized this "genre" too, if we may call it that, even if the modern reader does not. In fact, unlike other more memorable tales, this one is told almost completely in Lauretta's own voice. Aside from Restagnone's initial proposal that the three couples pool their money and elope (§§12–14), only Folco's scattered suggestion to Ninetta that they escape from the duke's men as fast as possible is recounted in direct speech (§31). The voice that tells us absolutely everything else belongs solely to the narrator. A rough review of the *Decameron* suggests that no other novella is more thoroughly entrusted to the narrative voice than this one. The single vantage point, typical of medieval exempla, explains both the lack of dialogue (which always accompanies character development elsewhere in Boccaccio's works) and the matter-of-fact recounting of the unfortunate events that take place in the wake of an initial ethical lapse. The story's puppet-like characters are not meant to make us cry as much as to encourage reflection. This kind of artistic aesthetic belongs, at least in part, to a medieval didactic tradition that is simply not as easily appreciable nowadays. Like the lion's share of religious art of the fourteenth and earlier centuries, moral stories did not depend on realistic representation to get their messages across; it was often enough to give the impression of verisimilitude against a backdrop of traditional imagery and let the reader fill in the gaps, as necessary.

Only when we recalibrate the novella as an illustration of sin (or moral error), as Lauretta unequivocally affirms, can we appreciate some of its often-overlooked value. This is not to suggest, however, that the story is superficial or, indeed, easily "decoded." It simply means that we must make an attempt to look beyond the tale's literal meaning, or plot, to find its greater allegorical usefulness. Boccaccio, consistently mindful of the interconnectedness of morality and mimesis, explicitly chose the tale of the three sisters – including everything that earlier seemed adventitious – to illustrate the perils of anger. Upon hearing Lauretta's introduction, his ideal (coeval) readers surely knew what to expect. Roundly speaking, the pleasure provided by a text like ours derived not from unexpected originality, but instead from the creative combination and/or recombination of ideas and adages that were already familiar. The medieval fascination with the writings of *auctoritates* (moral, poetic, and intellectual precursors) led not only to the endless repetition of *sententiae* (pearls of wisdom) but also to the creation of *florilegia* (collections of wise thoughts) and to an enthusiasm for anecdotes. The more readers knew, the more easily they could participate in the intellectual *divertissement* of identifying links among the text's allusions and kernels of the common cultural legacy. Thanks to longstanding tradition in allegorical and scriptural exegesis, moreover, commentaries of respected works often relied on what would seem nowadays to be a surprisingly large amount of interpretation based on analogy, etymology, and easy moral parallels. Perhaps inevitably, the six and half centuries or so that separate us from Boccaccio's masterpiece have made it more difficult to engage in the erudite call-and-response allusive play that its ideal reader would have anticipated. Hence, we must resort to scholarship and footnotes.

In the next few pages, we shall attempt to identify some of the traditional ideas and assumptions that, though once regularly repeated, have since faded from memory. In normal medieval fashion, Lauretta begins by decrying anger as an irrational "movimento" ("motus," emotion or impulse, §4), caused by sadness, that leads to temporary insanity. The notion that anger is "subito e inconsiderato" [§4: sudden and thoughtless] was practically a commonplace in Boccaccio's wide-ranging readings. For instance, Bede had explained, and was often quoted as having said, that "ira repentino motu nascitur," anger is born of a sudden impulse.[4] What makes this maxim most interesting, however, is the fact that it lies – as is often the case in Boccaccio's writings – at the intersection of the ancient and medieval worlds. The sudden wrathful impulse, when unimpeded by reason, produces a fury that is as old as civilization itself. Boccaccio explains: "con ciò sia cosa che manifesto sia l'ira, poi che il consiglio della ragione ha tolto dell'uomo, col furor suo molti n'abbia già in misera e detestabile ruina condotti" [It is manifestly clear that wrath, after depriving men of their powers of reason, has in its fury already driven many to miserable, detestable ruin],[5] and this particular furor has quite a pedigree. As a matter of fact, the very first word of the *Iliad* – and indeed, of Western literature at large – is Achilles' "menis." Cassian (who had set up one of the first Western European anchorite monasteries precisely in Marseille, where our tale begins) reminds his readers that "irae conterendus est furor, tristitiae superanda dejectio" [the fury of wrath must be quashed, and the dejection of sorrow overcome].[6] Hugh of St Victor likewise warns that "Ira est furor injustus, vel illicita insania mentis commotae" [Anger is unjust fury, or the illicit madness of a distressed mind].[7] Horace's clever quip that "ira furor brevis est" [anger is short-lived madness][8] even finds its way into Petrarch's *Canzoniere*, "Ira è breve furore" [anger is brief madness],[9] and its prose equivalent pops up in Seneca's *De ira*: "Quidam itaque e sapientibus viris iram dixerunt brevem insaniam" [Certain wise men, therefore, have claimed that anger is temporary madness].[10] Whether Greek or Roman, ancient or "modern," each of these authors addressed the universal emotion of anger together with its consequences. Although a lot of fourteenth-century religious prose overlooks it, the contemplation of emotions was a mainstay not only of medieval Christian morality, but also of ancient philosophy.

The two main pre-Christian schools of thought regarding anger were the Stoic and the Aristotelian. The Stoics, whom Boccaccio knew through Seneca directly, and indirectly by way of Cicero, believed in the

4 Bede, *De orthographia*, col. 90.136a.
5 Boccaccio, *Esposizioni*, VII.all.125 (trans. Papio).
6 Cassian, *Instituti*, 225b.
7 Hugh of St Victor, *Expositio moralis in Abdiam*, 401a.
8 Horace, *Epistles*, I.2.62.
9 Petrarch, *Canzoniere*, 232.12.
10 Seneca, *De ira*, 106–7.

principle of *apatheia*, according to which all emotional extremes were to be avoided (including hilarity, unfortunately). More specifically, they taught that the wise sage must never allow reason to be subsumed by the intellectual anarchy of anger. Aristotle, however, felt that a certain measure of anger was a healthy and even necessary part of *eudaimonia*. He wrote: "Non irasci enim in quibus oportet, insipientis esse videtur, et qui non ut oportet, neque quando neque quibus oportet. Videtur autem non sentire neque tristari" [A man seems to be foolish who does not get angry at the things he should both in regard to the manner, the time, and the persons. Such a one appears not to feel things nor to be pained at them].[11] Of course, Aristotle sought wherever possible the *aurea mediocritas* or "golden mean" (the well-balanced state of mind that yields to neither extreme), also known as *metriopatheia*. This more measured approach was embraced by scholastics and entered easily into Catholic doctrine. One who exceeds the acceptable limits of anger falls prey to the evil of wrath, yet one who does not feel enough anger, at the right time and in proper measure, is equally blameworthy for the contrary defect, which is translated as *mansuetudo* in Latin and most often rendered as "meekness" in English. This delicate balance is the goal of ethical self-control, just as Aquinas explains in the opening pages of the twelfth *quaestio* in his *De malo*, where he clearly outlines the mistakes of the Stoics and corrects them according to a complex web of considerations on intentionality and inclination of appetite. Anger is attenuated by meekness, and the opposite is likewise true. The key to knowing whether one's anger is acceptable therefore meant knowing whether the *appetitus irae* was directed towards just ends and in proper measure.

These are the same considerations that underlie Boccaccio's notions of *ira bona* in his discussion of Filippo Argenti in *Inferno* 8 (and would presumably have returned in a discussion of Marco Lombardo and free will had his commentary stretched to the middle of *Purgatorio*). The wise man, as Boccaccio explains through the *Corbaccio*'s jilted lover, depends on reason in order to moderate his anger:

> Io dirò il vero: questo m'indusse a tanta indignazione d'animo che io fui alcuna volta assai vicino ad usare parole che poco onore di lei sarebbono state; ma pure alcuna scintilletta di ragione, dimostrandomi che molto maggiore vergogna a me, ciò faccendo, acquisterei che a lei, da tale impresa, non poco ma molto turbato mi ritenne. (115)

---

11 Thomas Aquinas, *Commentary*, 255.

> [I will tell the truth: this [the widow's derision] induced such indignation in my mind that I was often very close to using words that would have dishonored her; but since some small spark of reason still showed me that I would bring far greater shame upon myself than upon her by doing so, despite my great agitation, I restrained myself.] (trans. Cassell)

When the punishment fits the crime and is used properly towards righteous ends, as in Dante's angry reaction to Filippo Argenti or in that of the *Corbaccio*'s derided lover, it is not sinful anger but corrective indignation that flares up.

Lauretta, forced to tell a tale of sadness, simultaneously creates a cautionary one, perhaps more for the purposes of edification than entertainment, by pushing Ninetta over the line into blinding *mala ira*, which brings an avalanche of misfortune and death. If we are not particularly moved by the jealous rage that led to Ninetta's decision to poison her lover, we can nevertheless benefit from the thoughtful consideration of the universal emotions that drove her to it. While we are at it, we should also analyse its consequences. As all philosophers and theologians knew, the sudden impulse of anger is almost always directed towards retribution or vendetta in response to the injury that first caused the sadness. Boccaccio explains: "Dico adunque, che, secondo che ad Aristotele pare nel IIII dell'Etica, che l'ira, la quale meritamente si dee reputar vizio, è un disordinato appetito di vendetta; e per ciò pare questa essere causata da tristizia nata nell'adirato" [I say, then, that according to Aristotle's fourth book of the Ethics, wrath (which must deservedly be considered a vice) is an excessive desire for revenge. Thus, it seems that it is caused by an innate sadness in the wrathful man].[12] This instinctive sequence of sadness-wrath-revenge is played out quite intentionally in our tale. Convinced that Restagnone had betrayed her, Ninetta "in tanta tristizia cadde, e di quella in tanta ira e per conseguente in tanto furor trascorse, che, rivoltato l'amore il quale a Restagnon portava in acerbo odio, accecata dalla sua ira, s'avvisò con la morte di Restagnone l'onta che ricever l'era paruta vendicare" [§22: fell into a state of deep melancholy, which rapidly gave way to anger and finally to blazing fury. All her former love for Restagnone was transformed into bitter hatred, and in a paroxysm of rage she resolved to murder him and thus avenge the affront she believed him to have offered her]. We may conclude that it was inevitable, by the property of transitive relation (unhappy affairs cause sadness and sadness causes wrath), that

12 Boccaccio, *Esposizioni*, VII.all.111 (trans. Papio).

Filostrato's day would contain novellas featuring anger, precisely because they must end unhappily.

Lauretta's tale portrays Ninetta's abandonment of rational thinking in favour of an uncontrolled and excessive desire for vendetta (revenge on Restagnone for having gravely offended her). In the *Decameron*, this type of vengeance is almost always punished in dramatic contexts, as in the case of Bernabò, who explains Zinevra's murder ("Io, vinto dall'ira della perdita de' miei denari e dall'onta della vergogna che mi parea avere ricevuta dalla mia donna" [II.9.62: I was overcome with rage at the loss of my money ... and also with shame at the damage to my honour that I thought my wife had committed]), but is sometimes ridiculed in humorous tales, like that of Ciacco and Biondello (IX.8) or the two Ceccos (IX.4). Here in this tale, however, Boccaccio permits the plot to careen headlong into the kind of Old Testament misfortune that is impossible to defeat. In fact, the part of Lauretta's admonition in which she notes that anger "expels all reason, plunges the mind's eye into darkness, and sets our mind ablaze with raging fury" seems not to be solely the legacy of the Aristotelian-Thomistic line, but also of another, even older, series of motifs that fit very compatibly within the *predica* tradition. The fire-and-brimstone language echoes verses from Psalms: "Turbatus est a furore oculus meus" [Ps. 6:8: My eye is troubled through indignation] and "Miserere mei, Domine, quoniam tribulor; conturbatus est in ira oculus meus, anima mea, et venter meus" [Ps. 30:10: Have mercy on me, O Lord, for I am afflicted: my eye is troubled with wrath, my soul, and my belly], verses that were very commonly used to flesh out a *thema*, particularly one regarding the perils of anger. In fact, Gregory's "Ira quippe per vitium oculum mentis excaecat, ira autem per zelum turbat" [Anger blinds the eye of my mind with sin, and anger troubles it with jealousy][13] seems particularly relevant to our tale.

If Baratto was unmoved by "psychological elements and love story motifs that remain abstract,"[14] it seems unlikely that this "defect" similarly disappointed the members of the *brigata*. As soon as the other storytellers heard Lauretta's introduction, they likely knew that the plot would be somewhat secondary to the inherent moral message. At this juncture, it is important to consider the final lines of her introduction:

> Laonde, veggendoci naturalmente a ciò inchinevoli, e appresso raguardato come la nostra mansuetudine e benignità sia di gran riposo e di

13 Gregory, *Moralium in Job*, 726c.

14 Baratto, *Realtà e stile*, 100.

piacere agli uomini co' quali a costumare abbiamo, e così l'ira e il furore essere di gran noia e di pericolo, acciò che da quella con più forte petto ci guardiamo, l'amor di tre giovani e d'altrettante donne, come di sopra dissi, per l'ira di una di loro di felice essere divenuti infelicissimi intendo con la mia novella mostrarvi. (§7)

[Bearing in mind, then, that we [women] have a natural propensity to fly into a temper, that our meekness and goodness have a pleasing and very soothing effect upon our menfolk, and that anger and fury can bring about so much peril and anguish, I intend to strengthen our will to resist this vice by telling this story of mine, which, as I said above, concerns the love of three men and three young women, and which shows how, through the anger of one of these latter, their happiness was transformed into complete and utter misery. (translation modified)]

If we still had any doubt about the didactic style that Lauretta here assumes, the phrase "come di sopra dissi" [as I said above] should remove it. If women were more naturally disposed to compassion, it must have been all the more interesting to hear about an ideal wife who went so mad that she brought down her entire family. Like the myths of Phaedra and Medea (both treated by Seneca in plays that Boccaccio knew well), Ninetta's novella invites us to witness a family's undoing by wrath and to learn something from it.

Set, as we have noticed, in Marseille, her novella tells of a rich merchant named N'Arnald Civada, who has three daughters. The fact that it features three sisters – in addition even to all the foregoing – seems to beg the reader to look, as Boccaccio the commentator certainly did, for allegorical clues to decipher. In the light of the philosophical discourse provided by Lauretta's introduction to anger, we think immediately of the Furies, whose very name has just been defined. The Furies, also known (as Boccaccio himself explains) as the Erinyes, Dirae, Eumenides, Harpies, and Hounds of the Styx, are infernal female beings who specialize in anger and insanity, betrayal and vendetta, love and hatred. The following quotation comes from Boccaccio's explanation of the Furies' appearance in Dante's *Inferno* at a tower's peak above the walls of Dis. If we did not know better, though, we could very well take it as a moral reading of our novella. He writes:

Ma, acciò che noi possiam vedere quello che alla presente intenzione è di bisogno, si vuol guardare ciò che sotto così monstruose favole sentissono i poeti, e primieramente quel che volessero dire queste Furie essere state figliuole d'Acheronte e della Notte. Della qual cosa pare che questa possa

> essere la ragione: pare che sia di necessità che, avendo noi separata la ragione e seguendo l'appetito, che, non avvegnendo le cose secondo che noi disideriamo, ne debba turbazion seguitare, la quale ha a torre da noi e a rimuovere allegreza. La qual perturbazione non si riceve se non per malvagio giudicio, procedente da animo offuscato da ignoranza; e perseverando la perturbazione, e, come il più delle volte avviene, divegnendo per la perseveranza maggiore, conviene che proceda ad alcuno atto, sì come quella che continuamente molesta il perturbato: e questo atto, non regolato dalla ragione, sarà di necessità furioso. Per la qual cosa assai convenevolmente si può comprendere questo atto furioso esser nato dall'aver cacciata la letizia e la quiete della mente per la turbazion presa, e questo primo atto potersi chiamare Acheronte, che tanto vuol dire quanto "senza allegreza"; e, appresso, avere la perturbazion ricevuta essere avvenuto per ignoranzia d'animo: e la ignoranzia è simillima alla notte, e così questa seconda cagione, cioè la notte della ignoranzia, aver causata la furia della turbazion seguita.[15]
>
> [In order for us to be able to grasp what is essential to the author's intentions here, we must take into consideration what the poets represented beneath the surface of their monstrous fables, beginning with what they meant by saying that the Furies were the daughters of Acheron and Night. It seems that the reason for this assertion comes from the fact that, once we have cast away reason in order to follow our desires and then have seen that things do not happen as we would like, a great agitation must perforce arise that strips our happiness from us and destroys it. We are only assailed by this great distress, however, as a result of bad judgment, which derives in turn from a mind that is clouded by ignorance. When this agitation goes unchecked, it grows even greater (which is most often the case) and, because it incessantly disturbs whomever it afflicts, it eventually bursts forth in some sort of action, which, being beyond the control of reason, is inevitably one of fury. In this light, one can quite obviously see that this furious action was the result of having cast out happiness and mental serenity in exchange for agitation. This initial act can be called Acheron, which means something like "without happiness." Hence, once this agitation is discernible, we can see both that it came about from mental ignorance, which is very similar to night, and that this second cause (the night of ignorance) is what brought about the fury that arose from the agitation.]

In both the *Esposizioni* and the *Genealogie*, Boccaccio's comments regarding these three sisters go on at some length. What is most important for our purposes here, as in nearly all cases of medieval allegorical

---

15 Boccaccio, *Esposizioni*, IX.all.23–5 (trans. Papio).

interpretation, is that the principal moral components of our story are suitably aligned with traditional hermeneutic patterns. As medieval commentators knew, the Furies are a literary personification of a deeper moral crisis, but so too must our three sisters be, especially as their moral interpretation (the danger of wrath) is so very similar to the Furies'. What, then, caused the avalanche of disasters in Ninetta's tale? Boccaccio has already told us: "this furious action was the result of having cast out happiness and mental serenity in exchange for agitation." He who intentionally seeks agitation and unhappiness, as Filostrato does in mandating the theme of unhappy love throughout Day Four, obviously runs the risk of falling into anger, fury, and calamity. Lauretta's tale very cleverly abides by the rules but simultaneously provides a cautionary novella about the error of vice.

We shall now review our story's plot in the light of what we have been considering in these last few pages. Three sisters from southern France (an excellent geographical setting for jealousy, considering the prominent role of that emotion in Capellanus, the Provençal poets, the French romances, and even the *fabliaux*) become involved with three young men. And it is jealousy, as the rubric shows, that lights the powder keg of trouble. Lauretta specifically tells us that Ninetta becomes enraged upon believing that she has been betrayed by Restagnone; however, the narrating voice also refuses to confirm that the adulterous love has actually been consummated. (This odd detail must surely have been added in order to accentuate the perils of impetuousness and a loss of self-control.) Gravely offended by the injury of his treachery, Ninetta feels overpowering sadness and loses her mind. A victim of sudden fury (or brief insanity), enveloped in the darkness of ignorance and now untethered from reason, she chooses vendetta over meekness, killing her lover with poison. The remaining plot elements are then given to us, one falling domino at a time, until the inevitable destruction of the three couples is complete.

What may have initially seemed to be a hodgepodge of plot elements can now be reorganized into a convincingly coherent whole. Briefly put, we see two acts of infidelity, two murders, and two innocent family members brought down by uncontrollable forces that we are tempted to call fate. The chain of events begins with Restagnone's ill-advised flirtation (described with Dantean tones as "folle amore" [§34: reckless love]), which causes Ninetta to murder him. Her twin sister, Magdalena, who magnanimously gives herself to the duke in exchange for Ninetta's freedom, thereby repeats the same betrayal of love, causing her own husband to lose his mind too in what symmetrically amounts to the male version of the same cause-and-effect relationship (or, from a prescriptive perspective, moral shortcoming). The two murderers disappear into the night, but poor Ughetto and Bertella, the most blameless of the victims, are imprisoned and tortured before managing at last to bribe the guard and to flee penniless still farther from home. Why? Because the consequences of anger logically may extend beyond those immediately involved.

We may wonder, in conclusion, what this tale means for the others of its day and, in fact, for those of all the other days. As usual, the *Decameron* offers no definitive answers. Instead, the story of the ill-starred sisters is simply one single tile of the *Decameron*'s entire mosaic, which seems, from one angle, to portray one thing and, from another, something else. At best, we may say that it is but one perspective on destructive anger that belongs in the line running from the *Fiammetta* forward. There are, of course, many other points of view and many other ways of examining anger, even within the *Decameron* itself. For example, we realize that Andreuccio has begun to learn only once he gets angry (II.5.48). Similarly, we see in the behaviour of the lady from Gascoigne that there are other ways to deal with the desire for vendetta (I.9.6), and from King Agilulf we learn that jealous anger can be assuaged without any suffering at all (III.2). Currado Gianfigliazzi controls his anger, in the most admirable of ways, and forgives Chichibio (VI.4). Another Currado is convinced not to kill his daughter in rage (II.6.38), and Lizio da Valbona likewise eschews anger in favour of a peaceful resolution (V.4). And, oddly enough, Dioneo tells Fiammetta to reveal the name of her lover, lest he be stolen from her and she be forced to get angry (X.Concl. §15). Perhaps most interesting, though, is what the novella of the ill-starred sisters – being a prescriptive lesson on moderated anger – can teach us about those tales in the *Decameron* that spring to life from the extremes of the Aristotelian ethical spectrum: sinful wrath and sinful meekness. As Tolstoy observes on the first page of *Anna Karenina* (beneath the epigraph "Vengeance is mine"), "All happy families are alike; each unhappy family is unhappy in its own way." For our purposes, we could rephrase this as: all tales that conform to the rules are quite similar, whereas those that break them are different each in its own way. The tale of the scholar and the widow (VIII.7) is an example of excessive anger that goes unpunished, and the story of Griselda (X.10) is the opposing example of excessive meekness. Both of these tales are easily classifiable as *capolavoretti*, or mini-masterpieces, far more memorable than ours. Nevertheless, and even despite its adherence to the aesthetic norms of a genre of short fiction that may no longer appeal to modern tastes, Lauretta's novella certainly does possess a beauty of its own. One simply has to know where to look for it.

Love, Heroism, and Masculinity in the Tale of Gerbino (IV.4)

GUR ZAK

Story IV.4 of the *Decameron*, which tells about the tragic love of "il bel Gerbino" [IV.4.14: gallant Gerbino] and the Saracen Princess of Tunis, has received relatively minimal critical attention. Scholars who have offered analysis of the tale have outlined its epic and chivalric roots and the emblematic conflict between love and duty that characterizes it.[1] Torn between his love for the princess and the pledge of honour given by his grandfather, King William II of Sicily, to the King of Tunis, Gerbino chooses to follow his heart – to devastating effect, as both his beloved and himself pay with their lives. For critics such as Giovanni Getto, Victoria Kirkham, and Guido Ruggiero, this demonstration of the disastrous consequences of *amore* offers a universal warning about the perils of unbound desire: "the fourth tale explores how love can become literally a mad passion destroying a young man completely, making no crime too great to commit."[2] In its focus on the perils of uncontrolled passion, as Ruggiero perceptively suggests, *Decameron* IV.4 continues a theme that was also central to the previous tale, *Decameron* IV.3.[3]

1 While the story, as Branca has noted, does not have a specific literary antecedent, it is filled with allusions and parallels to works such as Virgil's *Aeneid* and the twelfth-century *chanson de geste l'Histoire de Huon de Bordeaux*, as well as medieval retellings of "the matter of Britain." See Branca's note in his edition, 516n2. Studies of the tale include Baratto, *Realtà e stile*, 324–7; Francillon, "Quelques observations"; Getto, *Vita di forme*, 123–6; Paden, "Elissa," 144–5; Psaki, "The One and the Many," 241–3; and Ruggiero, "Getting a Head," 1168–9.

2 Ruggiero, "Getting a Head," 1168. According to Kirkham, *Decameron* IV.4, like the other tragedies of Day Four, shows how "disaster is certain when love and marriage are driven apart." See Kirkham, "Love's Labors," 89. See also Getto, *Vita di forme*, 125, and Alfano's remarks in Boccaccio, *Decameron*, ed. Quondam et al., 671.

3 Ruggiero, "Getting a Head," 1168. While IV.3 and IV.4 concentrate on the particular role of desire in bringing about tragedy, other stories of Day Four emphasize the tragic potential of attempts by authority figures to curb love among the young. See especially IV.1 and IV.8.

While the demonstration of the destructive potential of desire is undoubtedly essential to the tale, in this chapter I would like to argue that *Decameron* IV.4 explores the nature of heroism and masculinity as they pertain to love. The relationship between heroism, masculinity, and desire was a major concern for Boccaccio, starting early on in his writings, receiving its most elaborate treatment in his early vernacular prose epic, the *Filocolo*. In this work, Boccaccio established the active, daring, and relentless pursuit of one's object of desire as the cornerstone of heroism and masculinity, bringing together in the figure of his protagonist Florio traits associated with the heroes of both epic and romance. In *Decameron* IV.4, Boccaccio returns to this ideal from his youth but engages in a critical dialogue with it, stressing the dangers of amorous heroics and subtly pointing to an alternative model of heroism and masculinity, one that exalts moderation and self-control. The dialogue with the *Filocolo* in *Decameron* IV.4 thus has both ethical and poetic dimensions, as it points to Boccaccio's later critique of the genre of romance and the heroic ideals associated with it. To fully appreciate the significance of the tale of Gerbino, we need to examine it not only in the context of the *Decameron*'s stories, but also as it is situated within Boccaccio's overall literary oeuvre, a frame of reference that is often ignored in *Decameron* scholarship.

The following discussion of heroism and masculinity in *Decameron* IV.4 will begin with a short summary of the tale; we will then turn to the critical dialogue the story of Gerbino holds with the model of heroic masculinity introduced in the *Filocolo*, discussing its emphasis on the disastrous effects of Gerbino's heroics and his general propensity to emotional excess. The final section will offer some reflections on the way the story of Cimone in *Decameron* V.1 revisits issues raised in IV.4, complicating further the dialogue on heroic masculinity in Boccaccio's works. The exploration of the trajectory Florio-Gerbino-Cimone will thus allow us to appreciate the nature and methods of "the ethical work" occurring within Boccaccio's fictions: his narratives tend to introduce an ethical dilemma and then return to it over and over again from various angles, perspectives, and literary genres, without ever offering a definitive answer to the issue at hand.

~

Narrated by Elissa – one of the names of Carthaginian Dido and thus a fitting choice for an epic-like tale taking place in the Mediterranean – the tale of Gerbino begins with a historical genealogy that places us within the courtly context of the medieval Kingdom of Sicily. Elissa introduces King William II, the renowned King of Sicily from 1166 to 1189, who, "come i ciciliani vogliono" [§4: according to the Sicilians], had two children. (King William II is an actual historical figure; however, in actuality he had no children – a point to which we shall return.) One of the children, Ruggieri, died young and left a son – Gerbino. The king raised his grandson with much diligence, turning him into the finest knight, "famoso in prodezza e in cortesia" [§4: famous for his daring and courtesy]. The renown of Gerbino's qualities reached the ears of the beautiful and noble Saracen Princess of Tunis (who is left unnamed in the tale). Following the courtly convention of *amor de lonh* – the falling in love from afar – she fell deeply in love with him. The princess's reputation had similarly reached the ears of Gerbino, who fell for her in a like manner. The story, as F. Regina Psaki has pointed out, takes care to describe their falling in love through parallel constructions that underscore the reciprocal nature of their love: "non meno che di lui la giovane infiammata fosse, lui di lei aveva infiamato" [§7: no less than the young woman was enflamed by love for him, he was burning with a love for her (my translation)].[4]

Unable to meet in person, owing to the geographic – and likely religious – circumstances, the two young lovers manage to communicate their love through messengers and the exchange of precious jewellery.[5] This state of affairs continues until the princess's father, the King of Tunis, decides to marry his daughter to the King of Granada. Before sending his daughter to her future husband, the latter, who has become aware of Gerbino's ardent love, asks King William for a guarantee that nothing unbecoming will take place during his daughter's sea-voyage to Granada. The elderly King William, who is completely oblivious of his young grandson's love, willingly gives the pledge in the form of a glove – a mark of total obligation in the romance tradition.[6]

4 Psaki, "The One and the Many," 241. On Boccaccio's critical engagement with the courtly convention of love by hearsay in *Dec.* IV.4, see Asaro, "Unmasking the Truth."

5 Although Boccaccio's attitude towards Muslims in the *Decameron*, as Smarr has shown, is strikingly positive, it is worth noting that encounters of Christian men and Saracen women in the work generally end with the demise of the men (whether physical or spiritual). Consider, in this regard, the fate of Alatiel's lovers in *Dec.* II.7 and the hermit infatuated with Alibech in III.10. At the same time, as Smarr points out, the men's fall is generally attributed to their own inability to control their desire – a point which is highly relevant also to IV.4 (which Smarr does not discuss). See Smarr, "Other Races and Other Places."

6 See Branca's note in his edition, 520n9.

The young lovers, as we expect, are devastated. The princess decides to send a messenger to Gerbino, prompting him to prove both his manhood and his love – "se cosí fosse valente uomo come si diceva e se cotanto l'amasse" [§14: whether he was as daring a man as people reported, and whether he loved her as deeply]. True masculinity, for the princess, consists of actively and daringly pursuing one's desires. Yet, aware of his grandfather's pledge, Gerbino is now torn between his beloved's promptings and his familial duties. Just like Virgil's Aeneas, who is torn between his love for Dido and his destiny as the founder of Rome, or the chivalrous Tristan, who is conflicted about whether to pursue his love for Iseult or remain dutiful to his uncle, King Mark, so Gerbino has to make the fatal choice between love and duty. "[P]er non parer vile" [§15: not wishing to appear a coward], Gerbino chooses love, to disastrous effects.

When Gerbino attacks the ship that carries his beloved to Granada, the Saracen sailors show him the glove his grandfather gave as a pledge, yet Gerbino, infatuated with passion, scornfully rejects it. In response, the Saracen sailors murder the princess in front of his eyes and throw her body into the water. Later, when King William II hears the novella (§26) of his grandson's transgression, he sentences him to death without hesitation: "volendo avanti senza nepote rimanere che esser tenuto re senza fede" [§26: preferring to lose his only grandson rather than gain the reputation of being a monarch whose word was not to be trusted]. While Gerbino chose love over familial duty, his grandfather chooses duty over family ties, and the story ends on the grim note of Gerbino's decapitation.

There are several important parallels between the "mini prose epic"[7] of Gerbino and Boccaccio's earlier vernacular epic, the *Filocolo*, composed likely in 1336–8: similar to Gerbino, Florio is a prince who falls in love with a foreigner, the Roman-Christian Biancifiore, who was raised as an orphan in Florio's parents' court in Marmorina (Verona). Unhappy with their son's choice, Florio's pagan parents try to impede his love in various ways. Florio too is thus torn between love and familial duty, ultimately deciding – like Gerbino – to disobey his parents and embark on a heroic expedition at sea in pursuit of his beloved. Before they embark on their respective heroic missions, both Florio and Gerbino address their men in an elevated speech, in which they demonstrate not only their daring but also their rhetorical prowess (*Decameron* IV.4.16; *Filocolo* III.67.3). Gerbino's speech is closely reminiscent of

7 Baratto, *Realtà e stile*, 324.

Florio's earlier address, both beginning with an invitation to their men to recall from their own experience the immense power of *amor*.[8]

Boccaccio's lengthy narrative of Florio's love in the *Filocolo* offers key insights on two conflicting views of heroism and masculinity that govern his works. In the first half of the work, Florio is mostly the epitome of the elegiac lover, ceaselessly lamenting his enforced separation from his beloved and passively waiting for his fortune to change. However, at the end of Book III, the mid-point of the work, Florio is transformed: upon learning that his parents have sold Biancifiore to Italian merchants, the furious Florio decides to take matters into his own hands and undertake a sea-voyage in pursuit of his beloved, directly confronting his fortune.[9] From a passive and "effeminate" figure[10] Florio is transformed into an active and daring hero. His heroic mission allows him not only to obtain his beloved, but also to be converted to Christianity through her mediation, ultimately bringing Christianity to his kingdom. The pursuit of individual desire, characteristic of romance, facilitates in the work the attainment of collective and national goals typical of epic, thus allowing Boccaccio to fashion in the *Filocolo* a new type of hero – the epic hero of love.

Yet while establishing Florio as a new model of heroic masculinity, Boccaccio's lengthy narrative also questions this very model at several junctures in the narrative: in Book II, Florio's father, King Felice, accuses his son of loving "oltre misura" [II.14.3: beyond measure], claiming that being carried away by passion in such manner is in fact the mark of the loss of one's "virile animo" [II.14.3: manly soul]. Towards the very end of the work, it is none other than Florio himself who wonders whether his entire

8 Florio's address to his men near the end of Book III begins as follows: "Cari amici e compagni, quanta forza sia quella d'amore a niuno di voi credo occulta sia, però che ciascuno, sì com'io penso, le sue forze ha provate" [III.67.3: Dear friends and comrades, I believe it is not hidden from any of you how great is the force of love, for I believe each of you has experienced its power]. Gerbino's speech to his companions – a group of "valenti uomini" (IV.4.15) he assembled in Messina – begins thus: "Signori, se voi così valorosi siete com'io vi tegno, niuno di voi senza aver sentito o sentire amore credo che sia, senza il quale, sì come io meco medesimo estimo, niun mortal può alcuna vertù o bene in sé avere" [IV.4.16: Gentlemen ... if you are as gallant as I conceive you to be, I doubt whether there is a single one of you who has never been in love. It is my conviction that no mortal thing who is without experience of love can ever lay claim to true excellence].

9 On Florio's transformation and maritime journey, see also Morosini, "Per difetto rintegrare," 56–108, and "Penelopi in viaggio," 8.

10 Near the beginning of Book III, Florio's host tells him bluntly: "lascia il piangere, il quale è atto feminile e di pusillanimo cuore" [III.3.5: leave off your weeping, which is a womanish act and one showing a pusillanimous heart (modified)].

heroic mission was not a "lunga follia" [V.75.5: long folly], indicating that his subjection to passion was "oltre al ragionevole dovere" [V.75.5: beyond all reasonable measure]. The model of active heroism in the name of love embodied in the figure of Florio is thus challenged in the work by another model, which suggests that the ability to control passions – including love – rather than being carried away by them is the true mark of manhood.

In *Decameron* IV.4, as the close parallels between Gerbino's and Florio's heroic whims and elevated motivational speeches indicate, Boccaccio returns to the model of amorous heroism embodied by the figure of Florio, yet this time solely in order to highlight its perils. The critique of Florio's passion, as it is expressed in the warning of King Felice in the *Filocolo*, takes centre stage in Gerbino's story, posing him as a counter-example to Florio. Not only does *Decameron* IV.4 elaborate on the disastrous effects that Gerbino's actions have on both his beloved and himself, but it also subtly alludes to the wider political implications of his actions, which are also disastrous, the mirror image of Florio's.

In an insightful analysis of the role of Elissa in the *Decameron*, Michael Paden highlights the way in which Elissa's telling of the tale of Gerbino in effect describes the end of Norman rule in Sicily and the beginning of the conflict between Guelfs and Ghibellines in the Italian peninsula.[11] Though Elissa's claim that the Norman King William II had two children was historically incorrect, her story about Gerbino's tragic end gives a dramatic reason why the king had no successor. In reality, King William II produced no heirs, a fact which led to the end of Norman rule in Sicily and the rise of the Hohenstaufen line to the throne. With the rise of the Hohenstaufens, the conflict between Guelfs and Ghibellines in the Italian peninsula ensued.[12] By inventing the figure of Gerbino and his tragic end, Elissa's tale turns his *folle amor* into the very reason why King William II remained without heirs, thus casting Gerbino's desire and actions as the root cause of the demise of Norman rule in Sicily.[13] Whereas Florio's amorous quest was the source of a national triumph in the form of the arrival of Christianity

11 Paden, "Elissa," 144.

12 The House of Staufen, whose castle was at Waiblingen (the origin of the Italian word *ghibellino*), was the traditional foe of the German House of Welf (the origin of the Italian *guelfo*). The ascendancy to power of the Staufen Henry VI and later Friedrich II was thus the beginning of the immense political conflict between Guelfs and Ghibellines in Italy. See Paden, "Elissa," 144–5.

13 The fact that the king's decision to execute his grandson ultimately caused the demise of his kingdom inevitably raises the question whether the execution itself was not excessive. Choosing to be lenient and merciful, the story implies, might have been more appropriate under the circumstances.

to his kingdom, Gerbino's parallel heroism was the cause of a political catastrophe. As opposed to the *Filocolo*, *Decameron* IV.4 thereby asserts the incompatibility of romantic love and the collective or national ends of epic, suggesting that in matters of love moderation and self-control are preferable to unbound daring.

The story's critique of Gerbino's heroism is made further apparent by the way his speech to his men eventually departs from Florio's. When rallying their companions to action, as we have seen, both Florio and Gerbino first urge them to take note of the power of love from their own experience. Following his initial reference to love, Florio goes on to tell his friends that as humans they were not born to live like brutes but rather to pursue virtue and glory – closely echoing Dante's Ulysses' own speech to his companions in *Inferno* 26: "noi non ci nascessimo per vivere come bruti, ma per seguire virtù, la quale ha potenza di fare con volante fama le memorie degli uomini etterne, così come le nostre anime sono" [*Filocolo* III.67.12: we were not born to live like beasts, but to follow virtue, which has the power by means of soaring fame to make the memories of men eternal, just as our souls are (slightly modified)].[14] While Florio echoes the elevated words of Dante's Ulysses, Gerbino chooses to add to his lofty statements on love an invitation to plunder the ship they are about to attack: "e ciò che io amo nella nave che qui davanti ne vedete dimora, la quale, insieme con quella cosa che io piú disidero, è piena di grandissime ricchezze; le quali, se valorosi uomini siete, con poca fatica, virilmente combattendo, acquistar possiamo" [*Dec.* IV.4.17: The object of my love dwells out there upon that ship, which not only holds that which I desire above all else, but is crammed to the gunwales with treasure. If you are brave, and fight manfully, it will not be too difficult for us to take possession of these riches]. Although Gerbino then specifies that he himself is interested only in his beloved, leaving the booty to his companions, the fact that he urges them to attack the ship for its booty casts a negative light on his entire expedition and inevitably calls the reader's attention to the fact that Gerbino himself is about to abduct what is in effect not his. Rather than a virtuous undertaking, Gerbino's amorous heroism is presented as a type of piracy. Again the slight differences in Boccaccio's presentation of his two parallel protagonists underscore his negative view of romantic heroes who chase love at all costs in *Decameron* IV.4.

14 Dante's Ulysses' words are: "Considerate la vostra semenza: / fatti non foste a viver come bruti, / ma per seguir virtute e canoscenza" [*Inferno* 26.118–20: Consider well the seed that gave you birth: / you were not made to live your lives as brutes, / but to be followers of worth and knowledge (trans. Mandelbaum)].

In addition to the stress on the questionable nature and devastating outcomes of Gerbino's heroic whims, *Decameron* IV.4 repeatedly emphasizes his propensity to emotional excess and lack of self-control, a trait that is specifically cast as unmanly and perilous. In the description of Gerbino's *innamoramento* in the beginning of the tale, the narrator describes his desire for the princess as "beyond measure": "disideroso *oltre modo* di vederla" (§8; emphasis added). Later, after Gerbino hears the news of the princess's coming marriage, it is stated that he grieved "senza misura" [§11: without measure (my translation)]. The words "oltre misura" were used, as we have seen, by King Felice in Book II of the *Filocolo* when he critiqued Florio's passion as excessive and hence unmanly. These terms, moreover, are associated from the very beginning of the *Decameron* with perilous lack of reason: in the Proem, the author-narrator describes how from his early youth he was enflamed with a passion "oltre modo" [Proem. §3: beyond measure], describing this passion as a "soverchio fuoco nella mente concetto da poco regolato appetito" [immoderate fire engendered within the mind by ill-restrained appetite (translation modified)]. This unbridled passion, as he specifies, almost brought him to death. From the very beginning of *Decameron* IV.4, Gerbino's desire is thus associated with dangerous lack of self-control.

Gerbino's tendency to emotional excess and lack of control is made further apparent by the description of his reaction to his beloved's horrific death. After the Saracen sailors murder the princess in front of his eyes and throw her body into the water, Gerbino becomes filled with rage and ferociously seeks revenge. Jumping on the enemy's ship and indiscriminately cutting down the sailors, Gerbino is compared to a wild, hungry lion: "non altramenti che un leon famelico nell'armento de' giovenchi venuto or questo or quello svenando prima co' denti e con l'unghie la sua ira sazia che la fame, con una spada in mano or questo or quel tagliando de' saracini crudelmente molti n'uccise Gerbino" [§24: he started laying about him with his sword, cutting down Saracens without mercy on all sides, as though he were a starving lion falling upon a herd of young bullocks and tearing and ripping them apart one after another, intent on appeasing its anger rather than its hunger]. These lines not only portray Gerbino as a raging animal,[15] but they also

15 Branca identifies Virgil's *Aeneid* 9.339 ff. – portraying Nisus's bloody raid in the Rutulians' camp – as the source of Boccaccio's image of the raging lion (see Branca's edition, 523–4n10). The depiction of Gerbino as a lion possibly recalls also the comparison of Turnus to a raging lion in *Aeneid* 12.5–11, a parallel which would further accentuate the uncontrolled and negative nature of his "furor." I thank William Robins for pointing out this parallel to me.

establish a clear parallel between the Saracen sailors' horrendous murder of the princess and his thirst for revenge: his lion-like "svenando" [§24: tearing] of the sailors repeats the way they "svenarono" [§23: slit the veins] of the princess; the use of the adverb "crudelmente" [§24: without mercy] to describe his killing repeats the description of their murder as an act of "crudeltà" [§24: cruelty].

Immediately following his violent revenge, Gerbino recovers his beloved's body from the sea and mourns over it with an abundance of tears: "Quindi, fatto il corpo della bella donna ricoglier di mare, lungamente e *con molte lagrime* il pianse" [§25: He then saw to the recovery from the sea of the fair lady's body, which he mourned over at length, shedding a great many tears (emphasis added)]. The description of his tears anticipates that of tender Lisabetta's weeping in the following story: "*con molte lagrime* della sua lunga dimora si doleva" [§11: she would burst into tears because of his failure to return (emphasis added)]. Following the death of the beloved, Gerbino thus wavers between the extremes of animalistic rage and intense mourning. And while such an extreme display of emotions may be understandable given the horrific unfolding of the events, it also underscores Gerbino's lack of self-control throughout the story.

Such an oscillation between the extremes of sorrow and vengeful rage, we should remember, also defines the two central – and highly volatile – male figures of the day: the king of the day, Filostrato, and the central protagonist of the opening tale, Tancredi. In the case of both, a form of excessive and frustrated love leads to an oscillation between extreme sorrow and cruel rage. In the conclusion to Day Three, Filostrato bemoans his sorrows in love and chooses the theme of the day – tragedies of lovers – because of his view that such tragedies mostly resemble his own miserable condition.[16] However, the members of the *brigata* consider his choice of theme to be an overly cruel revenge upon lovers: "Troppo siete contro agli amanti crudele" [IV.3.3: you are being too cruel towards lovers (slightly modified)]. Tancredi, on his part, first responds to the discovery of his beloved daughter's illicit affair with uncontrolled weeping: "piagnendo sí forte come farebbe un fanciul ben battuto" [IV.1.29: began to wail as though he were a child who had been soundly beaten]. His tearful response is strategically contrasted with the self-control of his daughter, who, as the story specifies, manages to

16 "[C]he io prima per altro abandonato e poi non sia sempre di male in peggio andato; e così credo che io andrò di qui alla morte" [III.Concl. §5: I have invariably been forsaken to make way for another. Things have gone from bad to worse for me, and I do not suppose they will improve to my dying day].

remarkably overcome her "feminine" propensity to tears and laments (IV.1.30). Tancredi's excessive tears are thus specifically presented as unmanly and anticipate the eventual lack of control exhibited in his vengeful act of "crudeltà" (IV.1.44) – the decision to execute Guiscardo and cut out his heart. Gerbino's oscillation between the extremes of sorrow and vengeful rage therefore recalls the emotional volatility of Filostrato and Tancredi, further highlighting his tendency to perilous excess.

The grouping together of unbound love, sorrow, and vindictive anger, as Michael Papio demonstrated in the previous chapter, is also central to the preceding tale in the collection, *Decameron* IV.3. This emotional linkage, as Papio further highlighted, has strong Aristotelian and Thomistic roots. However, while in IV.3 the tale's narrator, Lauretta, specifies that women are particularly prone to such emotional volatility (IV.3.5–7), the example of Gerbino – like those of Filostrato and Tancredi – shows how men are no less susceptible to such precariousness. Rather than a model of heroic masculinity, Gerbino emerges as yet another example of damaged manhood over the course of Day Four.

The story's negative commentary on Gerbino's love and actions culminates in the grim depiction of his death, with which the story ends. As opposed to other examples of romantic heroes, such as Tristan and Iseult and several other tragic couples of Day Four (IV.1, IV.6, IV.7, IV.8, IV.9), at the end of *Decameron* IV.4 there is no mention of a shared grave or a cathartic public mourning of the couple's death, and only a brief reference to their "mala morte" (IV.4.27).[17] While Gerbino ostensibly chose the same path as Tristan, pursuing his love at all costs, Elissa's austere conclusion suggests that there was nothing romantic about Gerbino's love and death. The lovers' death is nothing but grim, and it is perhaps for this reason that Elissa's story is the only one in Day Four that the king of the day, Filostrato, somewhat commends; its bleak outcome is tragic enough for his taste.[18]

In the Proem of the *Decameron*, after the author-narrator describes the excessive love which has plagued him since his youth, he states that at present, with the healing passage of time, he is able to enjoy the delectable feeling which "[amor] è usato di porgere a chi troppo non si mette ne' suoi più cupi pelaghi navigando" [Proem. §5: love habitually

17 On Boccaccio's dialogue in Day Four with this romantic convention, see Francillon, "Quelques observations," 27, and Picone, *Boccaccio e la codificazione*, 192–3.

18 "Finita la novella d'Elissa e alquanto dal re commendata" [IV.5.2: When Elissa's story came to an end, the king bestowed a few words of praise upon it].

reserves for those who refrain from venturing too far upon its deepest waters]. Gerbino, we may therefore surmise, is precisely an example of the danger of venturing too far into the sea – both metaphorically and literally – going into excess in both love and the heroics performed in its name. Whereas the example of Florio highlighted the merits of heroic action in the name of love, Gerbino's story alerts the reader to the possibility that self-control in matters of love is the true mark of heroic masculinity.[19]

As is always the case with Boccaccio's works, however, Elissa's portrayal of the dangers of amorous heroism in IV.4 is by no means the final word on the issue in the *Decameron*. The opening story of Day Five, immediately following the tragic Day Four, repeats almost verbatim crucial features from the tale of Gerbino and engages in a dialogue with it – a dialogue that appears to reaffirm the value of active heroism embodied in the figure of Florio. Narrated by Panfilo, the story takes place in ancient Cyprus and deals with Galesus, a.k.a. Cimone ("simpleton"). While a noble-born young man like Gerbino, Cimone is presented in the beginning of the story as a complete imbecile, the opposite of "il bel Gerbino." All of his father's efforts to cultivate and educate Cimone fail, and he leads a brutish life in the woods. This state of affairs continues until one day Cimone happens upon the beautiful Iphigenia near a secluded fountain in a meadow. The sight of her physical beauty (rather than the princess's reputation, which Gerbino only heard about) instils love in Cimone's heart. It is the quickening of love that finally manages to transform him into a "gentiluomo," becoming "il piú leggiadro e il meglio costumato e con piú particulari virtú che altro giovane alcuno che nell'isola fosse di Cipri" [V.1.20: the most graceful, refined, and versatile young man in the island of Cyprus].

As in the case of Gerbino, however, Cimone's beloved is betrothed to another, a certain nobleman from Rhodes. Further like Gerbino, Cimone refuses to accept his misfortune and decides to boldly confront it head-on, planning an attack on the Rhodian ship that carries his beloved to her future husband. When he and his valiant men catch the

19 It is worth noting, in this regard, that in the beginning of *Dec.* X.7, King Charles's successful effort to control his destructive desire for the two young daughters of his host is described as "virile magnificenzia" (X.7.2).

ship at mid-sea, Cimone jumps upon the enemy's deck and strikes his adversaries "con maravigliosa forza" [V.1.28: with astonishing vigour]; he is compared – exactly like Gerbino – to a "fiero ... leone" [V.1.28: raging lion]. In stark opposition to the Saracen sailors in *Decameron* IV.4, however, the Rhodians surrender on the spot, and instead of murdering Iphigenia, they hand her over to the raging Cimone (V.1.33).

Cimone's heroic conquest is followed by various setbacks, until he finally manages to violently abduct Iphigenia one last time and return triumphantly with her to Cyprus. Thus, even though his love and heroism are no less extreme than Gerbino's – the narrator refers to the way he "in alcune cose ... trasandasse" [V.1.23: was inclined ... to carry his love for Iphigenia to extremes] – his story ends *in bono*. Although Cimone does not break a pledge like Gerbino, his repeated abductions of Iphigenia and extremely violent actions towards the end of the story undermine the social and political order no less than Gerbino's actions. The fact that in Cimone's case amorous heroics prove triumphant thus opens up again the question of the *Decameron*'s view of active heroism and the nature of masculinity, leading the reader to wonder whether in matters of love one should be measured and prudent, avoid perilous excess, or rather do everything in one's power to obtain the object of desire, no matter the cost.

While the answer to this dilemma is ultimately left without a definitive answer in the *Decameron*, the text itself still raises serious doubts regarding Cimone's actions. Unlike in *Decameron* IV.4, however, in V.1 these doubts relate especially to the fate of the female protagonist Iphigenia: while Cimone's heroics end well as far as he is concerned, in the case of Iphigenia the issue is much less certain.[20] Whereas in *Decameron* IV.4, as we have seen, the narrator took care to emphasize from the beginning the reciprocal nature of the protagonists' love, in *Decameron* V.1 the love is clearly one-sided, as Iphigenia repeatedly objects to Cimone's advances and responds with horror to his recurring abductions of her.[21] Tellingly, the ending of the story associates its happy outcome only with the male figures: "Cimone con Efigenia lieto si tornò in Cipri e Lisimaco similmente con Cassandrea ritornò in Rodi; e ciascun lietamente con la sua visse lungamente contento nella sua terra" [V.1.70: Cimone with Iphigenia returned happily to Cyprus, and Lysimachus similarly returned to Rhodes with Cassandra. And each lived happily

20 On this aspect of *Decameron* V.1, see also Sherberg, *Governance*, 132–7.

21 "[P]iagnendo Efigenia a Cimon concedettono" [V.1.33: handed over the weeping Iphigenia to her captor] and "Le novelle spose cominciarono a piagnere e a gridare" [V.1.66: The brides began to cry and scream].

ever after with his lady in the land of his birth (translation modified)]. As to the women's view of their situation, the story leaves us in the dark, thus possibly alerting our attention to the one-sided nature of Cimone's heroics.

But it is not only the condition of Iphigenia that raises concern about Cimone's actions. As Michael Sherberg pointed out, Cimone's violent and ruthless attack on Iphigenia's wedding towards the end of the tale suggests that his transformation into the perfect gentleman through the meditation of love was only superficial.[22] Inwardly, he remained a brute. Rather than an emblem of stilnovistic notions of the ennobling power of love and a model of active heroism, Cimone emerges as yet another example of the destructive power of *amor* and the actions done in its name. Even though Cimone succeeded where Gerbino failed, the story still raises grave doubts regarding his heroic undertaking, developing further the critical dialogue with the heroic model of Florio that was central to *Decameron* IV.4. In matters of love, *Decameron* IV.4 and V.1 suggest, self-control and regulated desire should be seen as the true marks of heroism and masculinity, thus possibly pointing to Boccaccio's transition in the *Decameron* from chivalric and romantic codes of manhood to more middle-class ones. At the same time, the attainment of such a balanced disposition, as the tales of the *Decameron* indicate over and over, is quite hard to navigate.

22 Sherberg, *Governance*, 134–7.

The Tale of Lisabetta da Messina (IV.5)

KRISTINA M. OLSON

For a novella whose protagonist is renowned for the silence with which she confronts her tragic destiny, the *fortuna* of the fifth tale of Day Four, the tale of Lisabetta da Messina,[1] has suffered no such fate. Its critical reception can be described as polyvocal, as it is distinguished by a variety of approaches: structuralist, formalist, sociological, and psychological – just to name those that appear, for example, in the edited volume dedicated to IV.5, *Il testo moltiplicato: Lettura di una novella del "Decameron."* The *fortuna* of this tale – claimed by Terzoli to be the first to inaugurate the motif of a dismembered head placed into a vase[2] – also includes literary, visual, and cinematic adaptations over the centuries. Authors and artists ranging from the poets Hans Sachs (whose interpretations of the tale between 1515 to 1548 inspired the folkloric ballad "The Bramble Briar")[3] and John Keats ("Isabella, Or the Pot of Basil," 1818)[4] to the Pre-Raphaelite artists inspired by

1 Lisabetta's name also appears as Ellisabetta and Elisabetta in the tale, though more frequently as Lisabetta.

2 Terzoli makes this affirmation on the basis of studies by S. Thompson and D.P. Rotunda: "the lover's head, detached from the body and put in a vase ... does not appear either in the song or in other preceding popular texts. And in fact the first recorded occurrence in the great repertories of narrative types and motifs is precisely this novella" ("La testa," 198). As for the sources of the novella, Branca, in the notes to his edition, offers a parallel for Lorenzo's apparition in Apuleius's *Metamorphoses*, VIII, 8 and IX, 31, beyond gesturing towards the *canzone* at the end; see Boccaccio, *Decameron*, 526n3. Forni claims that the motif of the decapitated head that Boccaccio weaves into IV.5 actually belongs to the Provençal sources behind IV.9; see Forni, *Adventures in Speech*, 4.

3 See Belden, "Boccaccio," 327–95, and Lee, *The "Decameron,"* 137.

4 See MacCracken, "Source," 147–8, where MacCracken maintains that Keats read Boccaccio in Italian, and Ford, "Note on a Line," for an assessment of the presence of Petrarch in the seventh story of George Turberville's *Tragical Tales* (1587), which is a creative rewriting of *Decameron* IV.5.

his poem – John Everett Millais (*Isabella*, 1849), William Holman Hunt (*Isabella and the Pot of Basil*, 1866–8), and the "modern" Pre-Raphaelite John William Waterhouse (*Isabella and the Pot of Basil*, 1907) – to Pier Paolo Pasolini (who adapts this tale in his *Decameron*, 1971)[5] have added their voices to Boccaccio's narrative (vis-à-vis Filomena, its narrator) in rewriting his tale to the sonnet form, canvas, or movie screen.[6] This rich afterlife affirms IV.5's status amongst the most studied and interpreted of the *Decameron*, such as those of Alatiel (II.7) and Griselda (X.10).

In the pages ahead I synthesize and expand on several of the conclusions that have been previously reached by the numerous scholars of this tale. I begin by discussing how this novella shows the fate of various hybrids that populate the story on thematic and formalist levels (the basil plant and the head; the love affair of a Pisan and a Messinese whose ancestry is Tuscan; the *canzone* and the novella). While most of the hybrids that exist within the world of the novella are undone with violence, only the integrity of the generic hybrid of the novella and the *canzone* survives, thriving, as it does, in the satisfied reaction of the *brigata* at the beginning of IV.6. The essay then moves to read the novella within the macro-textual context of the *Decameron* while taking historical and sociological contexts into consideration.[7] *Decameron* IV.5 not only highlights the brutal logic of the merchant class, as Vittore Branca famously stated,[8] but it also evokes the physical structures of the merchant world, namely in the evocation of the merchant colonies called *fondaci* that appear in few other canonical texts from that time. In further contemplating the symbolism of Lorenzo's decapitated

5 See Lawton, "Boccaccio and Pasolini."

6 See Lee, *The "Decameron,"* 136–7, who lists the examples of the *Canzoni a ballo* by Lorenzo de' Medici and Poliziano (1568), Hans Sachs, George Turberville's *Tragical Tales*, B.M. Ranking's *Streams from Hidden Sources* (1872), and Martin Montanus's *Wegkürzer* (1608). Maiorana proposes the case of Anatole France's *Le basilic*, from the *Poèmes dorés* (1873), to this list in the essay; see "Un conte de Boccace." In the same volume as Maiorana's piece, Devoto adds the case of Paul Claudel's *Le Père humilié* (1916), in "Quelques notes." Terzoli suggests a passage from Ugo Foscolo's *Ultime lettere di Jacopo Ortis* (1801), in which the lovelorn Lauretta carries a skull buried in a basket amongst roses, as well as a character from Don DeLillo's *Underworld* (1999) who decapitates his lover and then carries her head in a box on the subway; see Terzoli, "La testa," 198–9.

7 The most notable approaches of this nature are the interventions by Baratto, "Struttura narrativa e messaggio ideologico," and Marcus, "Cross-Fertilizations."

8 Branca writes of IV.5, "The theme of the novella is precisely the pious, disconsolate wilting and death of the flower of love in the hardened earth of the absolute dominion of 'mercantile logic'" (*Boccaccio medievale*, 156).

head, which has been interpreted as a saintly remain (Branca, Marcus, Terzoli),[9] I read this novella as a tale of relics, from the unsettled fate of Lorenzo's head to the false relics of San Lorenzo in IV.10 that form an unlikely counterpart. In conclusion, this essay treats the character of Lisabetta as a literary hybrid figure of sorts, whose identity is split between those of the restricted women of the Proem and that of an author herself.

It seems ironic, yet fitting, to begin an analysis of the complex structure of IV.5, a novella that conflates the tropes of textual, corporeal, and geographic origins, not at the onset of the story but at its truncated ending, where the folkloric origins of IV.5 are briefly evoked. Boccaccio would have us believe that this tragic love story is the unabridged history to another *testo*, the Sicilian folksong at its ending, which is only cited in its first two verses. This is the conclusion that the reader is meant to reach when she reads the *brigata*'s reaction to the tale at the beginning of IV.6: "Quella novella che Filomena aveva detta fu alle donne carissima, per ciò che assai volte avevano quella canzone udita cantare né mai avean potuto, per domandarne, sapere qual si fosse la cagione per che fosse stata fatta" [IV.6.2: The story related by Filomena was much appreciated by the ladies, for they had heard this song on a number of occasions without ever succeeding, for all their inquiries, in discovering why it had been written]. The purported reason why the tale of Lisabetta and Lorenzo exists, as Millicent Marcus has claimed, dwells in this "metatextual clue" of the *brigata*'s reaction, as it "resolves a mystery and it does so by explaining the meaning of a Sicilian song which evidently enjoyed immense popularity in Tuscany at the time of Boccaccio's writing."[10] The sentimentality of Filomena's tale does not tug at the heartstrings of its listeners in the *brigata*, whose reaction

9 See Marcus, "Cross-Fertilizations," 391. Branca alludes to this when he describes the dream vision in which Lorenzo indicates the location of his corpse to Lisabetta: "Lorenzo reveals to Lisabetta where he is buried, with a gesture analogous to the traditional one of martyrs who indicate to the devout where their body or some relics of theirs lie" (*Decameron*, ed. Branca, 529n9). Terzoli also notes that the presentation of Lorenzo in the text recalls the legends of saints: "è però soprattutto presente in morte, quando – se si esclude l'unica azione dell'apparire – non agisce ma subisce una serie di operazioni: è ucciso, sepolto, invocato, trovato, dissepolto, decapitato e fatto oggetto di venerazione. Soprattutto le modalità del suo ritrovamento e le pratiche che ne derivano richiamano da vicino quelle relative ai corpi dei martiri, morti per amore del Cristo e della Chiesa per mano di brutali persecutori" ("La testa," 200). Getto notes that "we witness the celebration of a true and proper cult, transferred from the world of religion to that of love" (*Vita di forme*, 129).

10 See Marcus, "Cross-Fertilizations," 384.

raises the following question: did Boccaccio compose IV.5 as a meditation upon literary origins?[11]

The function of IV.5 as a "solution" to the riddle of the *canzone* gestures to the ways in which stories can and cannot compensate for the *lacunae* of their source texts. The relationship between Filomena's tale and the folksong is not a neat correspondence whereby the former tale picks up the narrative threads of the latter, since many of the elements introduced in Filomena's tale do not begin to take shape in the song. "Qual esso fu lo malo cristiano," as scholars of the *canzone* have noted, does not boast the narrative intricacies of a love affair thwarted by possessive brothers, recounting as it does only the loss for a woman whose beloved basil plant was stolen.[12] More than explaining the background of the *canzone*, the tale of Lisabetta and Lorenzo, when seen as the "source" text for the song, invents the song's origins out of whole cloth. The specificity of the tale determines the song's reception. As well, for the reader, who is bereft of the entire text of the *canzone*, Filomena's tale dominates the pages of the *Decameron*, only alluding cursorily to the song at its end. Thus, though Filomena's tale resolves the *canzone* for the *brigata*, for the reader of the *Decameron* it *decapitates* the *canzone*, both in content and in form, leaving only its first two verses intact. At the same time, it grafts onto it the intricate story of Lorenzo and Lisabetta, like the robust basil plant that takes root in Lorenzo's dead head, adding *fogli* (pages) of text where the basil plant would add *foglie* (leaves). The end result is a forced joining of literary origins that differ as much in genre as they do in substance, just like the basil plant that takes life from a decomposing head.

The analogies of *testo/testa* with the literary texts at hand and Lorenzo's head are suggestive of the fluidity with which hybridity can be poetically conceived.[13] But it is a hybridity that is cleft by the violence of Lisabetta's

11 In a similar way, Marcus states that IV.5 is where Boccaccio offers "his most rigorous and sustained commentary on the relationship between folklore and literature" (ibid.). Forni (*Adventures*, 21–2) discusses the focus of IV.5 in terms of the concept of *inventio* in the *Decameron*: "Boccaccio's game of gloss entails a displacement: the focus is not on the sources of the story, but on the story as source. We are being told how the song was born of the story, or, more precisely, of the events contained in it. This strategy leaves the reader wondering about the origin of the story itself. We cannot help entertaining the possibility that the declared creative sequence from story to song must be reversed in order to begin to understand the story's processes of *inventio*."

12 For the full text of the *canzone*, see the Appendix in Marcus, "Cross-Fertilizations," 397–8, who cites the text from Carducci's *Cantilene e ballate dei secoli XIII e XIV*.

13 In a related note, Segre notes that IV.5 is dominated by two metonymies: the first being that of Lorenzo's iconic image in the dream vision and the second one, the

brothers. If IV.5 stands for the basil plant that Lisabetta lays over Lorenzo's head, which, in turn, symbolizes the *canzone*, then we should also recall that the vase is abruptly emptied of its contents by Lisabetta's brothers, who then replant it, thus rending the connection between source and product. Overturning the assertion that the *Decameron* proposes, that the story is the historical antecedent to the *canzone*, is easy as well; the *brigata* might find Lisabetta's tale to be a resolution, but the informed reader of the *Decameron* can become quickly aware of the fact that the text of the *canzone* predates the text of IV.5. As Marcus saliently argues, the complex relationship between the song and the novella for the reader (but not for the *brigata*) casts IV.5 as a tale about "problematic filiation."[14] I would add to this point that the novella, at formal and textual levels, highlights the distance between textual and geographic origins and their products. This holds true for the novella on the meta-textual level, as regards the interpretation of sources, and also for the story itself, which features the first generation of an emigrated merchant family that uproots itself from Messina at the end of the tale. Geographic and corporeal detachments and reconciliations are significant features of the plot, as they touch upon the sense of estrangement at the heart of the tale.

Geographical origins are of great importance in this novella, which foregrounds place names and modifiers in a noteworthy way. One would only need to evoke the fraught matter in the critical reception of the kind of basil Lisabetta plants over the disembodied head of Lorenzo, which is identified, curiously, by its origin of Salerno in the novella ("di bellissimo bassilico salernetano" [§17: the finest Salernitan basil]), but not necessarily in the *canzone* ("del bassilico mio selemontano?"). No such species of basil – noted by either the modifier "salernetano" or "selemontano" – exists.[15] Antonio Mazzarino, based upon his studies of the twelfth-century Arab author Ibn-Al-Awam and his treatise *Kit-al-Falahah*, found that the type of basil located at the top of its category is in the shape of a skull, and thus presents the possibility that this kind of basil is a "fossile della presenza araba" in the story.[16]

---

head. He writes, "the head for the body and the cadaverous body for the beloved's body. It is not hard to think, with regard to this contemplation of the vase with the head in it, of an act of fetishism. Fetishism is an erotic metonymy ... the real, in the end, can also be manipulated, transformed by means of language (and we are always fairly close to metonymy)" ("I silenzi," 84).

14 See Marcus, "Cross-Fertilizations," 387.

15 See Mazzarino, "Il basilico," 460.

16 See ibid., 471. If this is emblematic of an Arabic presence in this novella, then IV.4 shares a similar encounter between Christian and Muslim worlds in the character of the Tunisian princess.

The explanations that have been offered for the basil all seem to involve a geographic designation or reference; either the basil is, as just noted, a reference to the Arabic presence in Messina at the time, or Boccaccio meant to evoke Salerno, or, as Mazzarino also argues, it is a form of "siler montarum": herb of the mountain.[17] In other words, the *canzone* in itself highlights the question of geographic origins by means of the modifier "salernetano."

Yet another indication of a concern with origins and geographic distance lies in the origins themselves of Lisabetta's family, which are somewhat ambiguous as regards the generation of Lisabetta and her brothers. Filomena claims that the father came from San Gimignano, but the birthplace of his children is not specified. This has resulted in some critical disagreement. Marcus and Baratto believe that the children were distanced from their origins, with Marcus further asserting that the children suffer what she terms a "geographically induced paranoia."[18] If the family is not native to Messina, this could serve to explain, as she writes, the brothers' extreme fear of public opinion, manifested both in their murder of Lorenzo and their hasty departure from the city (as she cites from the text, "senza danno o sconcio di loro, questa vergogna, avanti che più andasse innanzi, si potessero torre dal viso" [§7: it was safe and convenient for them to rid themselves of this ignominy before it got out of hand]). Picone, on the other hand, maintains that the children were most likely born and raised in Sicily; Cirese asserts that Messina is insignificant to the story because all of the characters are Tuscan.[19] The text, however, is not entirely specific either way. Whatever the case may be, one could argue that the connection that Lisabetta and her brothers feel to their surroundings is precarious; this would be supported by both the extreme reactions of the young men and the ways in which Lisabetta's neighbours monitor her from a distance, never intervening directly to assist her but simply noting her curious behaviour to the brothers: "e servando la giovane questa maniera del continuo, piú volte da' suoi vicin fu veduta. Li quali, maravigliandosi i fratelli della sua guasta bellezza e di ciò che gli occhi le parevano della testa fuggiti, il disser loro: 'Noi ci siamo accorti, che ella ogni dí tiene

17 See ibid., 467–8.

18 See Baratto, "Struttura narrativa," 41.

19 Picone writes, "And the sociological line does not seem very coherent either, as it tends to justify the characters' behaviour with this unrooting: such a situation, if it is true for the 'Pisan' Lorenzo, surely cannot be applied to Lisabetta and her brothers, who are probably born and raised on the island (only of the father is it said that his 'native town was San Gimignano')" (Picone, "La 'ballata' di Lisabetta," 181; see also Cirese, "Lettura antropologica," 107).

la cotal maniera'" [§20–1: The young woman constantly followed this same routine, and from time to time she attracted the attention of her neighbours. And as they had heard her brothers expressing their concern at the decline in her good looks and the way in which her eyes appeared to have sunk into their sockets, they told them what they had seen, adding: "We have noticed that she follows the same routine every day"]. Lisabetta's estrangement from the social worlds of both family and neighbours reaches its climax once she is bereft of her vase and abandoned by her brothers, both events that sever her from the transplanted *testa* and her familial roots.

The best indicator of Lisabetta's nativity for Filomena's purposes resides in her modification of Lisabetta's name: "da Messina." The reader's knowledge of Lisabetta's existence takes place exclusively in the world of Messina, in a bustling Mediterranean merchant enclave in this Sicilian port. That Boccaccio means to draw our attention to the location of this tale is clear;[20] the fifth tale of Day Four, the day during which stories of love with an "infelice fine" are featured, names Messina not once, but four times (a notable frequency for a city in the *Decameron* that is not Rome, Florence, Bologna, or Genoa, the highest-ranking cities in terms of frequency within one story). Filomena credits her evocation of this city to the preceding novella, the tale of Gerbino (who, like Lorenzo, is also decapitated) in IV.4, with the inspiration for her narration:

> La mia novella, graziose donne, non sarà di genti di sí alta condizione come costor furono de' quali Elissa ha raccontato, ma ella per avventura non sarà men pietosa: e a ricordarmi di quella mi tira *Messina* poco innanzi ricordata, dove l'accidente avvenne. Erano adunque in *Messina* tre giovani fratelli e mercatanti ..." (IV.5.3–4; emphasis added)
>
> [This story of mine, fair ladies, will not be about people of so lofty a rank as those of whom Elissa has been speaking, but possibly it will prove to be no less touching, and I was reminded of it by the mention that has just been made of Messina, which was where it all happened. In Messina, there once lived three brothers ...]

Messina is also referenced when the brothers return from having assassinated Lorenzo in the countryside (§9). When the brothers depart from the city towards the very end of the novella, Messina comes to be

---

20 Thus I agree with Marcus when she writes, "Boccaccio is too artful and self-conscious a writer to let anything as significant as geographic location remain extrinsic to his storytelling design" ("Cross-Fertilizations," 388).

replaced by Naples, that other city where Boccaccio lived for several years (1326–39),[21] and more precisely, where he spent time in a *fondaco*, as I will discuss below.

Messina's brief and unflattering appearance in IV.4, the novella that prompts Filomena to recall this city, first draws an association between Messina, merchants, and avarice, all elements that are inherent to the tale of Lisabetta. In IV.4, Gerbino departs with a ship from Messina in order to intercept the ship of the daughter of the King of Tunis at Sardinia. The passionate *messinesi* who have accompanied Gerbino on his trip become invigorated by his reminder that they will themselves earn all of the plunder on the ship. They are *not*, however, motivated by his words regarding the ennobling power of love; Elissa refers to them as "vaghi della rapina" [IV.4.18: avid for plunder]. If this is the Messina that inspires Filomena in telling IV.5, it seems fitting, then, that the reader associates its people not with a stilnovist sensibility but with greed. The only other appearance of Messina in the *Decameron*, VIII.10, again features it in a negative light. Here Jancofiore, who dupes the merchant Salabaetto (only to be duped herself by Salabaetto), claims to have received a letter from her brother in Messina, a lie that is a part of her deception.

If, like the tragic tales of Day Four, Messina is another kind of *infelice fine*, then it should be noted that these themes surface elsewhere in the *Decameron* in contexts other than Messina but still in tales told by the same narrator, Filomena, before IV.5: I.3, II.9, and III.3. The tale of Melchisedech the Jew and the Saladin (I.3) explores the competition that ensues from the ambiguous inheritance received by three brothers of three rings from their father, thus presenting a group of brothers in the context of greed. As regards the battle of the sexes amongst members of the merchant class, Bernabò lauds his wife, Zinevra (in II.9), for her ability to perform the gender-specific activities of women and men, as scripted in the Proem and in this tale. Not only can she embroider, she can hunt, ride a horse, read, write, and gather accounts better than if she were a merchant (II.9.6). The tale of Bernabò also features a *fondaco* (like IV.5) of Venetian merchants at the city of Acre, a place where Zinevra, as Sicurano, recognizes her possessions. After a discussion with Ambrogiuolo in the *fondaco* there, she swears to avenge herself and correct the wrongs done to her marriage. It is this tale that shows yet another side of the "ragion de mercatura," when the competition into which merchants enter attempts to claim women as the victims of a cruel wager unfairly

21 See Torraca, *Giovanni Boccaccio a Napoli*, for more information about this period in Boccaccio's life.

executed.[22] In III.3, Filomena narrates the wit of a young woman who dupes a friar into permitting her to commit adultery with a young man; in describing the young man's unseemly conduct towards her, she remarks that she has thought of informing her brothers. Yet because men can be tactless in their handling of such matters, the lady claims to have thought it in the interest of the welfare of others to stay silent: "Hommi posto in cuore di fargliele alcuna volta dire a' miei fratelli; ma poscia m'ho pensato che gli uomini fanno alcuna volta l'ambasciate per modo che le risposte seguitan cattive, di *che nascon parole e dalle parole si perviene a' fatti*" [III.3.12: I have made up my mind on several occasions to inform my brothers about him. But then it has occurred to me that men are apt to be tactless in their handling of these matters, and when they receive a dusty answer they start bandying words with one another and eventually somebody gets hurt (emphasis added)]. The subtext here of the brutal act of Lisabetta's brothers in IV.5 is evident: from words they arrive at deeds ("dalle parole si perviene a' fatti").

The brothers in the *Decameron* under discussion here (III.3, IV.5, and VII.8) are often potential or real instruments of revenge, though their actions, however hastily designed, are not effective, as Sherberg argues.[23] One case in point, the tale of VII.8 as narrated by Neifile, recounts the failure of the merchant Arriguccio Berlinghieri to avenge his lost honour by enlisting Sismonda's three brothers against her. One could perceive this tale as a version of IV.5 rewritten *in bono* for the female protagonist, since the woman in question is not a victim of the violence of her brothers. Importantly, in VII.8, Monna Sismonda does not succeed in turning the tables on Arriguccio by means of her own *ingegno*, but her mother comes immediately to her rescue, expressing her disapproval of Arriguccio and even of her own sons, who failed to marry Sismonda into a better family. Alas, much more silent than Sismonda, and quite contrary indeed to the adulterous escapes of the "heroine" of VII.8, Lisabetta is also deprived of a source of maternal support in fending off the violence of her brothers. Marcus argues that it is the maternal absence in IV.1, the tale of Ghismonda, that "went far to explain Ghismonda's tragic plight," as she states.[24] Deprived of both

22 See Barolini's analysis of how Zinevra "crosses the bridge from words to deeds" in "Le parole," 179–85.

23 Sherberg writes that "this story [IV.5], like the others, denies the full efficacy of the repressive actions that powerful men undertake. The brothers kill Lorenzo in secret and then quietly flee Messina, making every effort to hide their guilt. But never mind, for as the tale's conclusion makes clear, the story comes out anyway, in the form of the *canzone*, whose first lines Filomena cites" (*Governance*, 126n18).

24 See Marcus, "Cross-Fertilizations," 389.

mother and father in IV.5 – the father's death is at the head, so to speak, of the story – Lisabetta is entirely at the mercy of her brothers.

In comparison with the female audience identified in the Proem, the female protagonists of Day Four who are "ristrette da' voleri, da' piaceri, da' comandamenti de' padri, delle madri, de' fratelli e de' mariti" [Proem. §10: forced to follow the whims, fancies and dictates of their fathers, mothers, brothers and husbands] are most vehemently confined by just one set of these *paterfamilias* figures: either father, brother(s), or husband.[25] One would only need to recall the tales of Tancredi, Guiscardo, and Ghismonda (IV.1), and of Guiglielmo di Rossiglione, his wife, and Guigliemo Guardastagno (IV.9), as examples of how the stories of Day Four illustrate the repression exerted by patriarchal rule upon women, a pattern that Sherberg sees as a larger discourse on the three types of *paterfamilias* relations.[26] He argues that the monarchical rule imposed by Tancredi in IV.1 switches to a timocracy in the tale of Lisabetta da Messina, whose brothers form a community of equals as defined by Aristotle in the *Ethics* (1161a4): "The community formed by brothers resembles a timocracy, since brothers are equals, except to the extent that their ages differ."[27] They deliberate and act together, though their actions are rash and ineffective. Sherberg believes that the brothers are shamed by Lisabetta's sexual conquest of Lorenzo because it reminds them of their failure as *paterfamilias* to secure her marriage ("che che se ne fosse cagione, ancora maritata non aveano" [§6: for some reason or other they had failed to bestow her in marriage]).[28] Serpieri argues that the brothers are reluctant to marry their sister because they fail to see her as a sexual creature; this denial, in turn, becomes a source of revulsion.[29]

Though he disagrees that the story's illustration of the "ragion de mercatura" contains a logic for the actions of the brothers (Baratto, Marcus), arguing convincingly that the proper source of the scandal in this situation resides with Lisabetta being unwed, Sherberg's identification

25 Despite these repressive forces, the women of Day Four are not the direct victims of male violence, as Migiel points out. She writes, "Unlike men, who meet death mainly because of their own crimes, or because of political and sexual strife, the women of Day 4 tend to die of natural causes ... or by their own doing (Ghismunda in *Decameron* 4.1, Lisabetta da Messina in 4.5, Simona in 4.7, the wife of Guglielmo Rossiglione in 4.9)," arguing that Lisabetta "allows herself to waste away" (*Rhetoric*, 148).

26 See Sherberg, *Governance*, 119–20.

27 See ibid., 125.

28 See ibid., 126.

29 Serpieri writes, "The discovery of the erotic infraction upsets them exorbitantly, because they feel their sister's sexuality as a personal shame, a contamination that marks *their* repressed faces" ("L'approccio psicoanalitico," 65).

of timocracy vis-à-vis Aristotle for the tightly knit community of the brothers harmonizes with a sociological reading of the novella on a different level.[30] Aristotle presents timocracy as based upon a principle of property (*Ethics* VIII, x), as Solon defined *timokratia* in the constitution for Athens in the sixth century BC, according to which the four tiers of the population could possess political power depending upon their possession of property.[31] In the language of the novella, Lisabetta and Lorenzo are the property of the brothers:

> Erano adunque in Messina tre giovani fratelli e mercatanti, e assai ricchi uomini rimasi dopo la morte del padre loro, il quale fu da San Gimignano; e *avevano* una loro sorella chiamata Elisabetta, giovane assai bella e costumata, la quale, che che se ne fosse cagione, ancora maritata non aveano. E *avevano oltre a ciò* questi tre fratelli in un lor fondaco un giovinetto pisano chiamato Lorenzo, che tutti i lor fatti guidava e faceva ... (IV.5.4–5)
>
> [In Messina, there once lived three brothers, all of them merchants who had been left very rich after the death of their father, whose native town was San Gemignano. They had a sister called Lisabetta, but for some reason or other they had failed to bestow her in marriage, despite the fact that she was uncommonly gracious and beautiful. In one of their trading establishments, the three brothers employed a young Pisan named Lorenzo, who planned and directed all their operations ...]

Note the double usage of the verb *avere* in this context that signifies possession; these wealthy brothers not only had a sister, but they also had a young Pisan. The parity of their objectification transitions with ease into the equally reciprocal emotions they experience; the love begins with Lisabetta, but then Lorenzo abandons his other love interests to bend his soul towards hers, culminating at the point at which "piacendo l'uno all'altro igualmente" [§5: they were equally in love with each other].[32] The novella thus conflates the coercive forces that

30 Baratto, as mentioned earlier, argues that the shame felt by the brothers more directly relates to their status as disenfranchised merchants: "the logic of merchants abroad, exposed to dangers, damaged in any event by eventual scandals and therefore worried about their honour, used to thinking long and hard before deciding" ("Struttura narrativa," 41).

31 See Grote, *A History of Greece*, vol. 3, 121.

32 Segre notes, in this respect, that "Lorenzo is never an autonomous figure, he is little more than a pretext for what happens. There is something more of note, however: it seems to me that there is a sort of specularity between Lisabetta and Lorenzo" ("I silenzi," 78). Terzoli draws attention to the rapid interchange of Lisabetta and

impose order within a patriarchal structure and the merchant logic, to evoke Branca's "ragion de mercatura," which regards the laws of desire without sympathy. Lisabetta and Lorenzo are kindred spirits who are suffocated by a family structure whose views are dictated by the social and the political.

These relationships of power are represented within the rubrics of IV.5, IV.1, and IV.9 as well.[33] Lisabetta begins as the pawn in a story in which her brothers are in control, a dominance that is established syntactically within the rubric itself. The brothers are situated first as the subjects of the vicissitudes of the plot, and Lisabetta as the conclusive victim:

> *I fratelli d'Ellisabetta uccidon l'amante di lei*: egli l'apparisce in sogno e mostrale dove sia sotterato; ella occultamente disotterra la testa e mettela in un testo di bassilico, e quivi su piagnendo ogni dí per una grande ora, i fratelli gliele tolgono, e *ella se ne muore di dolor poco appresso*. (§1; emphasis added)
>
> [Lisabetta's brothers murder her lover. He appears to her in a dream and shows her where he is buried. She secretly disinters the head and places it in a pot of basil, over which she weeps for a long time every day. In the end her brothers take it away from her, and shortly thereafter she dies of grief.]

If Lisabetta and her brothers seem to alternate in the quest for dominance of the actions of the plot – with Lorenzo intervening only once – the rubric tips the balance of power in favour of the brothers: her brothers "uccidono" and "tolgono," whereas Lisabetta "disotterra" and "se ne muore." Lorenzo, on the other hand, only *appears* and *shows*: "apparisce" and "mostrale," both of which are consonant with the quality of his function from the mid-point to the end of the tale; he appears to Lisabetta in a dream, instructs her as to the location of his remains, but then disappears, only to finish as a hidden presence in the vessel, the *testo*, at the end of the novella. None of the rubrics for the earlier

---

Lorenzo's names, which unites them: "It is almost a verbal and symbolic linking: underscored also by the alliteration Lisabetta-Lorenzo, which connects the two names as it had already connected those of the tragic lovers of the first *novella*, Ghismonda-Guiscardo" ("La testa," 197).

33 For a study of the hermeneutic challenges posed by analysing the rubrics of the *Decameron*, see D'Andrea's "Le Rubriche," 41–67. Like D'Andrea, I believe that the rubrics are best analysed as a narrative in their own right, and that they cannot be read as summaries of their respective *novelle*, given the generic differences involved.

novelle in the *Decameron* shifts subjective authority between three parties with this kind of syntactic tension.[34]

The tale of Lisabetta da Messina is the second tale whose rubric will feature the verb "uccidere" as its initial verb. The rubric of IV.1, the tragic tale of Ghismonda, is the first: "Tancredi, prenze di Salerno, *uccide* l'amante della figliuola e *mandale* il cuore in una coppa d'oro; la quale, messa sopr'esso acqua avvelenata, quella si bee, e cosí *muore*" [IV.1.1: Tancredi, Prince of Salerno, kills his daughter's lover and sends her his heart in a golden chalice; she besprinkles the heart with a poisonous liquid, which she then drinks, and so dies]. Just as this rubric begins with "uccidere," it ends with the closing verb of IV.5's rubric, "morire." Tale IV.9 will feature a murder as well, though, just as it is executed clandestinely within the story itself, the murder of Guillaume de Cabestanh is hidden within the syntax of the first sentence of the rubric, where "uccidere" appears in the passive form: "Messer Guiglielmo Rossiglione dà a mangiare alla moglie sua il cuore di messer Guiglielmo Guardastagno *ucciso da lui* e amato da lei; il che ella sappiendo, poi si gitta da un'alta finestra in terra e *muore* e col suo amante *è sepellita*" [IV.9.1: Guillaume de Roussillon causes his wife to eat the heart of her lover, Guillaume de Cabestanh, whom he has secretly murdered. When she finds out, she kills herself by leaping from a lofty casement to the ground below, and is subsequently buried with the man she loved]. To be noted here is the closure for the murder that burial provides in the sentence, unlike the rubrics that end with an unburied death, as in IV.1 and IV.5. The tale of Lisabetta introduces exceptionally, in the rubric itself, a syntactic tension and a brutality in deeds that have yet been unparalleled in the rubrics of the preceding stories narrated by the *brigata*.

That the brutality in IV.5 is symptomatic of the "ragion de mercatura," the pitiless and anti-sentimental merchant world as depicted, for instance, in the cold calculations of Ser Cepperello, was argued first by Branca and sustained by Baratto and Marcus. According to this reading of the novella, the "mercantile logic" explains the actions of the brothers as motivated by the quest to preserve their family's reputation. Additionally, the geographical precision made in this novella of the *fondaco*, a merchant colony, in Messina lends itself to a wider interpretation of this *locus non amoenus*, so to speak, in the *Decameron* where

34 In contrast, Serpieri reads the brothers as entirely passive and incapable of action and Lisabetta as active: "Fin dall'inizio, il suo modo di agire reca indizi di intraprendenza: è lei ad assumere l'iniziativa con Lorenzo ... È capace di fare e di amare. È attiva di fronte alla pasività dei fratelli, dei quali infrange il divieto implicito" ("L'approccio psicoanalitico," 62).

the brothers of Lisabetta, and Lorenzo, belong, and where Lisabetta's love is stifled. The world of the *fondaci*, the merchant colonies that were widespread in the Mediterranean before and during Boccaccio's time, are given a prominence in the *Decameron* that cannot be found in many other Italian literary texts of the fourteenth century.[35]

Fondaci, a term employed by Boccaccio in the *Decameron* to signify variously a colony, a trade-shop or store, a warehouse, or simply a stand, appears in five tales in the *Decameron*. In all of their appearances, they are the sites where dissimulation ("dissimulazione") is executed in order to avenge love wronged, to exploit the idea of love, or to spite love itself. I have discussed one of those *novelle* earlier: Filomena's other story of the deception of merchants, II.9. Here, Zinevra, disguised as the male Sicurano, discovers the deception of Ambrogiuolo when she is looking through his wares at a *fondaco* of Venetian merchants. It is the time of the customary fair, the *fiera* in which both Christian and Saracen merchants congregate. Because of her proficiency in the language, she is a court dignitary in charge of protecting the merchants and their merchandise. When she comes across the wares of merchants from Sicily, Pisa, Genoa, and Venice, she marvels to find her own belongings – a bag and a belt – at a "fondaco di mercatanti viniziani smontato" [II.9.48: stall of some Venetian merchants]. She engages Ambrogiuolo in conversation, during which he, deceived by her disguise, lies about having slept with her and reveals the terms of the wager he had placed with her husband. Swearing to avenge herself, she dupes Ambrogiuolo in order to cultivate their friendship to her advantage, thus demonstrating her prowess in the mercantile/masculine skill of dissimulation, which Lisabetta's brothers also perform. As Segre notes in regard to the behaviour of the brothers, "opera una strategia astuta, sostanzialmente ipocrita, che ha come strumento principale la dissimulazione. I fratelli non agiscono mai d'impulso, ma dopo aver calcolato bene situazioni e consequenze delle azioni corrispondenti."[36] Whether or not, as Sherberg has argued, their calculations are the best ones possible, there is an undeniable element of deception executed for personal gain in their actions.[37]

35 Constable writes, "Although Boccaccio was using the term *fondaco* more in its fourteenth-century Tuscan sense – as a branch of a privately owned commercial firm, with its own manager – his contemporary audience would have appreciated the verisimilitude of his setting" (*Housing the Stranger*, 210n33). For another treatment of *fondaci* in the medieval period, see Concina's *Fondaci*.

36 See Segre, "I silenzi," 80.

37 Sherberg writes, "Their dispatch in resolving the problem only makes them look worse" (*Governance*, 126).

The other stories of the *Decameron* that feature a *fondaco* as the location for a turning point in the plot are IV.8, VII.7, and VIII.10. In Neifile's tale, IV.8 (just like VII.8, where the mother's role is paramount to the outcome of the plot), the mother of Girolamo Sighieri, son of wealthy merchant Leonardo Sighieri, sends her son off to another city in the service of the *fondaco* in order to extinguish his love for Salvestra, the daughter of a tailor. The enforced absence from Salvestra while working at the *fondaco* will purge him, the mother believes, of this love for a member of a lower class. In VII.7, narrated by Filomena, Lodovico, though born to a nobleman-turned-merchant, is specifically *not* sent to a *fondaco* as a means of launching him towards a career in business, but instead lives a life in the French royal household, where he becomes a gentleman and, importantly, falls in love with a certain Beatrice, wife of Egano de' Galluzzi.

The tale of Jancofiore and Salabaetto, VIII.10, takes place in Palermo, though it refers to Messina. Here, a Palermitan *fondaco* is the stage for the novella. A discussion of the practice of merchants who arrive in a port and load their cargo into a *fondaco* or warehouse, which is often called a *dogana*, opens the novella itself. This change in terms came with the Christian appropriation of *fondaci* in the fourteenth century, according to Constable, from *funduq* to *dogana*:

> Soleva essere, e forse che ancora oggi è, una usanza in tutte le terre marine che hanno porto cosí fatta, che tutti i mercatanti che in quelle con mercatantie capitano, faccendole scaricare, tutte in *un fondaco il quale in molti luoghi è chiamato dogana*, tenuta per lo comune o per lo signor della terra, le portano. (VIII.10.4; emphasis added)
>
> [In the seaports of all maritime countries, it used to be the practice, and possibly still is, that any merchant arriving there with merchandise, having discharged his cargo, takes it to a warehouse, which in many places is called the *dogana* and is maintained by the commune or by the ruler of the state.]

The seaport at Palermo is notable, Dioneo states, for the dishonest women there who court foreign merchants in order to fleece them for their merchandise. Hence the love in the *dogana* in Palermo is false; it is, as in the case of Zinevra, simply women who are skilled in the mercantile art of *dissimulazione*.

Boccaccio thus not only fictionalizes the historical realities of the *fondaci* in the world of the *Decameron* but also deliberately draws a relation between the mercantile activity of these areas and erotic adventure.

The *fondaco* of the tale of Lisabetta is noteworthy in that it does not just present the potent combination of commerce and eros, but conflates the restrictions placed on lovelorn women as described in the Proem. Specifically, the world of the *fondaci* reveals those restrictions not placed by fathers or mothers, but by brothers, the least diplomatic (to echo the words of the young woman in III.3) in negotiating the affairs of the heart for their sisters within the economy of the *Decameron*. The potential historicity of the *fondaco* of Lisabetta's brothers is unique in this theme, and more complex than the critical tradition has credited. As Branca has noted, Messina was home to various merchants from San Gimignano, the fatherland of Lisabetta and her brothers, and the city had a vibrant wool guild there.[38] The presence of *sangimignanesi* in Messina was of such prominence that the *Libro di Provvisioni* from San Gimignano notes that, in 1296, Charles II of Naples asked them for assistance against his adversaries (who would have been led by James II of Aragon, the former King of Sicily).[39] Additionally, a *curiosa coincidenza* has been noted by Branca, namely that of the merchant family of the Ardinghelli from San Gimignano, who moved from Messina to Naples in the mid-thirteenth century, just as Lisabetta's brothers do at the end of the novella.

There is another interesting historical tension that Boccaccio embeds in the novella and that has not yet been explored: that of Lorenzo's Pisan origins, which could be interpreted as a potential sign of his status as an independent merchant. According to Constable, Pisa also had one or several *fondaci* in Messina during the time, which tended to collaborate with the city of San Gimignano during the first half of the thirteenth century, before, perhaps, San Gimignano itself had its own *fondaco* in that city.[40] Relations with Genoa, on the other hand, were strained, as the Pisans stayed faithful to Emperor Frederick II and overtook one of their *fondaci* in 1194. As Constable writes, "A contract written in San Gimignano in 1232 concerned local merchants trading pepper in Messina and mentioned that they went to the Pisan *fondaco* in that city. Ten years later, in 1243, another contract from San Gimignano was sent to the Pisan *fondaco* in Naples, a city where Florentines also had a *fondaco* of their own."[41]

38 *Decameron*, ed. Branca, 527n1.

39 See *Il testo moltiplicato*, 19–20n5.

40 Constable writes, "Instead, Genoese, Pisan, and Florentine merchants had establishments in Messina by the last decade of the century, and Italian consuls appear in Messina in 1189" (*Housing the Stranger*, 208).

41 Ibid., 209.

Filomena does not present Lorenzo as having his own *fondaco*, but as a Pisan youth who held a high managerial presence within the *fondaco* of Lisabetta's brothers ("un giovinetto pisano chiamato Lorenzo, che tutti i lor fatti guidava e faceva" [§5: a young Pisan named Lorenzo, who planned and directed all their operations]). However, in the critical reception of the novella he is often interpreted as a man of a lower class who brings shame to their household by means of this affair. The story itself would imply that Lorenzo had a certain business acumen that allowed him to direct all of their affairs. In fact, nowhere does the novella present the idea that the brothers killed Lorenzo because of the shame that would ensue from a relationship between Lisabetta and a man of lesser social stature, as Alessandro Serpieri notes;[42] it only indicates that they were determined that no shame should be brought upon their reputation ("e con loro insieme, dopo lungo consiglio, diliberò di questa cosa, acciò che né a loro né alla sirocchia alcuna infamia ne seguisse, di passarsene tacitamente e d'infignersi del tutto d'averne cosa veduta o saputa infino a tanto tempo venisse" [§7: and the three of them talked the thing over at considerable length. Being determined that the affair should leave no stain upon the reputation either of themselves or of their sister, [one of the brothers] decided that they must pass it over in silence and pretend to have neither seen nor heard anything until such time]). Could Lorenzo's managerial skill have posed a threat to the brothers that was then exacerbated by his affair with Lisabetta outside of matrimony? Did Lorenzo threaten the brothers by "possessing" in the conquest of their sister that which they thought to have possessed? And why did Lorenzo not work in a Pisan *fondaco* in the first place? These questions, which are unanswerable,[43] gesture to the novella's own historical realism, which highlights the level to which the story is dependent upon the contingencies of history while maintaining a self-consciousness about literary form. In other words, the tale of Lisabetta reads like a chronicle without a wide spectrum of historic specificity for the vicissitudes of the plot.

Two other elements address the historical correlations of IV.5 that can be extrapolated from Boccaccio's own biography: Boccaccio's possible experience in a *fondaco* and the nearby location of the Basilica

42 Serpieri writes: "Here there exists a social disparity, of a mercantile-bourgeois type, but to a relative degree: Lisabetta is not noble, Lorenzo is the administrator of the holdings of the merchant brothers" ("L'approccio psicoanalitico," 62).

43 Serpieri (ibid., 62–5) convincingly argues that Lorenzo functions as a surrogate father for the brothers, who burden him with all of the managerial responsibilities of the *fondaco* ("*tutti* i lor fatti *guidava*"). Thus the shame that the brothers feel upon learning of Lisabetta's affair with Lorenzo reads as the taboo of incest.

of San Lorenzo.[44] Based upon Davidsohn's records and the text of Boccaccio's Epistle XIX to Iacopo Pizzinga, Branca conjectures that the Boccacci family went to live in the Florentine *fondaco* in Naples that was not far from the "Laurentii sacram edem" – the "pleasant and beautiful temple" of San Lorenzo.[45] The Basilica of San Lorenzo of Naples, located at the present-day intersection of Via Tribunali and Via San Gregorio and itself built on the remains of a Roman market, is also where Boccaccio saw his mythical Fiammetta in the form of Maria, daughter of King Robert. What seems to be an uncanny coincidence between Boccaccio's possible experience in a Neapolitan *fondaco* and the name of the nearby basilica, San Lorenzo, does, however, confirm a reading of the function of the character Lorenzo in IV.5 as a saint, and, moreover, similarities between merchant and sacred worlds at large.[46]

Several critics have interpreted Lorenzo and his death allegorically in terms of religious symbolism. Giovanni Getto was the first to identify Lisabetta's behaviour around his corpse as resembling that of a religious cult ("si assiste alla celebrazione di un vero e proprio culto, trasferito dal mondo religioso a quello dell'amore").[47] If saints are to be dismembered, as Marcus argues, then Lisabetta, after decapitating Lorenzo, fulfils the terms of his martyrdom.[48] The life of Lorenzo in IV.5 does not neatly parallel the life of the third-century saint, nor does Lorenzo "behave" as a saint during her dream vision, however.[49] He instructs Lisabetta in nothing more than the location of his body, in the same brusque speech that shuns dialogue which her brothers use earlier. Lorenzo does not express any wish to become a saint – in fact, we do well to recall that, in his dream appearance, he seems to complain to Lisabetta about her incessant weeping: "O Lisabetta, tu non mi fai altro che chiamare e della mia lunga dimora t'atristi e me con le tue lagrime fieramente acusi; e per ciò sappi che io non posso più ritornarci, per ciò che l'ultimo dí che tu mi vedesti i tuoi fratelli m'uccisono" [§13: Ah,

44 Constable (*Housing the Stranger*, 210n33) writes, "Boccaccio was familiar with his subject since he had himself been an apprentice in a commercial firm in Naples as a young man."

45 See Branca, *Boccaccio: The Man and His Works*, 16–19.

46 Lorenzo's decapitation also functions as a reminder of another martyrdom, that of John the Baptist. Again, Lorenzo's life might not parallel the Baptist's, but Lisabetta – Elizabeth – is also the name of the mother of the Baptist, who, as we read in various biblical sources (the books of Mark and Luke, for example), was beheaded at the request of Salome, stepdaughter of King Herod. See Terzoli, "La testa," 198.

47 See Getto, *Vita di forme*, 129.

48 See Marcus, "Cross-Fertilizations," 391.

49 Valerio Cappozzo identifies an interpretive key to her dream vision in the *Somniale Danielis*: "Chol morto favellare significa lite." See Capozzo, *Dizionario*, 49–50.

Lisabetta, you do nothing but call to me and bemoan my long absence, and you cruelly reprove me with your tears. Hence I must tell you that I can never return, because on the day that you saw me for the last time, I was murdered by your brothers]. He indicates to her where his body lies, with the gesture of a martyr, and then tells her not to call on him or wait for him any longer. Unlike a saint, he wishes not to receive any prayers in the afterlife and does not perform any divine aid on her behalf; he wishes to be left in peace. The "sanctification" of Lorenzo, the extraction of his *testa* in order for it to be placed in a *testo,* to be made into a relic, is exclusively Lisabetta's project of mourning. And alas, it is a relic that is ultimately destroyed, compounding her loss.

The tale of Lisabetta hence draws attention to the emptiness of the "relics" of the sacred and merchant worlds, which exist in juxtaposition to each other. It is not coincidental, then, that the other appearance of San Lorenzo in the *Decameron,* the story of Frate Cipolla (VI.10), emphasizes the empty significance of relics.[50] Here, relics are instruments of deception meant to procure money for the corrupt *frate;* as the rubric reads: "Frate Cipolla promette a certi contadini di mostrar loro la penna dell'agnolo Gabriello; in luogo della quale trovando carboni, quegli dice esser di quegli che arrostirono san Lorenzo" [VI.10.1: Friar Cipolla promises a crowd of country folk that he will show them a feather of the Angel Gabriel, and on finding that some bits of coal have been put in its place, he proclaims that these were left over from the roasting of Saint Lawrence]. Frate Cipolla carries these coals in a *cassetta,* a casket, and not a *testo.* Upon chanting a hymn to San Lorenzo, whose feast day occurs two days later, he unveils the coals to the "stolta moltitudine" [VI.10.53: foolish multitude], who receive them with great reverence. Lisabetta's relic of San Lorenzo will be hidden from the masses, though her incessant weeping is noted by her neighbours. Lisabetta's relic and solitary ritual of mourning hold value, ultimately, for one individual; Frate Cipolla's fake relic brings meaning to many, despite its false significance. In both cases, however, the nature of relics remains arbitrary.

From *fondaco* manager to martyr, the character of Lorenzo in IV.5 carries a multiplicity of interpretations that can only be matched by Lisabetta. Critics have interpreted her alternatively as the protagonist of tragedy and elegy,[51] with Branca and Getto incorporating sociological

50 Terzoli discusses the life of the saint and draws a parallel with *Decameron* VI.10 ("La testa," 207–8).

51 Momigliano pronounced that Lisbetta was "that young woman closed up in her gloomy pain, in her tender and tragic contemplation" (*Storia,* 85). In contrast, Luigi Russo reads the tale as elegy (*Letture critiche,* 166–7).

insight into their conclusions.[52] Most recently, Simone Marchesi has also argued for a reading of Lisabetta as a tragic figure, but one that is elaborated by Boccaccio under the influence of the complex textual tradition behind Dido.[53] On a different note, scholars have been reluctant to view the "cold calculations" of the decapitation of Lorenzo as comparable to the act of her brothers. But do not her deeds also indicate another kind of logic, perhaps the *ragion* of the women of the Proem? Unlike Ghismonda, Lisabetta does not dwell in the world of words, nor is she a Zinevra, able to engage in both words and deeds. In fact, Lisabetta patently refuses to enter into the world of words: even if she asks her brothers insistently about Lorenzo's whereabouts, after the dream vision she takes up her own plan to visit the corpse without saying anything to them: "non avendo ardire di dire alcuna cosa a' fratelli" [§14: She dared not mention the apparition to her brothers].

If Lisabetta lives in the world of deeds and silence, she is ultimately frustrated in that regard as well: the transformation of the *testa* into a *testo* is not as successful as the *testo* of the *canzone* at the end of the novella in endowing her with an afterlife of her own. Lisabetta's final words, in this respect, are never her own, but belong to her biographers: Filomena and the anonymous author of the *canzone*. Indeed, the structure of IV.5 lends itself to comparison with the troubadour *razos*, where Lisabetta is the poet whose life is chronicled.[54] In this light, the lovelorn woman bears a resemblance to the authorial voice in the Proem, who also depends upon his poetic imagination to make her story flourish and grow, just like the plant of basil. Or, perhaps, she is more like the character of Girolamo (IV.8), suffocated by the bourgeois world, unable to protect, even with violence, "la natura delle cose" [IV.8.3: the laws of nature] of which Neifile speaks. Her silence and her unwillingness to dissimulate, as in the case of Jancofiore, Zinevra, or others, in the mercantile world, which was marked by its multilingualism (one only need think of the term *funduq* upon which *fondaco* is based),[55] or

52 Branca writes, "But this final elegy of love and death, abandoned and very sweet, becomes more chaste and fascinating because it is projected against the background of the brothers' calculating stubbornness" (*Boccaccio medievale*, 156). Getto writes, "The tragedy of the great aristocratic lovers is thus transformed into the elegy of the humble Lisabetta" (*Vita di forme*, 128).

53 Marchesi writes, "The structure of the events of Lisabetta da Messina is conceived along the same lines and constructed with the same elements as that of Dido, just as it is told in a spider-web of texts, all surely known to Boccaccio, at the centre of which is the Vergilian 'tragedy'" (*Stratigrafie*, 68).

54 See Terzoli, "La testa," 195.

55 I would like to thank Dennis Looney for this insight.

to enter into the changeable world of words, seals her fate. Words endlessly transform themselves in this novella: from the *testa* to a *testo*, as from the *pianto* to the *pianta*, which then, once gone, becomes the *pianto* of her death. Lisabetta does not live within the world of words, because those words betray their own instability as well – or her impermanence in that world. They are words that reveal the frustrated transposition of Lisabetta into the world of men, of Lisabetta into Lorenzo.

In solving the riddle of Lisabetta, one might consider this novella in light of its recent appearance in a very different work of literature: Steven James's 2009 detective thriller, *The Knight*. In this thriller, a number of serial killers base their murders upon the means of death for the lovers of the *Decameron*'s Day Four. It is once they come across the pots of basil with heads inside that the detectives break the case, linking this unusual "evidence" to the text of "John" Boccaccio. What the thriller conflates and multiplies, of course, is Lisabetta's decapitation of Lorenzo with the assassination executed by her brothers. Yet what the novel suggests is the extent to which Lisabetta can be seen – contrary to the numerous arguments offered here – as the primary agent in IV.5. For in Filomena's tale, she *solves* the murder of Lorenzo, with the help of his spirit, and makes possible his rebirth as a plant. She is, just like the author of the *Decameron*, an author of hybridity, creating new forms to give meaning to the past.

The story of Lisabetta links relics and objects to a series of individuals, embedded in a particular time and place, and to origins. Lisabetta desperately attempts to connect with her lover by planting his head in a mobile vase, creating a symbol reminiscent of the transitory world of commerce. But her attempt to reconcile these origins is too challenging a task for our protagonist. Unlike the author of the *Decameron*, she is closed in her grief as much as the women of the Proem are closed within their rooms, only to pine away. She does not write poetry; she did not even write the *canzone*, though it is allegedly sung in her voice. For a character whose existence takes origin in a literary text, she is disempowered of the very element of her existence: words. In this respect, she is the kindred spirit of Alatiel, the silent inhabitant of Boccaccio's multilingual Mediterranean whose voice remains inaccessible to readers, existing only within the form of literary biographies composed by others. These women's silent existence feeds the literature that circulated in the mercantile world, as *teste/testi* that feed *fogli*.

The Dream of the Shadow (IV.6)

F. REGINA PSAKI

No *Decameron* tale is an island. Each novella resonates with a widening circle of intertexts: with the other tales in its *giornata;* with analogous tales across the *Decameron;* with other tales told by the same narrator; with its sources and analogues; with later materials in our mental horizon but beyond the author's ken. Though this is true of the entire collection, it is particularly true of the Day Four tales, already exceptional for their "fiera materia di ragionare" [IV.1.2: cruel topic for discussion]. These tales are braided with particular intricacy: they parallel each other so systematically, with divergences so strategically deployed, that it is more difficult than usual to extract a single tale for examination. Each Day Four tale glosses the others, as much through analogy and parallel as through alteration and disparity. The sixth tale must be read in dialogue with the other Day Four *novelle* which inform it and which it illuminates in its turn.

Filostrato imposes his painful subject matter motivated by his own morose lovesickness and his desire for company in his misery. His mandate does not, however, result in stories that parallel his lovesickness; the *brigata* narrators do not like the topic, which violates their prohibition on reporting "novella altro che lieta" [I.Intro. §101: any but happy tales]. They squirm under it; some indeed squirm their way around it and out of it, with the result that IV.2 and IV.10 are in no way heart-rending. *Decameron* IV.1, IV.5, and IV.9 (still not love betrayal stories) set up a kind of scaffolding for the day's narration, a backdrop which the other tales will recall, mirror, and oppose. The primary narrator's elaborate Introduction to Day Four sets up the futility of barring "nature" (IV.Intro. §29) and its resulting human desire and does so in the context of a partial response to putative criticisms already levelled at this partial book. Filippo Balducci's putatively incomplete tale is comic in tone and outcome; no disaster results, or at least is reported, from his son's overriding desire for a "gosling." Most of the tales of Day Four, on the other hand, explore in the minor key of tragedy the futility of barring "nature" (IV.Intro. §29) and its resulting human desire.

Tales 1, 5, and 9 have featured in criticism as the scaffolding of Day Four.[1] With their deliberately spaced positioning, shared thematic palette, and shared lexicon, they give a structure to the *giornata* and a baseline plot profile which the other tales reproduce and adapt. Their thematic overlap includes forbidden and secret love, obscure familial motivation, violated class categories, bodily mutilation, and anthropophagy (literal, metaphorical, or metonymic); their lexical overlap plays on etyma such as *dolore, piangere, triste, crudele, fiero, amore,* and *cuore*. Both thematic and lexical echoes link them tightly across the span of Day Four, and make them reach backward and forward to the tales of other days such as *Decameron* II.7 (Alatiel) and V.8 (Nastagio); and most vividly, many *richiami* link them to the other tales of Day Four. Michael Sherberg notes that *Dec.* IV.1, 5, and 9 feature "three types of *paterfamilias* relations, namely father, brother, spouse, which Aristotle treats in Book VIII of the *Ethics*."[2] Sherberg aligns these with "the political models [Aristotle] discusses – monarchy, aristocracy, and timocracy and their negatives, tyranny, oligarchy, and democracy – [which] actually mimic, to his mind, the relationships, functional and dysfunctional respectively, found in families."[3] This is a compelling layering, and Sherberg shows neatly how these models interact with degrees and kinds of love and friendship in the three scaffolding tales. Given the power vested in the patriarch or his proxy, the plots of Day Four are most often framed in terms of masculine prohibition and female resistance (IV.8 is the main exception). In IV.1, 5, and 9, the bond the patriarch (father, brothers, husband respectively) feels for female family members (daughter, sister, wife) is somehow dubious, whether over-motivated, under-motivated, or perverse. Because of that extra impetus – an unstated but demonstrated investment in the woman whose sexuality is under contest – in each case the woman and her lover die. The remaining Day Four tales dissever themselves from the model of IV.1, 5, and 9 to become part of a metanarrative gloss on them, illuminating their

1 Fedi calls them the "ossatura" of the storytelling day ("Il 'regno' di Filostrato," 51); Mercuri the "spina dorsale" ("Per una lettura," 199); and Sherberg, similarly, the "backbone" (*Governance*, 119).

2 Sherberg, *Governance*, 120.

3 Ibid., 2–3.

darkness by the lighter strokes of lighter plots and personas, in what Marga Cottino-Jones calls a calculated chiaroscuro.[4]

Although *Dec.* IV.6 is a kind of intersection of all three of the "scaffolding tales" of Day Four, the tale of Tancredi and Ghismonda is a particularly domineering precedent. The template of IV.6 deliberately echoes IV.1: a noble daughter, a humble lover (husband), a secret liaison, a disappointed father, the death of the lover. But if the template is parallel, its details diverge; indeed, the initial similarities only highlight the divergences from the scaffolding tales and characters. In IV.6, instead of illicit sex we have a secret marriage; instead of a possessive and vengeful father, a compassionate and forgiving one; instead of a defiant and contemptuous daughter, a contrite and affectionate one; instead of nightmares in real life, premonitions in dreams. Boccaccio explores the *fiera materia* of Day Four not only through the explicit horror of the scaffolding tales, but also through the unlike signs of solicitude, generosity, propriety, and honour which illuminate that horror, and these unlike signs are amply on display in IV.6.

The rubrics of the three scaffolding tales, intriguingly, begin with the repressive male family members as the agents of the tale: "Tancredi, prenze di Salerno, *uccide* l'amante della figliuola" [IV.1.1: Tancredi, Prince of Salerno, kills his daughter's lover]; "I fratelli di Lisabetta *uccidon* l'amante di lei" [IV.5.1: Lisabetta's brothers murder her lover]; "Messer Guglielmo Rossiglione dà da mangiare alla moglie sua il cuore di messer Guiglielmo Guardastagno *ucciso* da lui e amato da lei" [IV.9.1: Guillaume de Roussillon causes his wife to eat the heart of her lover, Guillaume de Cabestanh, whom he has ... murdered]. The women then become the grammatical subjects of active verbs (including *muore*) as they respond to the domination and violence of their male family members. These three rubrics are relatively short (thirty words to fifty-four) and replicate the basic plot: the men kill;[5] the resistant women determine to die.[6] The rubric of *Decameron* IV.6 by contrast opens with a female subject, a reciprocal narration of dreams, and her husband's spontaneous death, all within the first twenty words:

---

4 See Cottino-Jones, "The Mode and Structure of Tragedy." While Cottino-Jones's assignments of value (what is *chiaro* and what is *scuro*) may perplex, her insights into the effects of darker and lighter tales of Day Four are acute.

5 The rubrics limit the men's actions to two: murder, and the giving or withholding of the lover's corpse. Tancredi "uccide," "mandale"; the two brothers "uccidon," "tolgon"; Guiglielmo Rossiglione "dà da mangiare" ("ucciso da lui").

6 The rubrics give more space to the women's response: Ghismonda ("messa"), "si bee," "muore"; Lisabetta "disotterra," "mettela," "piagnendo," "se ne muore"; the unnamed lady "sappiendo," "si gitta," "muore, è seppellita."

> L'Andriuola ama Gabriotto: raccontagli un sogno veduto e egli a lei un altro; muorsi di subito nelle sue braccia; mentre che ella con una sua fante alla casa di lui nel portano, son prese dalla signoria, e ella dice come l'opera sta: il podestà la vuole sforzare, ella nol patisce: sentelo il padre di lei e lei innocente trovata fa liberare, la quale, del tutto rifiutando di star piú al mondo, si fa monaca. (IV.6.1)
>
> [Andreuola loves Gabriotto. She tells him of a dream she has had, and he tells her of another. He dies suddenly in her arms, and whilst she and a maid-servant of hers are carrying him back to his own house, they are arrested by the officers of the watch. She explains how matters stand, and the chief magistrate attempts to ravish her, but she wards him off. Her father is informed[,] her innocence is established, and he secures her release. Being determined not to go on living in the world, she enters a nunnery.]

In all four tales the women choose and engage their lovers; only in IV.6 is this move not fatal to both parties. That divergence in plot is marked in the verbs as well: Andreuola is the subject of eight verbs in the (seventy-four-word) rubric;[7] her lover, of two; the *podestà*, of one; her father, of two. A great deal more plot follows Gabriotto's death than in the scaffolding tales, where once the lover dies the only question is how the woman will achieve her own death. The succession of Andreuola's tale, powered by no patriarchal punishment but rather by Gabriotto's spontaneous death, will cover the continued concealment of the marriage, the disposal of a body, an encounter with the law, an attempt by the *podestà* first at blackmail and then at force, the revelation to her father, and her deliberate retreat from the world. Indeed, the phrase "rifiutando di star piú al mondo" echoes indirectly the deliberate death of the scaffolding tales' ladies, but again the parallel only makes the divergence more marked: Andreuola may die to the world, but by her own choice "si fa monaca."

As always, between the rubric and the beginning of the new tale there is the connective tissue to the previous novella, Filomena's story of Lisabetta and the pot of basil. Despite the king's direction to tell heart-rending tales, no compassionate response to IV.5 is depicted in the frame narrative. Despite the insistence on Lisabetta's weeping in IV.5, the primary narrator mentions only the ladies' pleasure at learning the source of the song "Qual esso fu lo malo cristiano" [IV.5.24:

---

7 Two of these verbs are plural, as Andreuola acts with the assistance of her *fante* ("portano," "son prese").

Whoever it was, / Whoever the villain], making no reference to any vicarious sorrow or compassion they might have felt (or been expected to feel) for Lisabetta and Lorenzo. Panfilo's connective tissue too is made up of strictly analytical, non-affective matter: the truth-value (or not) of dreams. Lisabetta's dream in IV.5 made him choose this tale to tell, he says; he notes no substantial difference between her dream and those of his two lovers, Andreuola and Gabriotto, except that their dreams refer to the future ("di cosa che a venire era") and hers to the past ("di cosa intervenuta" [IV.6.3: relating to a future event as distinct from something ... that had already taken place]).

Panfilo's page-long discussion of dreams and their relation to reality is philosophically nuanced and rhetorically polished, with elegant alliterations and parallel constructions. While all three narrative dreams were confirmed in the waking world (§§3 and 6), Panfilo's analysis explores the degree to which different people put stock in dreams (§§4–5) before passing to the truth-value of dreams (§§5–6) and the moral choices that should or should not result from pondering their content (§7). In other words, Panfilo begins with the conviction that a dreamer feels within a dream and, once awakened to reality, sees "varie cose nel sonno, le quali quantunque a colui che dorme, dormendo, tutte paian verissime, e desto lui, alcune vere, alcune verisimili e parte fuori da ogni verità giudichi" [§4: various things in his sleep. And although whilst he is asleep they all seem absolutely real, and after waking up he judges them to be real, others possible, and a portion of them totally incredible ...]. He considers the affective disposition of certain dreamers, which makes them believe their dreams and rejoice or grieve over their content (§5). This describes Andreuola's reaction to her dream. Panfilo also considers the precognitive assumptions of those who will believe in *no* dreams until they correspond concretely to the truth: "e in contrario son di quegli che niuno ne credono se non poi che nel premostrato pericolo caduti si veggono" [§5: At the other extreme there are those who refuse to believe in dreams until they discover that they have fallen into the very predicament of which they were forewarned]. Gabriotto will be one of these. Panfilo approves neither the rush nor the refusal to believe that dreams can be a medium of understanding truth: "de' quali né l'uno né l'altro commendo, per ciò che *né sempre son veri né ogni volta falsi*" [§5: In my opinion, neither of these attitudes is commendable, because dreams are neither true every time nor always false (emphasis added)]. His balance between the two extremes is syntactically reenacted in this play of "né ... né" and in his repetition "che essi non sien tutti veri ... e che essi tutti non sien falsi" [§6: dreams are neither true every time nor always false]. He invokes universal experience for proof that not all dreams are true, and his own tale and Filomena's for proof that not all dreams are false (§6). His reflection concludes with the injunction never to let what appears in dreams sway us away from our "buoni proponimenti" [*good* intentions] and towards "cose perverse e *malvage*" [perverse and *wicked* matters (modified)]; moral choices should be made on the basis of verifiable truth, not chancy interpretations of what may be wholly fictitious (§7). "Ma vegniamo alla novella" [§7: But let us turn now to the story].

Part 1: Andreuola and Gabriotto (§§8–21)

We have seen that though Boccaccio's introductory sketches (or more properly, his narrators' sketches) of his protagonists are succinct, they are significant. The descriptors assigned to characters are always carefully chosen, and for the pairs of unhappy lovers of Day Four Boccaccio chooses parallel terms. Andreuola, already identified as "gentile," is described as "giovane e *bella assai* e senza marito" [§8: an *exceedingly beautiful* young woman ... as yet unmarried (emphasis added)]; her beloved is described as of opposite social standing but similar appeal, a "*uomo di bassa condizione* ma *di laudevoli costumi pieno* e della persona *bello* e *piacevole*" [§8: A man of *low estate* but full of admirable qualities, as well as being handsome and pleasing in appearance].[8] Young, noble, and beautiful, Andreuola falls in love and takes the initiative to let the lucky man (but not her father) know it (§9). In doing so she acts like Ghismonda and Lisabetta, but she and her beloved actually marry in secret, to keep anything but death from separating them.

Both before and after the marriage, the couple meet in secret in a "bel giardino del padre di lei" [§9: a beautiful garden ... of her father's]; more on this, below. The text emphasizes the reciprocity of their affection and pleasure as their "congiugnimenti," couplings, continue "furtivamente," in secret, in the garden.[9] One night Andreuola has a dream, the details of which are essential, set in that very place:

---

8 Narrator Panfilo's description of Gabriotto echoes Fiammetta's of Guiscardo, a man similarly low-born whose virtue makes him noble: "*uom di nazione assai umile* ma *per virtú e per costumi nobile*, piú che altro le *piacque*" [IV.1.6: she was attracted to ... a man of exceedingly humble birth but noble in character and bearing].

9 "a diletto dell'una parte e dell'altra" [§9: to the mutual joy of the two parties concerned]; "con grandissimo piacere di ciascuno" [§10: giving and getting intense pleasure]; "grande e assai lunga festa insieme avuta" [§12: they disported themselves merrily together for a long while] "abbracciandolo e basciandolo alcuna volta e da lui essendo abbracciata e basciata" [§18: embracing and kissing him while being embraced and kissed by him (modified)].

parve in sogno vedere sé essere nel suo giardino con Gabriotto, e lui con grandissimo piacer di ciascuno tener nelle sue braccia; e mentre che cosí dimoravan, le pareva veder del corpo di lui uscire una cosa oscura e terribile, la forma della quale essa non poteva conoscere, e parevale che questa cosa prendesse Gabriotto e mal grado di lei con maravigliosa forza gliele strappasse di braccio e con esso ricoverasse sotterra, né mai piú riveder potesse né l'uno né l'altro. (§10)

[she seemed to see herself in the garden with Gabriotto, giving and getting intense pleasure as she held him in her arms: and whilst they were thus occupied, she seemed to see a dark and terrible thing issuing from his body, the form of which she could not make out. The thing appeared to take hold of Gabriotto, and, by exerting some miraculous force, to tear him away from her despite all she could do to prevent it.]

Andreuola is chary of what she saw, enough to cancel her tryst with her husband that evening – meeting him the next day only to keep him from worry or suspicion (§11). She believes in dreams enough to evaluate them according to her hopes and fears, like those dreamers Panfilo had mentioned first (§5).

But when Andreuola meets Gabriotto the next night and relates her dream, he denies its veracity. As proof he offers his own eerie dream, equally rich in symbolism, which he says still did not keep him from visiting her:

a me pareva essere in una bella e dilettevol selva e in quella andar cacciando e aver presa una cavriuola tanto bella e tanto piacevole quanto alcuna altra se ne vedesse giammai; e pareami che ella fosse piú che la neve bianca, e in brieve spazio divenisse sí mia dimestica, che punto da me non si partiva. Tuttavia a me pareva averla sí cara che, acciò che da me non si partisse, le mi pareva nella gola aver messo un collar d'oro, e quella con una catena d'oro tener colle mani. E appresso questo mi pareva che, riposandosi questa cavriuola una volta e tenendomi il capo in seno, uscisse non so di che parte una veltra nera come carbone, affamata e spaventevole molto nella apparenza, e verso me se ne venisse; alla quale niuna resistenza mi parea fare; per che egli mi pareva che ella mi mettesse il muso in seno nel sinistro lato, e quello tanto rodesse che al cuor perveniva, il quale pareva che ella mi strappasse per portarsel via. (§§14–16)

[I seemed to be out hunting in a fine and pleasant wood, and I captured the most beautiful and fetching little doe you ever saw. It was whiter than the driven snow, and it quickly grew so attached to me that it followed me

> about everywhere. For my part, I was apparently so fond of the animal that I put a golden collar round its neck and kept it on a golden chain to prevent it from straying. But then I dreamt that, whilst the doe was asleep, resting its head upon my chest, a coal-black greyhound appeared as if from nowhere, starving with hunger and quite terrifying to look upon. It advanced toward me, and I seemed powerless to resist, for it sank its teeth into my left side and gnawed away until it reached my heart, which it appeared to tear out and carry off in its jaws.]

After Gabriotto mocks his own dream (and worse ones) as insubstantial, Andreuola continues to worry, even more now that she has heard his dream, and "talvolta per lo giardin riguardava se alcuna cosa nera vedesse venir d'alcuna parte" [§18: Every so often she cast her eyes round the garden to make sure that there was no sign of any black thing approaching]. Just as their two dreams are parallel, so are the dreamers' reactions on waking – fear and the need to check (§11, §17) – though she tends to believe in dreams and he forcefully makes the opposite claim: that there is never any truth in dreams ("tutti vani" [§13: invariably ... meaningless]). In his introduction Panfilo had judiciously offered that we cannot conclude that dreams are all true or all bogus, since the evidence is mixed (§§5–6). But despite Gabriotto's derision, both dreams were true presages of events in the waking world, and his sudden death parallels his own dream as well as Andreuola's.

Although Panfilo had acknowledged no difference between Lisabetta's dream and those of his two lovers beyond chronology (§3), Boccaccio's readers might remember a more substantial difference. Lisabetta's dream was utterly literal, mimetic, explicit: Lorenzo appears to her exactly as she would later find him, "pallido e tutto rabbuffato e co' panni tutti stracciati e fracidi" [IV.5.12: pallid-looking and all dishevelled, his clothes tattered and decaying]. The flat literalness of Lisabetta's dream becomes *unheimlich* precisely because in it Lorenzo tells her what no one but her brothers knew: not only that they had killed him, but where they had buried him. Her dream features none of the mystification, elision, or substitution that moderns consider characteristic of dreams, but it does correspond to the medieval category of the *visio*.[10]

The dreams in IV.6 are of quite another order. Andreuola's dream features an indeterminate black mass ("una cosa oscura e terribile, la forma della quale essa non poteva conoscere" [§10: a dark and terrible thing issuing from his body, the form of which she could not make out])

10 Marchesi, "Dire la verità," 174.

that came out of Gabriotto's own body. Gabriotto's dream features a black hound that came from somewhere indeterminate and tore out his *heart*, linking IV.6 to IV.1 and IV.9. Both black presences stand in for Gabriotto's death.[11] His dream also features the beautiful little white doe, a word which essentially combines the names Gabriotto and Andreuola into "cavriuola." This white doe, so dear to him that he binds it with a golden collar and chain, so fond of him that it never leaves him and rests its head on his heart, figures both Andreuola and their love – the joining of both parties in a marriage. The black hound attacks Gabriotto alone, while the white doe ("tanto bella e tanto piacevole" [§14], as Gabriotto is "bello e piacevole" [§8]) is not mentioned again. Now this is how we moderns think of dreams working, with imagistic transpositions and wordplay, not like a scene beamed from real life into the dreamer's head; and this category of medieval dream is a *somnium*.[12]

Panfilo tells us that Gabriotto "fu menato" [§9: was conveyed] into that beautiful garden of Andreuola's father, and that space takes on the contours of an eroticized landscape, or better, a specific erogenous zone made into a landscape. Gabriotto penetrates the intimate space of the family garden, as Guiscardo climbs up the disused "grotta" to enter the intimate space of Ghismonda's bedroom. Both lovers' dreams are set in the garden, though in Gabriotto's version it is slightly disguised (first a "bella e dilettevole selva," then an unspecified location). The garden is described schematically, but as a *locus amoenus*: "E avendo molte rose bianche e vermiglie colte, per ciò che la stagione era, con lui a piè d'una bellissima fontana e chiara, che nel giardino era, a starsi se n'andò" [§12: The roses were in flower, and she plucked a large number, some red and others white, before going to join him at the edge of a magnificent, crystal-clear fountain situated in the garden]. In this garden they compare their troubling dreams, so similar and so prescient; and it is in the garden that Gabriotto suddenly dies, in a position that blends their two dreams (§§19–20).[13] Gabriotto's death ruins the perfect

---

11 Myra Best discusses "the inevitable textual reappearance of repressed content" ("*La peste e le papere*," 158) in Day Four: "The references to the plague in the tales of the Fourth Day follow the dream-work model of repression and translation. Although the plague is not 'named' until Day VI, just as a dream tends to represent repressed material through veiled, visual references, the plague appears in Day IV through the visual signs associated with it: death, decomposition, the color black, and ... swelling and black marks" (166).

12 Marchesi, "Dire la verità," 174.

13 In Andreuola's dream she holds Gabriotto in her arms as he dies; in his dream he holds the "cavriuola" on his breast.

reciprocity of their love and he must be ejected from the garden, though covered with the silk and the roses of Andreuola. The nature of that eviction, and the new axis of Andreuola and her maidservant, occupy the next section of the tale.

Part 2: Andreuola and Her *fante* (§§22–30)

I noted that IV.6 conflates and varies the components of the scaffolding tales, and Part 2 of this novella most directly echoes IV.5. Like Lisabetta, Andreuola has a trusted *fante* who has assisted the lovers in their secret and transgressive love affair (§§9 and 20), and in the absence of a living mother she functions to some degree as a protective, maternal accomplice. In the face of their beloved's death, Lisabetta and Andreuola, both devastated, turn to this figure for support and practical help. Lisabetta's *fante* is a walk-on, present only when they dig up Lorenzo's body and remove his head (IV.5.15–16) and then vanishing from the novella. Andreuola's *fante*, by contrast, is present through the end of the tale.

Andreuola's reaction to Gabriotto's sudden death is first and foremost emotional, and Panfilo renders it in a carefully wrought series of hendiadys and doublets. On the one hand she is at a loss in practical terms ("non sappiendo che far né che dirsi" [§22: not knowing what to do or say]), and on the other she is in great need of solace ("cosí lagrimosa come era e piena d'angoscia andò la sua fante a chiamare ... e la sua miseria e il suo dolore le dimostrò" [§22: her tears streaming down her cheeks, she ran to fetch her maidservant ... and revealed to her all her sorrow and misery (modified)]). The *fante* joins wholeheartedly in her distress and in weeping over Gabriotto's dead face ("miseramente insieme alquanto ebber pianto sopra il morto viso di Gabriotto" [§23: The two women wept for some time, gazing down together upon Gabriotto's lifeless features]). Andreuola then declares for the first time that she does not mean to go on living, but before she kills herself she wants them both to contrive an honourable burial for Gabriotto that will help preserve her honour and their secret love.

On religious grounds the *fante* tries to talk Andreuola out of killing herself: why end up in hell for suicide, when the good Gabriotto surely has not gone to hell? Why not live to assist him with her prayers instead? As for the concrete challenge of the tell-tale corpse, she recommends burying him in the garden (the quickest solution and the most securely secret) or leaving him out in the street for his relatives to find. At this point the tale flirts with the comic potential of the inconvenient corpse motif, which will recur in IV.8 and (in a fully slapstick version) in IV.10. Panfilo quickly deflects that comic undertow not only by

Andreuola's continual weeping[14] but also by her sombre and honourable reasons for leaving Gabriotto outside his family's door: so that they too might mourn him; so that he not be buried clandestinely like a dog; so that she might honour their secret love and marriage. Here too, in her emotions and demeanour, Andreuola mirrors the heroines of the scaffolding tales: distraught and tearful like Lisabetta; determined to die but decisive and articulate, like Ghismonda and the lady of IV.9.[15]

Andreuola and her maid mirror Lisabetta and hers in the details of their care for the dead body. Gabriotto is wrapped in a "pezza di drappo di seta" [§27: a length of silk cloth], Lorenzo's head in a "bel drappo" or rich cloth (IV.5.17). Gabriotto is given a garland of roses and covered with them; Lorenzo is covered with fine basil from Salerno. Andreuola desires that Gabriotto "fosse *sepellito*" in a "modo *convenevole*" [§23: receive a proper burial (emphasis added)]; Lisabetta wishes for "più *convenevole sepoltura*," a more proper burial (§16). Andreuola "con molte lacrime chiusigli gli occhi e la bocca" [§27: weeping continuously ... closed his lips and his eyelids] and "con abondantissime lacrime sopra il viso gli si gittò e per lungo spazio pianse" [§29: she threw herself upon him once again, her tears streaming freely down her cheeks. She lay there sobbing for a long while]. Lisabetta "sopra essa [la testa] lungamente e amaramente pianse, tutta con le sue lacrime la lavò" [§17: cried bitterly, weeping so profusely that she saturated it [the head] with her tears]. The desperate tears, fine cloth, and roses give something of the garden to Gabriotto even as he is being cast out of it, and Andreuola re-enacts their wedding by putting her ring on his finger, as Gabriotto had placed a golden collar and chain on the doe in his dream. Lisabetta in IV.5 is assigned no direct discourse, and in her suffering becomes more passive and powerless. Andreuola, behaving now more like Ghismonda, apostrophizes her beloved (IV.1.51–4, 57), refers to her last gift, and falls in a deathlike faint over him: "'Caro mio signore, se la tua anima ora le mie lagrime vede, e niun conoscimento o sentimento dopo la partita di quella rimane a' corpi, ricevi benignamente l'ultimo dono di colei la qual tu vivendo cotanto amasti'" [§30: "[My] dear [lord], if your spirit is witness to my tears, and if there is any consciousness or feeling left in the human body after its soul has

14 Part 2 (§22–30) makes ten references to Andreuola's tears.

15 Panfilo emphasizes that Andreuola is not convinced by her maid's suggestions for disposing of the body, and decisively rejects the notion of burying Gabriotto in the garden "a guisa d'un cane" [§26: like a dog].

departed, receive fondly this final gift from the woman you loved so greatly when you were living on earth"].[16] Though Andreuola, like Ghismonda, wishes to die, she does not.

Part 3: Andreuola and the *podestà* (§§31–7)

Upon reviving, Andreuola with her maid carries Gabriotto's corpse towards his own house; she is intercepted by the *podestà*'s household and detained with the body. The *podestà* reflects the power of the state, in its investigatory function (§§33–4) and its enforcement function (§32). For reasons we shall see below, the entire purpose of the *podestà* in this tale is to embody the patriarch's power, and so schematic is his character that he is assigned no direct discourse at all that might characterize him in more nuanced fashion. In a few short lines the *podestà* twice deploys the threat of sexual coercion, both blackmailing Andreuola (promising to release her if she satisfies his desires) and attempting to take her by force. But he will also embody the threat of arranged (forced) marriage, and the constraining criteria of class and noble birth. In this section of the novella Andreuola's avatar is no longer Lisabetta (tearful but tenacious) at all, but Ghismonda.

Andreuola puts on her Ghismonda voice from the moment the night watch accosts her with her maid. Like Ghismonda, Andreuola is "piú di morte che di vita disiderosa" [§32: more eager to die than to go on living]; she too acknowledges their authority to detain her, but warns them commandingly: "'ma niuno di voi sia ardito di toccarmi ... né da questo corpo alcuna cosa rimuovere'" [§32: "let none of you be so bold as to lay a finger on me, or to remove anything from this man's body"]. With the imperious verbal power of a Ghismonda, Andreuola protects both her own person and the signs of their marriage on Gabriotto's body from being despoiled by force. She is brought before the *podestà* himself, who has the corpse examined for a cause of death. The doctors determine that Gabriotto died of natural causes, at which the *podestà*, since Andreuola was guilty of a minor crime ("in piccola cosa ... nocente," §34), abuses his power to coerce her: "dove ella a' suoi piaceri acconsentir si volesse, la libererebbe" [§34: if she would yield to his pleasures, he would set her at liberty]. At this Andreuola channels Ghismonda even more overtly: "da sdegno accesa e *divenuta fortissima, virilmente* si difese, lui con *villane parole e altiere ributtando indietro*" [§35:

16 Guiglielmo Rossiglione's furious accusations to his unnamed wife emphasize her love for Guardastagno and her pleasure in him (IV.9.20, 22) in similar language.

seething with indignation and summoning every ounce of her strength, [she] defended herself [manfully] (emphasis added)].[17] We are not shown when or how she told the *podestà* that Gabriotto was in fact her husband, but he clearly knows it by morning, when her father, Messer Negro, and his friends arrive at the palace.

When the *podestà* informs Messer Negro of the events, while trying to frame his own attempts at duress as a test of Andreuola's "costanza" [constancy] and "buona fermezza" [firm resolution] rather than as acts of sexual coercion and assault (§37), the old man grieves ("dolente a morte" [sick with anxiety], "dolendosi," §36). The *podestà* claims to have fallen powerfully in love with Andreuola ("sommo amore l'avea posto"), and to wish, with her father's permission and her own, to marry her ("dove a grado a lui, che suo padre era, e a lei fosse ... la sposerebbe," §37). If all this were not insult enough to Andreuola, the *podestà* emphasizes her husband's humble birth. By conjuring up the obstacle that had made Andreuola keep her marriage secret in the first place, he reaffirms that it really is a taint, though one he is willing to overlook. Messer Negro makes no reply at this juncture. Instead, the proposal remains in suspense when Andreuola enters, on stage with her father for the first time in the tale, and we learn how little in fact she understood his priorities and his reactions.

Part 4: Andreuola and Her Father (§§38–43)

In the context that Day Four is building, the oppressive prerogatives of the *paterfamilias* form an essential obstacle: the threats of sexual coercion and sexual violence; the unfreedom of arranged marriage; the burden of class categories conceived as an inflexible vertical hierarchy. It falls to the *podestà* to embody these prerogatives because, despite Andreuola's apparent expectations, her father declines to do so. In fact, Messer Negro sets aside the patriarchal criteria of absolute choice (for himself), obedience (for a daughter), and noble birth (for a husband); he applies instead the criteria of his daughter's happiness and her trust in him. Nothing Messer Negro says or does indicates that he would ever, in fact, have been intransigent or unforgiving had he learned of Andreuola's choice *before* the dramatic events of the night.

It is thus in the figure of Messer Negro that this tale departs most dramatically from its model, *Decameron* IV.1, and its parallels, IV.5 and 9. When Andreuola, weeping, interrupts the colloquy of the *podestà* and

17 Similar coercion occurs in IV.3 and IV.10 as well.

her father, Panfilo emphasizes details that already suggest that Messer Negro is no Tancredi: "'Padre mio ... quanto posso umilmente perdono vi domando del fallo mio ... non perché la vita mia sia perdonata, ma per morire vostra figliuola e non vostra nimica'" [§39: "Father ... pardon my transgression ... Nor do I crave this forgiveness in order that my life shall be spared, but so that I may die as your daughter and not as your enemy"]. Andreuola's weeping and contrition, calling Messer Negro "padre mio," addressing him as *voi*, and throwing herself before him – all are marks of affection and respect pointedly absent from Ghismonda's speech to Tancredi.[18] Unlike Ghismonda, Andreuola has of course nothing to upbraid her father for. Her plea is more honey than vinegar, which one could argue makes her father's reaction more accommodating than Tancredi's; but it seems clear that Andreuola's affectionate tone and behaviour are conditioned by her father's history with her rather than by any strategic intent on her part to manipulate him.

In this last section of IV.6 Messer Negro is described as elderly, kindly, and loving. That constellation of qualities, as we know, could conceivably not end well; Tancredi had been described as "assai umano" [most benevolent], "di benigno ingegno" [kindly of disposition] in his "vecchiezza" [IV.1.3: old age]. Fiammetta had described him as loving Ghismonda "tanto *teneramente* ... quanto alcuna altra figliuola da padre fosse giammai" [IV.1.4: as passionately ... as any father who has ever lived]. But again the parallels – lexical and thematic – mark the divergences, as Messer Negro is precisely the opposite of a Tancredi. His emotional profile was left undescribed at the beginning of IV.6, and only at this climax does Panfilo describe Messer Negro's emotions as Andreuola speaks: "Messer Negro, che *antico* era oramai e uomo di natura *benigno* e *amorevole*, queste parole udendo cominciò a *piagnere*, e *piangendo* levò la figliuola *teneramente* in piè" [§40: Messer Negro too began to *cry*, for he was by nature *generous* and *affectionate*, and he was *getting on* in years. And so, with *tears* in his eyes, he helped her *tenderly* to her feet (emphasis added)]. Messer Negro's emotion mirrors Andreuola's, not Tancredi's: he weeps for his daughter's suffering, not his own. What a real father does, in other words – one not pushed off balance by "scrambled desire" – Messer Negro willingly does. He comforts his daughter rather than accusing her. He suffers because she did not have faith in him ("[la] tua poca fidanza mi fa dolere" [§40: I am saddened to think that you did not trust me sufficiently]), rather than because she did not keep faith with him. He offers Gabriotto due honour as his son-in-law

18 Zak compares these two speeches in an illuminating article, "'Umana cosa,'" 18–19.

rather than murder and mutilation. Andreuola begs pardon for having "senza vostra saputa chi piú mi *piacque* marito preso" [§38: "without your knowledge, [taken as my husband] the man who was more pleasing to me than any other"]; to this her father replies, squarely, that while he would have preferred her to marry someone he had approved, still, "'se tu l'avevi tal preso quale egli ti *piacea*, questo doveva anche a me *piacere*'" [§40: "if you did indeed choose such a man, and he was pleasing to you, then [this must/should] have pleased me as well"]. This assurance – which must surprise Andreuola – is a far cry from Tancredi's tearful and accusatory reaction to Ghismonda's choice of a lowly lover. Messer Negro's paternal compassion, comprehension, and solicitude retrospectively recast Tancredi's possessive love in a queasy, greenish light.[19] When he promises to honour Gabriotto in death it is a heartfelt gesture made "per contentarti" [IV.1.41: to content you/satisfy you/console you], not the guilty reparation of a Tancredi responsible for the young man's death.

The axis of secrecy and knowledge subtends the whole of IV.6, as it does with the scaffolding tales. Messer Negro is the principal figure from whom Andreuola thinks that secrets must be kept,[20] and whose knowledge must remain imperfect; the flurry to dispose of the corpse in a way that would preserve the secret and Andreuola's honour resolves, with his recognition, into public participation in a ritual burial honouring the young couple. The fine cloth and the roses Andreuola had given in secret to the dead Gabriotto remain with him in his public burial, attended not only by his relatives but "quasi donne e uomini quanti nella città v'erano" [§42: nearly all the men and women in the city]. This secret, private bridegroom becomes an openly acknowledged member of a noble family, so that he "non solamente da lei e dai parenti di lui fu *pianto*, ma *pubblicamente* quasi da tutte le donne della città e da assai uomini" [§42: publicly received the tears, not only of Andreuola and of Gabriotto's [kin], but of nearly all the women in the city and many of the men]. Andreuola had made Gabriotto her *signore* and so addressed him (§§20, 30); her father's sorrow and pity "gentles his condition," so

19 In *Dec.* V.4, Messer Lizio da Valbona's love for his daughter, also a healthier and more equable love, offers another retrospective critique of Tancredi – though his motivation is coloured by his explicit calculation that Caterina's snared nightingale constitutes an advantageous alliance for his family.

20 "marito e moglie *segretamente* divennero" [§9: they *secretly* became husband and wife]; "il *segreto* amore tra noi stato" [§23: our *secret* love (modified)]; "*senza vostra saputa*" [§38: without your knowledge]; "prima che io l'abbia *saputo*" [§41: before I learned about it (modified)]; "che *saputa* avevano la novella" [§42: who had learned the news (modified and emphasis added)].

that in death Gabriotto is no longer an unfortunate *mésalliance* but an honoured son-in-law: "non a guisa di plebeio ma di *signore* ... sopra gli omeri de' piú nobili cittadini con grandissimo onore fu portato alla sepultura" [§42: in the style not of a plebeian but of a patrician ... borne on the shoulders of the highest nobles in the land (emphasis added)]. In IV.1 and IV.9, the tragic lovers are buried together with public acceptance, display, and mourning; Messer Negro's acceptance gives Gabriotto a similar status without the tragic double death.

The oppressive, manipulative *podestà* makes a last appearance, one that confirms his function in the tale: in the short coda after the burial he again asks Messer Negro for Andreuola as his wife. Hearing that she prefers to enter a convent, however, Messer Negro respects her wishes ("volendole in ciò *compiacere* il padre," §43), although presumably the *podestà* would have been a more socially acceptable match for Andreuola than the humble man she had chosen. At the level of plot, the *podestà*'s attempts to coerce Andreuola allow her to demonstrate the strength and eloquence of a Ghismonda, while his proposals of marriage allow Messer Negro to again express respect for his daughter's wishes, confirming him definitively as an anti-Tancredi. At the level of theme, the *podestà*'s title, role, and actions position him as the threatening shadow of patriarchal power, projected beyond the family and onto the force of the law – a shadow dissipated by Andreuola's actual father. His refusal to occupy the role of tyrant means that Andreuola, while ready to end her life, does not have to and indeed does not kill herself, neither actively like the women of IV.1 and IV.9 nor passively like Lisabetta in IV.5.

The deadly black figures in Andreuola's and Gabriotto's dreams could well have represented the patriarchal prohibition of Messer Negro, a prohibition in fact fatal to Guiscardo, Lorenzo, and Guardastagno.[21] In the event, however, Messer Negro's paternal love is one of altruistic care rather than selfish domination, and what the black figures presage is natural and unavoidable death. In the three scaffolding tales, the women resist or circumvent the patriarch's prerogative at their peril because their father/brothers/husband are more invested in that prerogative than in their daughter/sister/wife. Messer Negro, by virtue of a genuine benevolence and a genuinely parental solicitude, can carve

21 I owe this observation to Albert Russell Ascoli; and indeed it is plausible that the black mass and the black greyhound are imagistic references to their *fear* of Messer Negro, whom they conceive of as the opposite of (and opposed to) the white doe and the white roses associated with their love.

out the space first for his daughter's choice of a husband, and second for her choice to have no husband at all.[22] That the *fante* joins Andreuola in the cloister comports well with her earlier pious dissuasion from suicide, which she based on the probable fates of Andreuola and Gabriotto after death. For Andreuola herself, enclosure in the cloister may be a second-best solution, but the author of the *Decameron* – especially of the Proem – knew that for women in patriarchy, second-best solutions were often the best of a bad lot. *Decameron* IV.6 remains a tragedy, then, but one overtly not compounded by the imposition of patriarchal power and prerogative.

The parallels and divergences in themes, structures, and lexicon make IV.6 a dappling of light against the darker scaffolding tales. Such light patches will be the norm in Day Five, though the day will problematize the nature of its "happy endings."[23] When Panfilo has concluded his tale, the primary narrator specifies that Filostrato shows no compassion for Andreuola, as he had shown none for Lisabetta, or for anyone else in this woeful *giornata*, for that matter. Messer Negro's paternal compassion and clemency influence Filostrato not at all; instead he goes on oppressing the ladies in the frame tale as the patriarchs in IV.1, 5, and 9 had brutalized their female kin. Retaining his patriarchal prerogative, the king directs his next female narrator to get on with the misery for the benefit of his vengeful *Schadenfreude*. With no more discussion of the truth or untruth of dreams, the *Decameron* moves on to the next death of lovers in a garden.

22 Messer Negro will be countered in *Dec.* V.9 by Monna Giovanna's domineering brothers, who force her to remarry despite her strong reluctance.

23 Raymond Fleming points out that in *Dec.* V.8 and V.9 the endings are happy only for the men; see "Happy Endings?"

Spinning Yarns in *Decameron* IV.7

SUZANNE MAGNANINI

When it is Emilia's turn to tell the seventh tale of Day Four, she recounts the tragic affair of two working-class lovers, Simona, a wool spinner, and Pasquino, whose job it is to bring her the raw wool. Once their affair has begun, Pasquino suggests that the two meet in a garden, "che quivi più a agio e con meno sospetto potessero essere insieme" [IV.7.10: so that they could feel more relaxed together and less apprehensive of discovery]. One Sunday, in order to get out of the house, Simona lies to her father, telling him that she wishes to accompany her girlfriend Lagina to the Church of San Gallo to receive an indulgence. Her lie is not a particularly good one, for as Franco Sacchetti indicated, everyone knew that the real purpose for going to San Gallo was pleasure, not pardons: "Chi è uso a Firenze sa che ogni prima domenica di mese si va a S. Gallo, e uomini e donne in compagnia: e vanno là sù a diletto più che a perdonanza" [Whoever knows Florence, knows that every first Sunday of the month you go to San Gallo, men and women together: and they go up there more for pleasure than for the pardon].[1] Her father either trusts her fully or is not overly concerned for her honour, for he lets her go.

The two young women arrive instead at the garden and are met by Pasquino and his friend Puccino, whose street name is Stramba (Crooked). Each couple heads to a different part of the garden, with Simona and Pasquino settling themselves beside a large sage bush where they make love. Afterwards, the couple discusses sharing a *merenda*, or snack, that they plan to eat once they have rested. Pasquino changes the subject to praise the utility of sage for dental hygiene, and then rubs his teeth and gums with a leaf plucked from the bush only to return to speak

1 Cited in *Decameron*, ed. Branca, 1243n1. Sacchetti's Novella LXXV tells of two witty remarks made by Giotto, the first of which he makes after being knocked down by a pig on his way to San Gallo. See Sacchetti, *Trecentonovelle*, 224–5.

once again of their shared meal. Shortly thereafter, his face changes, his vision fails, he ceases to speak, and then falls dead. Simona's screams bring Stramba and Lagina, but rather than comfort her, Stramba loudly accuses her of having poisoned Pasquino. The uproar brings those who live around the garden out of their houses to investigate, and, on hearing Stramba's accusations met by Simona's silence and seeing Pasquino's swollen body, they lead Simona to the Palace of the Podestà. A judge begins his examination of the case immediately. Not convinced that she acted maliciously, he takes her back to the garden and to Pasquino's deformed corpse ("gonfiato come una botte" [§17: swollen up like a barrel]) so as to better understand her account. There she testifies once again, as Pasquino's friends mock her words and call for her to be burned; however, this time she also performs her testimony by wiping a sage leaf on her teeth. The sage kills her as well, much to everyone's surprise. The judge concludes that the usually innocuous, edible plant must somehow be poisonous. When he orders that the bush be dug up to prevent further misfortunes, a large toad is found at its roots. The judge deduces that the breath of the toad rendered the sage poisonous and orders both to be burned immediately.

In comparison to some of the tragic love stories of Day Four, the novella of Simona and Pasquino has received relatively little critical attention. Over the past fifty years, scholars have studied the tale as part of broader readings of the entire Day Four or of interpretations of the overarching tale of the *brigata*, oftentimes interrogating representations of gender. For example, highlighting the important role that the garden plays in this and other tales of Day Four, Marga Cottino-Jones reads the novella as demonstrating "the opposition between the private world of the individual in love and the outside society."[2] In her exploration of "the connections between plague and desire," Jessica Levenstein argues that the setting in the garden and Pasquino's swollen body, which resembles the sickened bodies described in the Introduction to the *Decameron*, suggest to the *brigata* that "their retreat does not guarantee their immunity from the plague."[3] Valerio Ferme considers the story of Simona and Pasquino alongside the other tragic tales told by the female narrators under Filostrato's rule and suggests that they reveal "the anxiety that comes from following one's natural desires in the patriarchal world, given the dangerous consequence they [women] can expect."[4] Another line of inquiry undertakes analyses of Boccaccio's literary style and his

2 Cottino-Jones, *Order from Chaos*, 75.

3 Levenstein, "Out of Bounds," 327.

4 Ferme, *Women*, 150.

use of literary antecedents in this tale. For example, Daniela Delcorno Branca explores Boccaccio's reworking of elements from the Ovidian (Pyramus and Thisbe) and courtly (Tristan and Isolde) traditions of love-death stories in this tale.[5] Mario Baratto includes his analysis of the working-class lovers in a chapter on Boccaccio's use of popular material and notes the tale's "duplice risonanza" [double resonance] as a story of lower-class characters who possess a tragic nobility.[6] More recently, taking a different tack, Justin Steinberg has focused on the judge's investigation during Simona's trial to support his argument that Boccaccio "employs the numerous 'procedural' tales in the *Decameron* to reflect critically on the nature of, and the increasing real-world power of, realistic narrative. Continually questioning the very realism he employs as a poet, he puts mimesis on trial."[7] Still other critics have examined the highly unusual death of the two lovers by sage and toad. In the eighteenth century, Domenico Maria Manni asserted that this aspect of the novella is "piuttosto favolosa che vera" [more fantastic than true].[8] This declaration, however, did not stop the nineteenth-century Neapolitan physician Giovanni Carusi from doggedly testing Manni's assertion empirically, by personally ingesting toads and scouring the Italian countryside for a poisonous variety of sage that he claimed to have identified.[9] In the twentieth century, a few scholars explained the poisonous sage-toad interaction as a folk belief that Boccaccio reworked to create his novella.[10] Some scholars searched for a literary or scientific source for Boccaccio's ingenious demise for his lovers, citing both an aphorism of the Schola Salernitana ("Cur moriatur homo cui salvia crescat in horto?" [Why should a man die while sage grows in his garden?]) regarding the positive medicinal effects of sage and other medieval medical texts that described poisoning by toad-infected plants.[11] More recently, Jonathan Usher has argued, convincingly to my mind, that the aphorism of the Schola Salernitana is not so much a direct source for Boccaccio's tale as

5 Delcorno Branca, *Boccaccio e le storie*, 24–7.

6 Baratto, *Realtà e stile*, 376.

7 See Steinberg, "Mimesis on Trial," 120.

8 Manni, *Istoria del "Decamerone,"* 294.

9 For a delightful account of Carusi's field work, see Pace, "Sage and Toad," 188–90.

10 In his commentary to this tale, Branca lists the following studies on the folklore that possibly informs it: Giuseppe Bonomo's *Scongiuri del popolo siciliano* and Maria Pia Giardini's *Tradizioni popolari nel "Decameron."* See *Decameron*, ed. Branca, 1242n1.

11 Manni indicates that the Schola Salernitana aphorism is cited in conjunction with this tale in sixteenth-century medical texts (*Istoria del "Decamerone,"* 295–6). Pastore Stocchi describes a passage in a commentary on the aphorism of the salutiferous effects of sage by a certain Bernard of Provence, who wrote in the mid-twelfth or early thirteenth century ("Altre Annotazioni," 195).

"a kind of vector, channeling and shaping other material and perhaps dictating certain choices of imagery."[12]

In the pages that follow, I begin by shifting the focus of analysis from the sage and toad at the end of the tale, compelling as they might be, to the beginning of the tale, specifically to the narrator Emilia's exordium and to Simona's occupation as spinner. The way in which Emilia binds her novella to certain others told on this day, as well as her narrative preferences throughout the *Decameron*, suggest that this tale represents not only a highly personalized and complex intervention in the ongoing protest against Filostrato's theme of "coloro li cui amori ebbero infelice fine" [IV.Intro. §1: those whose love ended unhappily] begun with Pampinea's comic tale of Frate Alberto (IV.2), but also, albeit more subtly, a revolt against her fellow female narrators and their own depictions of tragic love that create heroines out of victims. The surprisingly inarticulate spinner Simona, as well as the unsettling juxtaposition of Emilia's uplifting rhetoric and the grotesque burial of the doomed couple, offer an antidote to the potentially dangerous rhetoric hidden in the tragic love stories that precede hers. In her own way, Emilia, too, will reveal a poisonous toad lurking beneath a beautiful bush. As I undertake this reading, I will also suggest a new interpretation of the pestiferous toad as as a symbol of both the corruptibility of female flesh and the virtue of humility which could arise from the contemplation of such decay.

Emilia introduces her tale by stating, "Care compagne, la novella detta da Panfilo mi tira a doverne dire una in niuna cosa altra simile, se non che, come l'Andreuola nel giardino perdé l'amante, e così colei di cui dir debbo; e similmente presa, come l'Andreuola fu, non con forza né con vertù ma con morte inoppinata si diliberò dalla corte" [§3: My dear companions, having heard Panfilo's story I am impelled to narrate one that is dissimilar to his in every respect, except that, just as Andreuola lost her lover in a garden, so did the girl of whom I am obliged to speak. Like Andreuola, she too was arrested, but she freed herself from the arm of the law, not through physical strength, but by her untimely and unexpected death]. With these words, Emilia precisely describes how her tale relates to Panfilo's story of Andreuola and Gabriotto, a couple whose courtship and clandestine marriage take place in a garden. In both tales, the death of the male lover in the garden is followed by the female lover's appearance before a judge; however, in her exordium Emilia anticipates a very different outcome for her protagonist. Andreuola speaks "francamente" to the guards who seize her and she demands that her bodily honour be respected. With both words and

12 Usher, "Simona and Pasquino," 14.

deeds, Andreuola also valiantly resists the corrupt judge's attempt to sexually assault her: "da sdegno accesa e divenuta fortissima, virilmente si difese, lui con villane parole e altiere ributtando indietro" [IV.6.35: seething with indignation and summoning every ounce of her strength, [she] defended herself vigorously and hurled him aside with a torrent of haughty abuse]. And when, after Gabriotto's noble burial, this same judge wishes to marry Andreuola, she again exerts her agency by refusing his offer. Simona lacks both the *forza* and *virtù* to defend herself, for despite being afforded three different moments in which to speak, and having the good luck to appear before a just judge who does not jump to any conclusions, she fails miserably to make her case. Simona's failure is all the more remarkable when considered in the context of her identity as a lower-class woman and a spinner. These two groups were known for their loquacity and storytelling prowess, and so we might expect Simona to be a particularly competent narrator.

The quintessential female tasks of spinning and weaving have long been associated with storytelling in the Western literary tradition.[13] In Italian, as in English, the semantic fields for the needle and narrative arts overlap: *trama* can mean weave, weft, or woof, but also plot; the adjective *testo* means woven while the noun *testo* means text. In Book 6 of Ovid's *Metamorphoses*, the needle arts and a particular form of storytelling, testifying, are conflated in the story of the rape of Philomela. After being raped and having her tongue cut out of her mouth by her sister Procne's husband, Philomela "had a loom to work with, and with purple / On a white background, wove her story in, / Her story in and out, and when it was finished, / Gave it to one old woman, with signs and gestures / To take it to the queen [Procne]."[14] Unlike Philomela, Simona is a gifted spinner of wool, but a dismal teller of her own tragic tale.

Were she not a spinner, we still might expect Simona to be better able to sway the court to her side. Boccaccio's *Decameron* provides numerous examples in both the overarching narrative and the individual novellas of the loquacity of lower-class female workers: at the opening of Day Six, the servants Licisca and Tindaro's raucous argument over whether Sicofante's wife went to her marriage bed a virgin interrupts the *brigata*'s orderly amusements. Licisca silences Tindaro before arguing her point of view before the group that Tindaro is an idiot if he thinks young girls would squander their opportunities to enjoy themselves as they wait to be married off by their male relatives. Queen Elissa cannot seem to silence her: "la reina l'aveva ben sei volte imposto silenzio, ma niente

13 On this point see Rowe, "To Spin a Yarn," 72–3.

14 Ovid, *Metamorphoses*, trans. Humphries, 148.

valeva" [VI.Intro. §11: Six times at least the queen had told her to stop, but all to no avail], and she calls upon Dioneo to adjudicate the argument. He rules in favour of Licisca.[15] In Tale IV.5, as Gordon Poole argues, it must be Lisabetta's *fante,* or serving woman, who reveals what everyone else in that tale is trying desperately to hide. It must be the *fante*'s testimony, or gossip, that permits the tragic love story of Lisabetta and Lorenzo to become a well-known *canzone,* for she was the only one left in Messina who knew the truth. That she spilled the beans is no surprise, for as Poole observes: "Maidservants are of course, talkative, etymologically *fante* means precisely 'one who talks' (Latin *fans* from the verb *for*)."[16] Serving women also play key roles in other tales in Day Four by speaking persuasively and cleverly. It is Andreuola's *fante* who not only convinces her mistress not to commit suicide but also hatches the plan for removing Gabriotto's dead body from the garden. The *fante* in the tale Dioneo tells to close Day Four uses first her body "per essere meglio udita" [IV.10.48: knowing that she would obtain a better hearing] and then her words to convince the judge to reconsider the case against her mistress's lover, Ruggieri d'Aieroli. Her version of events triumphs and Ruggieri is eventually released. Certainly, Dioneo implicitly diminishes the power of the woman's words by noting that they require a sexual exchange in order to be efficacious with the judge; nonetheless, she and many others of her class utilize their speech either to convince others to act or to have their version of events heard and accepted as fact. Although born to the lower classes, Simona does not possess this gift of persuasive loquacity. Nor is she a competent female narrator of the sort that Boccaccio describes in the *Decameron* and other texts.

Many tales in the *Decameron* depict quick-witted working women who demonstrate considerable narrative skills. For example, the prostitute who tricks Andreuccio da Perugia does so with a *favola* that is "così ordinatamente, così compostamente detta da costei, alla quale in niuno atto moriva la parola tra' denti né balbettava la lingua" [II.5.25: She had told her tale very glibly and with great self-assurance, neither stammering at any point nor swallowing any of her words] that he cannot help but believe her. As mentioned above, the serving girl who secures Ruggieri's freedom in tale IV.10 manages to recount a complex series of events when speaking with the judge. In Book XIV of his *Genealogy of the Pagan Gods,* Boccaccio furthers his defence of poetic fictions by discussing the basest of narrators, a crazy old woman seated at the hearth and surrounded by young female servants, children, and old folks as she

15 On this "trial," see Steinberg, "Mimesis on Trial," 129–31.

16 Poole, "Boccaccio's *Decameron* IV.5," 4.

spins fantastic yarns of "ogres, fairies, and witches" on winter nights. Although generally dismissive of the crone's capacity to wrap an allegorical truth in her fantastic fictions, Boccaccio concedes that even these tales, despite the narrator's "feeble intellect," possess the power to frighten children, amuse young women, and perhaps illustrate the power of fortune.[17] In this sense, they are effective narratives that influence and shape the reactions of the audience or convey a message.

Emilia herself appears to be particularly appreciative of the talents of female narrators, for she depicts an elderly neighbour not only as the source for the tale she tells on Day Seven but also as cognizant of multiple variations of the stories she tells. In this tale, Emilia presents another Florentine woolworker, the gullible Gianni Lotteringhi, whose wife, Monna Tessa, plays upon her husband's superstitious belief in "la fantasima," a sort of folk demon, to explain her lover's knocking at their door late at night. Tessa invents a story with fantastic folk elements ("la fantasima") in order to save her reputation and her lover. Through a series of carefully worded "incantesimi" [spells], Monna Tessa dupes her husband and furnishes precise directions to her lover so that he may return another time. At the end of this tale, Emilia provides two variations on the plot, explaining,

> Ma una mia vicina, la quale è una donna molto vecchia, mi dice che l'una e l'altra fu vera, secondo che ella aveva, essendo fanciulla, saputo; ma che l'ultimo non a Gianni Lotteringhi era avvenuto, ma a uno che si chiamò Gianni di Nello, che stava in Porta San Piero, non meno sofficiente lavaceci che fosse Gianni Lotteringhi. E per ciò, donne mie care, nella vostra elezione sta di torre qual più piace delle due, o volete amendune: elle hanno grandissima virtù a così fatte cose, come per esperienza avete udito: appratatele, e portavvi ancor giovare. (VII.1.33–4)

> [However, there is a neighbor of mine, a very old woman, who tells me that both accounts are correct if there is any truth in a story which she was told when she was still a child, and that the second version refers, not to Gianni Lotteringhi, but to a man from Porta San Pietro called Gianni di Nello, who was just as great a dunderhead as Gianni Lotteringhi.
>
> I therefore leave it to you, dear ladies, to choose the version you prefer, or perhaps you would like to accept both, for as you have heard, they are extremely effective in situations like the one I have described. Commit them to memory, then, for they may well stand you in good stead in times to come.]

17 See the final line of Book XIV, Chapter X of the *Genealogia deorum gentilum, Opere in versi*, 970–1.

In this conclusion to her tale, Emilia creates a genealogy of competent female storytellers (Monna Tessa, the elderly neighbour, Emilia herself) and suggests that her female listeners might find storytelling useful themselves one day. Thus, it is quite curious that Simona, whose trade and socio-economic status Emilia highlights in her exordium and opening sentence ("di povero padre figliuola, la quale ebbe nome Simona: e quantunque le convenisse con le porprie braccia il pan che mangier volea guadagnare e filando lana sua vita reggesse" [§6: a young woman called Simona, a poor man's daughter ... Although she was obliged to earn every morsel that passed her lips by working with her hands, and obtained her livelihood by spinning wool], is a completely ineffectual storyteller.

Simona's narrative skills are so weak that she will testify three times without ever being understood. After Pasquino's unexpected demise, "ella, per lo dolore del subito accidente che il suo amante tolto avesse, quasi di sè uscita non sappiendosi scusare, fu reputato da tutti così come lo Stramba diceva" [§15: the girl herself, grief-stricken because of the sudden death of her lover, was so obviously at a loss for an explanation, they all concluded that Stramba's version of what had happened must be correct]. While we might attribute her inarticulateness to the shock of her lover's sudden death, things do not improve when she is brought before the judge. Although he believes her to be innocent, "volle, lei presente, vedere il morto corpo e il luogo e 'l modo da lei raccontatogli, per ciò che per le parole di lei nol comprendeva assai bene" [§16: he insisted that she should accompany him to the site of the occurrence, so that, by getting her to show him the manner of it and seeing the dead body for himself, he could form a clearer impression of the matter than he had been able to obtain from her words alone]. Her testimony has been so incomprehensible that the judge decides that her words do not suffice; he must also see what happened, she must show him rather than simply tell him. And once at the scene of the crime, Simona depends on gestures rather than words to finally get her point across: "Costei, al cesto della salvia accostatasi e ogni precendente istoria avendo raccontata, per pienamente darli ad intendere il caso sopravenuto, così fece come Pasquino aveva fatto, una di quelle foglie di salvia fregatasi a' denti" [§18: whereupon Simona walked over to the clump of sage, and, having told the judge what they had been doing together so as to place him fully in possession of the facts, she did as Pasquino had done, and rubbed one of the sage-leaves against her teeth]. Quite literally, Simona cannot tell a tale to save her life, and she dies from the fatal gesture meant to prove her innocence. As Emilia says at the beginning of the tale, she escapes from the clutches of the court, not with *forza* or *virtù*, but through death. Now it might be that

Pasquino's inexplicable and revolting passing – his body swells and is covered in dark blotches – is so horrifying that Simona is understandably left speechless, but, as I discuss below, Day Four of the *Decameron* provides numerous examples of women who speak up and speak out after the violent and/or unexpected death of their beloveds. In a text that celebrates the power of words to shape reality, Simona's narrative acts represent a colossal failure.

Simona's tragic death is followed immediately by Emilia's lengthy apostrophe-epiphonema that seems to ennoble the young working-class lovers by describing them with a rhetorical figure usually reserved for lofty epics such as the *Aeneid*.[18] Emilia exclaims:

> O felici anime, alle quali in un medesimo dì addivenne il fervente amore e la mortal vita terminare! E più felice, se insieme ad un medesimo luogo n'andaste! E felicissime, se nell'altra vita s'ama, e voi v'amate come di qua faceste! Ma molto più felice l'anima della Simona innanzi tratto, quanto è al nostro giudicio che vivi dietro a lei rimasi siamo, la cui innocenza non patì la fortuna che sotto la testimonianza cadesse dello Stramba e dell'Atticciato e del Malagevole, forse scardassieri o più vil uomini, più onesta via trovandole con pari sorte di morte al suo amante svilupparsi dalla loro infamia e seguitare l'anima tanto da lei amata del suo Pasquino. (§§19–20)

> [Oh, happy souls, who within the space of a single day were granted release from your passionate love and your mortal existence! And happier still, if your destination was shared! And happy beyond description, if love is possible after death, and you love one another in the after-life as deeply as you did on earth! But happiest of all, so far as we, who have survived her, are able to judge, is the soul of Simona herself, since Fortune preserved her innocence against the testimony of Stramba and Atticiato and Malagevole – who were certainly worth no more than a trio of carders, and possibly even less – and by causing her to die in the same way as her lover, found a more seemly way of ending her misery. For not only was she able to clear herself from their slanderous allegations, but she went to join the soul of her beloved Pasquino.]

Branca notes that Emilia's epiphonema is one of the rare moments before Day Ten in which a narrator intervenes to comment on his or her tale, and he views her use of this rhetorical figure as contributing to the

18 See Pastore Stocchi, "Altre Annotazioni," 197. He identifies the passage as an "apostrophe-epifonema," and notes its presence in Virgil's *Aeneid* (9.446).

development of what he perceives to be the theme of the tale, "il miracolo d'Amore eroicamente operante e trionfante anche nella più umile gente del popolo" [the miracle of Love working heroically and triumphing even in the most humble folks among the people].[19] Initially, it might seem that with this apostrophe-epiphonema Emilia simply tepidly joins the revolt against Filostrato. While he demands love stories with an *infelice fine*, she gives him one in which, as she states in her praise of Simona and Pasquino, the two young lovers are in the end *felici* because they die together on the same day. And yet the burial scene challenges this assertion of *felicità*. For Emilia's celebration, even if sincere and not ironic, is short-lived. She concludes her tale by shifting her focus from the happiness of the deceased lovers to the cause of their destruction: the sage and what lies beneath it, that "botta di meravigliosa grandezza" [§23: an incredibly large toad]. Once the mystery of their deaths is solved and the threat removed, the novella quickly ends with a grotesque funeral. In the final line of the novella, Pasquino, "insieme con la sua Simona, così enfiati come erano, dallo Stramba e dallo Atticciato e da Guccio Imbratta e dal Malagevole furono nella chiesa di San Paolo sepelliti, della quale per avventura erano popolani" [§24: whose swollen body, together with that of his beloved Simona, was buried by Stramba and Atticciato and Guccio Imbratta and Malagevole in the Church of Saint Paul, which happened to be the parish to which the two dead lovers belonged]. Initially, Emilia's epiphonema seems rhetorically to elevate these two lower-class lovers to heroic status, and to turn them into the exception to the rule of courtly love that true love manifests itself only in the hearts of lovers from the noble or upper classes. But soon after, the couple's grotesque cadavers are also literally borne aloft and into the church by a group of lowlifes, Pasquino's alleged friends, the same men who called for the death of his beloved Simona. These men show no remorse for their misguided actions in first accusing Simona and then calling for her execution, and Emilia berates them in her apostrophe by calling them "forse scardassieri, o vil uomini" [§20: worth no more than a trio of carders, and possibly even less]. Their nicknames, Stramba (Crooked), Atticciato (Potbelly), and Malagevole (Killjoy), recall those of Dante's devils. While there might be two Guccio Imbrattas running around Florence, Guccio Imbratta is one of the nicknames for Frate Cipolla's servant (VI.10), the same servant who allows Cipolla's relics to be stolen because he is too busy fornicating with the sweaty, greasy innkeeper's maid to keep an eye on them. He seems more a symbol of the sort of *amorazzo*, or base lust, that Stramba felt for Simona's

19 *Decameron*, ed. Branca, 1242n8.

friend Lagina, rather than an advocate of the dignified, courtly love that Simona and Pasquino seemed to have shared. Although the couple is buried together like Ghismonda and Guiscardo in the first tale of Day Four, no tears are shed over their demise, no one regrets their actions in the case, and they do not leave behind beautiful corpses.

In considering Boccaccio's tale of Nastagio degli Onesti (*Dec.* V.8) and its relations to a similar tale of an infernal hunt in the Florentine preacher Jacopo Passavanti's *Lo specchio della vera penitenzia* (1354), Olivia Holmes notes that the "Boccaccio's continual reworkings of inherited tales tend to make fun of normative readings, thereby dissuading us from interpreting his stories as illustrations of abstract principles or moral injunctions."[20] I would argue that in the final two sentences of the novella that juxtapose the poisonous toad and the lovers' swollen, decaying bodies, what Holmes calls Boccaccio's "recombinatory method"[21] plunges the humble woolworkers Pasquino and Simona to even lower depths. Certainly, during Day Four a number of tales conclude with poisoned and/or disfigured bodies. In the first tale, Tancredi cuts out Guiscardo's heart and Ghismonda will cover the organ with her tears and poison, before committing suicide by drinking both. In the ninth tale, Guglielmo Rossiglione will cut out the heart of his friend and his wife's lover, Guglielmo Guardastagno, and serve it to her. And in the fifth tale, Lisabetta decapitates her lover Lorenzo's corpse and hides the head in a pot of basil. These tales, however, feature members of the noble or merchant classes whose dismemberment involves noble body parts, the heart and the head, and whose self-poisoning is an act of agency. The focus on the humble characters, the poisonous toad, and corporeal decay in the final words of Emilia's tale recalls Jacopo Passavanti's "Trattato della umiltà" in *Lo specchio della vera penitenzia*. Passavanti provides multiple techniques for individuals to develop the virtue of humility, including considering their own shortcomings, meditating on Christ's humble origins and those of his disciples, and contemplating the vileness of burial and corporeal decay. He urges his readers, "Va, o uomo d'altura, quando vaneggi ne la mente tua, e considera la viltà della sepultura!"[22] [Go, man on high, when your thoughts turn to vanity,

20 Holmes, "*Decameron* 5.8," 36. In note 37, Holmes explains this concept: "This is what Guido Almansi calls Boccaccio's 'ars combinatoria' in which alternate versions of the same story can contain different messages"; see also Almansi, *Writer as Liar*, 63–107.

21 Holmes, "*Decameron* 5.8," 36.

22 Passavanti, *Specchio della vera penitenzia*, 396.

and consider the baseness of burial!] and describes in revolting detail the undoing of our mortal flesh:

> di certe membra dell'uomo, come dicono i savi esperti, nasce uno scorzone serpentino velenoso e nero, e di quelli della femmina una botta velenosa, fastidiosa e lorda. E di ciò pare che parlasse il savio Ecclesiastico quando disse: 'Cum mortuus fuerit homo, hereditabit serpentes, et bestias et vermes': quando l'uomo sarà morto, il suo retaggio saranno serpi e bestie e vermini.[23]
>
> [from certain of a man's members, the wise experts say, there is born a serpent, poisonous and black, and from a woman's a poisonous toad, bothersome and fat. And it seems that the wise Ecclesiasticus was talking about this when he said, "Cum mortuus fuerit homo, hereditabit serpentes et bestias et vermes": when a man dies, his legacy will be serpents, and beasts, and vermin.]

The immolated poisonous toad, the "botta velenosa," and its potential regeneration from Simona's decaying privates, bring our attention to ignoble organs, not the heads or hearts of tragic lovers found in other *novelle* of Day Four, thus adding to the debasement of the working-class lovers.

In the tale's jarring juxtaposition of aulic rhetorical figures and courtly metaphors with the revolting toad and swollen cadavers of the lovers borne aloft by Simona's thuggish accusers, a number of scholars have perceived a more complex vision of love and its possible manifestation across social classes than Branca allows. Giuseppe Petronio reads Pasquino and Simona's tale as a grotesque "caricature" of the tale of Andreuola and Gabriotto that precedes it.[24] Antonio Pace develops Petronio's idea as he examines the "contrastive machinery" in the tale, which he interprets as Boccaccio's negation of the possibility of "any notion of rustic, or proletarian, courtly love."[25] Certainly, Emilia's demeaning portrait of Madonna Piccarda's ugly maid Ciatuzza, who is willing to participate in a bed trick in exchange for a new shift (VIII.4), seems to suggest that she is not a champion of the lower classes. Jonathan Usher sees the contrasts in the tale (noble hearts in humble lovers;

23 Ibid., 397. I thank Michael Sherberg for pointing out this reference.

24 Petronio writes in his commentary to the *Decameron* (439) that this tale is "la trascrizione in stile caricaturale e grottesco della precedente" [the transcription of the preceding [novella] in a burlesque and grotesque style]. Cited in Pace, "Sage and Toad," 198n12.

25 Ibid., 197.

the move from a grim workshop to a garden of love; the joyous mood of the *compimento* undone by the grievous deaths of the lovers) as more a literary interrogation by Boccaccio of the received notions of courtly love than as a social commentary.[26] Emilia's apostrophe-epiphonema, which seems to elevate the lovers, however, is undone by the final two sentences of her tale, which describe the poisonous beast and the fate of the lovers' disfigured corpses. Though still linked to the virtue of humility, Pasquino and Simona are no longer Passavanti's positive examples of humble folk akin to Christ's disciples, but become instead negative examples of decaying flesh that should turn those who view them from vanity to embrace the virtue of humility. We do not know how the *brigata* itself viewed these contrasts in Emilia's novella because at the end of her tale no one comments; Neifile simply begins with her tale of Girolamo and Salvestra, another pair of lovers who will be buried together, albeit in a more noble, dignified manner.

In her exordium, Emilia explicitly links her tale to the one that precedes it, in part by recognizing the shared topography: in both tales the key narrative events unfold in gardens and courts. Justin Steinberg has noted that in Boccaccio's day, traditional accusatorial procedures (*accusatio*) that required the victim to make a formal accusation were supplanted by inquisitorial trials (*inquisitio*) in which "it was both the right and responsibility of the judge to proactively investigate and uncover crime whenever the 'clamor' of the populace 'reached his ears.'"[27] The judge's decision in Emilia's tale to return to the scene of the crime, however, is unique in the *Decameron*. Although medieval judges were advised by the jurist Gandinus to "examine the scene of the crime,"[28] no other judge or presiding official faced with adjudicating a crime will choose to do so. Once the judge enters the garden where Pasquino's corpse lies beside the sage bush, the garden becomes a courtroom. The inquiry continues with the judge considering the physical evidence now before him (Pasquino's body, the sage bush); testimony is pronounced and the accused is heard, if not completely understood, by the judge; the community, via Stramba, provides its opinion; and, eventually, a sentence of capital punishment is handed down to the culpable parties, the sage and toad. So despite the contrasts operating elsewhere in Emilia's tale, the spaces of the garden and the court are not so much contrasted or set in opposition to each other as they are merged or conflated.

26 See Usher, "Courtly Allusions."

27 Steinberg, "Mimesis on Trial," 121.

28 Ibid., 136.

In the courtly literature tradition, gardens tend to be the space of fulfilment, of the *compimento*, when after overcoming numerous obstacles the lovers are physically united. In this regard, gardens function as protective zones shielding the lovers from prying eyes and societal condemnation. In the *Decameron*, gardens play a key role, serving both as the locus for storytelling and chaste amusements for a *brigata* that flees the stricken city, and as the secretive space for illicit sexual encounters in individual tales, and thus become ambivalent symbols.[29] Metaphors of gardens and gardening, however, were also utilized in late medieval Italy to describe magistrates and the role that their just adjudications played in maintaining an orderly society. The historian Trevor Dean notes that fourteenth-century judges drew from a number of metaphorical fields to describe their work and its importance, and employed both medical and horticultural imagery: "they saw themselves as cleaners and weeders, removing dirt from the social fabric and digging out pernicious tares from the garden of state. Cleansing, weeding, healing all shared a restorative function."[30] When the judge in Emilia's tale enters the garden, he is not only furthering his investigation but also performing this metaphorical role of judge-as-gardener. In regard to his judicial duties, the judge presiding over Simona's case appears to be both diligent and assiduous; certainly he does not behave corruptly or foolishly as do judges in other tales.[31] Yet he has proven to be a very distracted gardener. Indeed, this judge presiding over Simona's case sees to ridding the garden of pernicious weeds only after two people have died, and then only by way of a proxy, by having "colui che del giardino era guardiano" [§22: the man in charge of the garden] uproot the plant before his eyes. By using this circumlocution to describe the sage's executioner, rather than *ortolano*, a word often used for other gardeners in the *Decameron*, Emilia suggests that no one is truly tending this garden. There are guardians but no gardeners. And

29 This contrast between the use of gardens in the frame tale and individual *novelle* is described in Usher, "Frame and Novella Gardens."

30 Dean, *Crime and Justice*, 90. In regard to the enforcement of the law being employed to discourage future illegality, Dean goes on to say, "Just as physicians working in the Hippocratic Galenic tradition saw disease as the outcome of humoral imbalance combined with environmental factors, so too legislators sought to restore and maintain a social balance by removing or confining contaminants and by reducing insolence through increased dosages of fear."

31 I have already discussed two tales in Day Four in which judges demand sexual favours from women appearing before them as defendants or witnesses (IV.6, IV.10). A *podestà* is cuckolded in III.5 and a judge has his pants pulled down in VIII.5. On these last two tales, see Dean, *Crime and Justice*, 76.

no one, not even the judge, has the courage to remove the true culprit, the monstrous toad, from the garden with his own hands, and so it is burned along with the sage bush.

By merging the garden and court in her tale, Emilia continues a discussion on women, love, and law woven throughout Day Four that began with the very first novella, that of Ghismonda and Guiscardo's doomed affair. Although Ghismonda never appears in court, she does plead her case before her father, Tancredi, who as the Prince of Salerno sits as the judge over both the public and private sphere, his kingdom and his home, and hands down both judgment and punishment. Emilia also implicitly links her tale to the third and fifth tales of Day Four. As in the stories of Simona and Andreuola, in Lauretta's tale (IV.3) love and the law intersect, albeit in a different way, when jealous Ninetta is jailed after murdering her wayward lover Restagnone. Her sister Magdalena secures her release by providing sexual favours to the duke who presides as the judge over the homicide. Emilia also associates her tale with Filomena's novella of Lisabetta and Lorenzo through the presence of the horticultural surprise at the end of both: the judge in Emilia's tale has the sage bush dug up to reveal a monstrous toad and Lisabetta's brothers unearth Lorenzo's head in their sister's pot of basil.

By joining her tale to all four of these *novelle* (IV.1, 3, 5, 6), Emilia strikes a discordant note in a group of tales about women who act to fulfil their own desires only to face dire consequences either before an actual magistrate or in the domestic tribunal where their male relatives sit as judges.[32] The women in the first four tales are all from the upper ranks of society: Princess Ghismonda in the first novella; the daughters of N'Arnald Civada of Provence, "uomo di nazione infima ma di chiara fede e leal mercatante, senza misura di possession e di denari ricco" [who, despite his exceedingly humble origins, had built himself a firm reputation as an honest merchant and amassed a huge fortune, both in money and capital goods], in IV.3; Lisabetta, a sister of "mercatanti, e assai ricchi uomini" [merchants who had been left very rich] in IV.5; and Andreuola, daughter of a "gentile uomo" in IV.6. Only Simona belongs to the lower classes. This descent from the upper to the lower rungs of society parallels a decline from the first four

32 Getto writes: "On the social level, with this novella, one descends a step with respect to the two previous stories and passes from the mercantile-industrial and citizen-magnate society into the midst of the humble folk to which both the young lovers belong, this time without any class distinction (an equality of class that one finds only, at the highest level of nobility, in the novellas of Gerbino and Rossiglione)" (*Vita di forme*, 133–4).

women's highly effective rhetoric or efficacious manipulation of the court to Simona's incomprehensibility. Ghismonda gives two lengthy speeches explaining her actions and criticizing her father. Magdalena sends word to the duke via a trusted ambassador indicating that she will yield to his heretofore rebuffed sexual advances, on the condition that her sister Ninetta is freed and the entire affair is kept secret. He agrees to both. Although Lisabetta weeps rather than speaks, the well-known *canzone* speaks for her, expressing her love and condemning her brothers' crime for eternity. Andreuola speaks authoritatively and effectively to all the men who may potentially exert control over her: the guards who seize her, the judge who attempts to sexually assault her, and her father who forgives her clandestine marriage to Gabriotto. But Simona, as we have seen, dies trying to make herself understood. Unlike in the tales of Ghismonda and Andreuola, none of what she says appears as direct discourse, so we have no way of knowing why her attempts to explain herself fail. In fact, the only words spoken in Emilia's tale are those of men: Stramba's accusation ("Malvagia femina, tu l'hai avvelenato!" [§14: Ah! You foul bitch, you've poisoned him!]) and the judge's less than brilliant assessment after Simona's death: "Mostra che questa salvia sia velenosa, il che della salvia non suole avvenire. Ma acciò che ella alcuno altro non offender non possa in simil modo, taglisi infino alle radici e mettasi nel fuoco" [§21: The sage is evidently poisonous, which is rather unusual, to say the least. Before it should claim any further victims, let it be hacked down to its roots and set on fire]. Simona's failure to testify persuasively on her own behalf, her inability to tell her own story, stand in stark contrast to the commanding words that Ghismonda and Andreuola speak to defend their desire and their agency. In order to understand fully Emilia's refusal to cast Simona's death as a heroic gesture, and to deny her the voice granted to many other female protagonists in the *Decameron*, it is necessary to read this novella in the context of the other tales that Emilia narrates. Those tales reveal Emilia to be a cynical realist who prefers to impart practical advice to her listeners, rather than supply them with uplifting fantasies.

We might be inclined to read the many ironic juxtapositions and contrasting elements in the novella of Simona and Pasquino as the work of an aristocratic narrator punishing lower-class workers for presumptuously aspiring to become courtly lovers. To read these contrasts only in this way, however, would be to ignore that the tale also functions as part of the broader discourse that Emilia constructs throughout the *Decameron* denouncing the corruption of the two institutions that established and enforced the laws in medieval Italy, the Church and the civic courts. Emilia begins her sustained denunciation of ecclesiastical and civic courts on the very first day of the *Decameron* (I.6), in which a "valente uomo" reveals the hypocrisy of the clergy by way of a witty retort he makes to a "frate minore inquisitore" (I.6.4), an examiner and judge of heretical practices. In Day Three, Emilia tells her companions of the adventures of Tedaldo, who secretly abandons Florence when rejected by his beloved lady. Returning to his native city seven years later, Tedaldo learns that the woman's husband, Aldobrandino, is in prison and facing execution for the murder of Tedaldo, an impossibility that leads him to reflect on the limits of judges and, more generally, a legal system dependent on the imperfect minds and testimony of men:

> Tedaldo, udito questo, cominciò a riguardare quanti e quali fossero gli errori che potevano cadere nelle menti degli uomini, prima pensando a' fratelli che uno strano avevan pianto e sepellito in luogo di lui, e appresso lo innocente per falsa suspizione accusato e con testimoni non veri averlo condotto a dover morire, e oltre a ciò la cieca severità delle leggi e de' rettori, li quali assai volte, quasi solleciti investigatori delli errori, incrudelendo fanno il falso provare, e sé ministri dicono della giustizia e di Dio, dove sono della iniquità e del diavolo essecutori. (III.7.16)

> [Having overheard the whole of this, Tedaldo began to reflect on how fatally easy it was for people to cram their heads with totally erroneous notions. His thoughts turned first of all to his brothers, who had gone into mourning and buried some stranger in his own stead, after which they had been impelled by their false suspicions to accuse this innocent man and fabricate evidence so as to have him brought under the sentence of death. This in turn led him to reflect upon the blind severity of the law and its administrators, who in order to convey the impression that they are zealously seeking the truth, often have recourse to cruelty and cause falsehood to be accepted as proven fact, hence demonstrating, for all their proud claim to be the ministers of God's justice, that their true allegiance is to the devil and his inequities.]

When later, disguised as a pilgrim, Tedaldo asks his beloved lady, Ermellina, why she ceased returning her suitor's affections, she replies that she was persuaded to do so by her confessor, a monk. Ermellina's admission spurs Tedaldo, who like the man in Emilia's anti-clerical tale on Day One is deemed a "valente uomo," to pronounce one of the longer anti-clerical tirades in the *Decameron* (III.7.33–44). In this novella, Emilia associates corruption in the church with corruption in the courts, although perhaps not directly or causally.

In the first half of the *Decameron*, Emilia expresses a dim view of inquisitors and the clergy more generally, as well as describing the ineptitude or corruption of the magistracy. It is perhaps no surprise, then, that Emilia claims not to have been listening when in Day Six Filostrato tells the well-known tale of Madonna Filippa's triumphal day in court. The other women in the *brigata* are initially embarrassed by Filippa's adulterous behaviour, but then cannot help laughing at Filostrato's tale. When called upon to narrate the next tale, "non altrimenti che se da dormir si levasse," Emilia admits that "un lungo pensiero molto di qui m'ha tenuta gran pezza lontana" [VI.8.4: as though she had just been awakened from a pleasant dream ... having been absorbed for a while in a distant reverie]. We do not learn where her mind went or for how long it was gone, but coming on the heels of Filostrato's tale regarding a theme dear to Emilia, female desire and the law, she appears to be dismissing his tale. Her companions find the novella amusing, but Emilia sees nothing to laugh at. Perhaps she wishes to contest Filostrato's vision of women rewriting the law in the courtroom before a judge, rather than using their bodies in private chambers to gain a favourable outcome. Despite Madonna Filippa's victory in having laws regarding adultery altered to remove the double standard and capital punishment for women in Filostrato's tale, historically, as Trevor Dean points out, the laws regarding adultery in many Italian cities evolved quickly over the course of the fourteenth century, with fines being imposed first on the man, and then on the woman via a loss of dowry. From the mid-fourteenth century onward, "more severe corporal punishments were introduced for the woman: shaving, whipping, death."[33] On account of this, Dean asserts that Filostrato's tale of Madonna Filippa's legal revolution runs counter to historical legal trends.[34] For this reason, at least, Emilia seems to have good reason not to laugh at Filostrato's tale.

As a narrator, Emilia has been considered a female counterpart to Dioneo, in part because when she is queen on Day Nine she loosens the narrative restraints by refusing to set a theme for the *brigata*'s storytelling. She does so, however, by arguing that after this bit of freedom, the rules may once again, and perhaps more effectively, be applied. She is under no illusion that any sort of momentary suspension of the law would lead to a sustained or permanent change in the status quo. In her obsessive returns to Florence through her tales, however, Emilia

33 Dean, *Crime and Justice*, 138.

34 Dean's discussion of this tale is part of his larger argument that historians must be careful when utilizing fiction as a source.

appears the opposite of Dioneo. He encourages his companions to sing and laugh in order to forget the stricken city, but Emilia returns to Florence, Fiesole, and the nearby countryside in six out of her ten tales.[35] She seems to be a narrator who recognizes the inescapability of certain realities and that the repressed almost always returns. While Dioneo apparently subverts societal and religious mores through his comic tales, Emilia seems to find it difficult to laugh at the ways in which corrupt institutions affect the lives of individuals, especially women.

It might seem that as the *brigata* draws closer to its inevitable return to Florence in the second half of the *Decameron*, Emilia, although never fully abandoning her anti-clerical opinions, softens her stance on women's unfair treatment before the law. In her exordium to the ninth tale, which she tells in Day Nine, Emilia openly states that "assai leggermente si conoscerà tutta la universal moltitudine delle femine dalla natura e da' costumi e dalle leggi essere agli uomini sottomessa e secondo la discrezione di quegli convenirsi reggere e governare" [IX.9.3: it will quickly be apparent that the vast majority of women are through Nature and custom, as well as in law, subservient to men, by whose opinions their conduct and actions are bound to be governed]. Through the tale she tells of two young men who seek advice from Solomon, she demonstrates herself to be well aware of how the law functions to coerce certain behaviours and punish transgressors. To the one who asks how to be loved, Solomon replies "Ama," and the other, who has inquired how to deal with his rebellious wife, Solomon instructs to go to the Ponte all'Oca. There the two men watch a muleteer viciously beat a mule into submission. The man then enacts the same violence on his wife, and, after a brutal beating that almost kills her, she meekly obeys his commands. Here, too, we see Emilia's cynicism and practical approach to her reality. As Michael Sherberg suggests, Emilia seems to recognize that the law, and particularly natural law, "serves men well, because it gives them the rhetorical props they require to rationalize violence – real and metaphorical – that they perpetrate against women." In his analysis of this tale, Sherberg observes, "Emilia's most important lesson, finally, is that women not be *oche*, because practical wisdom offers the only real chance for survival."[36] I would argue that Emilia's tale on Day Four, too, is a testament to her practicality when approaching the issues of female desire and agency and the law.

---

35 Emilia tells tales set in Florence on Days One, Three, Four, and Seven; in Fiesole on Day Eight; and in the Valdarno on Day Six.

36 Sherberg, *Governance*, 198.

Simona's inarticulateness serves as Emilia's reminder to her female companions that in the "real" world, in the Florence where the story takes place and to which the *brigata* will return, women's speech may be incomprehensible to or ignored by legal institutions, and female bodies can often be more efficacious than female voices in swaying the court to recognize female desire and agency. If women do dare to speak, their voices can be shouted down by the likes of Stramba and Malagevole. Paternal words and deeds do not always intervene to deliver women from punishment or abuse (Simona's father never appears to save or condemn her). Furthermore, Emilia's story of Simona and Pasquino's demise suggests the power of the court to penetrate the lovers' garden and that no space is completely safe for lovers even when their amorous actions are not directly censured. Finally, although in the end the judge convicts the toad and not Simona of poisoning Pasquino, if we read Emilia's conclusion to her novella while keeping in mind Passavanti's assertion that decaying female genitals can generate poisonous toads, the line separating the perpetrator from the victim begins to blur. Simona might not be responsible for the toad that killed her and her lover, but her body will potentially spawn other pestiferous creatures. She embodies the very harm that the court seeks to eliminate from the garden.

Emilia seems to recognize the way in which her companions' tales glorify their female protagonists, despite their tragic endings, by turning victims into heroines who defy the law enforced by fathers, brothers, and judges. She recognizes the seductiveness of the tragic love stories of these female rebels and the way they appeal to women, as they still do today. Notably, it is Ghismonda and Lisabetta, along with Griselda and Zinevra, who enter into Christine de Pizan's *City of Ladies*, not Simona;[37] and it is my experience that undergraduates reading the *Decameron* tend to remember easily Ghismonda and Lisabetta, but not Simona. With her apostrophe-epiphonema, an intervention that Branca describes as "the most emotional and keyed-up" by a narrator in the *Decameron*, Emilia performs a similar act of rhetorical seduction, elevating her humble lovers to the same heights as the other tragic couples that precede them. But then we experience a shocking fall from these noble heights. While Emilia's rhetorical figure assures us that the couple was "felice, felicissima," her final description of them

37 In the second book of Christine de Pizan's *Book of the City of Ladies*, Rectitude recounts to Christine Boccaccio's tales of Griselda (X.10) and Zinevra (II.9) as examples of female chastity and as "proofs to refute the view that women are lacking in constancy." On the "subject of women's constancy in love," Rectitude recites Boccaccio's tales of Ghismonda and Lisabetta (156–60; 163–8; and 178–86).

depicts swollen bodies being borne aloft by a company of scoundrels who shed no tears and show no remorse. Manlio Pastore Stocchi notes that this same rhetorical figure echoes Madonna Fiammetta's praise of the tragic lovers Pyramus and Thisbe in Boccaccio's *Elegia di Madonna Fiammetta,*[38] and so to some extent Emilia is providing an alternative ending not to just the tales told on Day Four but to a broader tradition of tales that celebrate or compensate for the tragic death of lovers with a shared tomb. Perhaps, then, Emilia provides practical advice for women not just regarding the law but also regarding literature: Beware of stories that make heroines out of victims, that glorify women whose momentary rebellion appears to transcend the law that in reality coerces them to punish themselves by taking their own lives or, like Andreuola, accepting the death of their secular selves. Beware, Emilia might tell us today, of Thelma and Louise. For women living in the real world, the examples of Ghismonda and Andreuola, although inspiring on some level, are ultimately dangerous, for underneath the beautiful rhetoric lurks a true threat.

38 Pastore Stocchi remarks that in the *Fiammetta* the protagonist/narrator uses similar words to elevate two tragic couples: Pyramus and Thisbe, and Tristan and Isolde. Rather than cite such stories as a source for the tale, Pastore Stocchi wishes "solo indicare la presenza già nell'ambito della tradizione tristaniana di spunti che troveranno un'eco nel commosso epicedio per Pasquino e per la Simona" ("Altre Annotazioni," 200).

Girolamo's Wicked Mother and the Setback of Reason in Taming Lovesickness (IV.8)

ANNELISE BRODY

The story of Girolamo and Salvestra, the eighth tale of Day Four of the *Decameron*, tells a tale of two young people who fall in love in childhood. As they grow into adolescence, their love becomes stronger. However, Girolamo's mother, concerned about the difference in social status between her son and Salvestra, objects to their love and manages to separate them by sending Girolamo to Paris. When he finally returns, his heart unchanged, he finds Salvestra married and rejecting his attentions. Broken-hearted, he resolves to let himself die next to her, in the wedding chamber where she and her husband sleep. When Salvestra and her husband realize that Girolamo is dead, they carry him home and leave him on the doorstep. The next day, upon her husband's suggestion, Salvestra goes to Girolamo's funeral wake and at the moment that she sees him in his coffin, she is overcome by love's pity and struck dead herself.

This essay aims to study the contextualization in the story of Girolamo and Salvestra of one of Boccaccio's central themes: the clash between parental and societal authority and love's raging force. This topic is particularly pivotal to Boccaccio as it spans the entirety of his works, including the *Filocolo, Amorosa visione, Decameron*, and *De mulieribus claris*.[1]

1 For *Filocolo*, see II.1–16. In the *Amorosa visione*, XXI.1, Boccaccio writes: "Or miri adunque il presente accidente / qualunque è que' che vuol legge ad amore / impor, forse per forza, strettamente. / Quivi credo vedrà che 'l suo furore / è da temprar con consiglio discreto, / a chi ne vuole aver fine migliore. / Vivean di questi i padri, ciascun lieto / di bel figliuolo: e perché contro a voglia / gli strinser, n'ebbe doloroso fleto". [Now let whoever wishes to put love / under law by intemperate force / contemplate this cruel event. / In it I believe he will see that love's furor / is to be tempered by discreet counsel / in one who hopes it will have a better consummation (trans. Hollander et al.)].

As Baratto has remarked, the tension in these stories springs from the contrasting interaction between the social environment of city life and the intimate world of emotions.[2] Boccaccio's concern about how to cure the pangs of love, displayed in the Proem of the *Decameron*, is focused here on the problem of how traditional education and parental authority ought to confront love's almighty power, which flows stronger in younger bodies. The *agritudo amoris* or lovesickness stems from Boccaccio's personal experience of distress and anguish over his being inflamed beyond measure with love. In this story, love's melancholy is defined by Girolamo's sick feeling ("non sentiva ben" [IV.8.6: could not bear]) in the absence of Salvestra. One could argue that Day Four, in which no lover rejoices in the end, is an extreme imaginary extension of the author's own possible death, as he himself affirmed in the Proem of the *Decameron*: "Nella qual noia tanto rifrigerio già mi porsero i piacevoli ragionamenti d'alcuno amico e le sue laudevoli consolazioni, che io porto fermissima opinione per quelle essere avenuto che io non sia morto" [Proem. §4: But in my anguish I have on occasion derived much relief from the agreeable conversation and the admirable expressions of sympathy offered by friends, without which I am firmly convinced that I should have perished]. In fact, the presence of compassionate friends in the life of the author establishes a dark contrast to the loneliness of the characters of Day Four, and of this story in particular. The admonition contained in Proem. §14, of taking useful counsel from the stories and of learning what ought to be avoided, is addressed to the abusive parental authority represented by Girolamo's mother.

However, the *fabula* in itself is not an original of Boccaccio's but rather represents a contemporary retelling of a plot taken from a Latin classic. The source of the story is to be found in Ovid's *Metamorphoses* 4.55–165, as Branca has already noted in a comment to the novella.[3] Boccaccio's use of this source is not unique to this particular story; he draws from it in other works, including the *Filocolo*, *Amorosa visione*, and *De mulieribus claris*. We also find a mention of this particular story in the *Teseida* and in the *Elegia di Madonna Fiammetta*.[4]

---

2 See Baratto, *Realtà e stile*, 133.

3 *Decameron*, ed. Branca, 1246n7.

4 *Teseida*: "Videvi istorie per tutto dipinte / intra le quai, con più alto lavoro, / della sposa di Nin vide distinte / l'opere tutte; e vide a piè del moro / Piramo e Tisbe / e già le gelse tinte" [Everywhere he saw stories painted / among which, with greater effort, / he saw Nun's wife among all the others; and he saw at the foot of the wall / Pyramus and Thisbe, / and the painted mulberries" (VII.62; my translation)]. *Elegia di Madonna Fiammetta*: "Considerate adunque costoro, mi viene la pietà dello sfortunato Piramo e della sua Tisbe, a' quali io porto non poca compassione, imaginandoli

The Ovid myth tells us of Pyramus and Thisbe, two Babylonian children who lived in neighbouring homes. Their love grows as they find a crack in the wall through which they communicate with each other. Their fathers oppose their marriage, and their decision to flee together brings on a series of unfortunate circumstances, which seal their doom. However, as Elsa Filosa points out, in Ovid's fable there is no mention of the parents' negative attitude or of their pain. It only says that they prohibited their children's wedding and that Thisbe's last prayer was for herself and Pyramus to be buried together. Her prayer moved the parents, who thus consented to the burial.[5] The manipulation of the story of Pyramus and Thisbe with the parental addendum is thus the starting point that allows Boccaccio to introduce the topic of parental harshness towards their children's love. Boccaccio started developing this theme in his earlier work the *Filocolo*. Its beginning shares many similarities with the story of Girolamo and Salvestra. The *Filocolo* opens with the king's adolescent son Florio falling in love with his playmate and the queen's servant Biancifiore. Like Girolamo and Silvestra, we have two children from two disparate social classes growing up together. Ramat notes that the story has its boundaries in the neighbourhood of the two young lovers, which, while spatially limiting, nevertheless give rise to a story that will reach "modi così eccezionali ed emblematici."[6] Therefore the words of Florio's father, a king, "'E certo io non mi dolgo che egli ami, ma duolmi di colei cui egli ami, perché alla sua nobiltà è dispari'" [*Filocolo* II.7: "And certainly I do not grieve that he should love; but I do regret that he should love someone inferior to himself in nobility" (trans. Cheney)], find echo in the thoughts of Girolamo's mother: "'Questo nostro fanciullo, il quale appena ancora non ha quattordici anni, è sì innamorato d'una figliola d'un sarto nostra vicina che ha nome la Salvestra, che, se non dinanzi non gliele leviamo, per avventura egli la si prenderà un giorno, senza che alcuno il sappia, per moglie, e io non sarò mai poscia lieta'" [§8: "This boy of ours," she told them, "who has only just reached the age of fourteen, is so enamoured of a local tailor's daughter, Salvestra by name, that if we do not separate them we shall perhaps wake up one

---

giovinetti, e con affanno lungamente avere amato, ed essendo per congiugnere i loro disii, perdere se medesimi" [ch. 8: After having reflected upon these ladies, I am filled with pity for the unlucky Pyramus and his Thisbe, and I feel no little compassion for them, since I imagine them losing each other when very young and after having painfully loved for a long time and being on the verge of fulfilling their desires (trans. Causa-Steindler and Mauch)].

5 See Filosa, "Intertestualità."

6 Ramat, *Saggi*, 73.

morning to find that he has married her without telling anyone about it, and I shall never be happy again"].

The parental approach of using punishments and threats does not prove effective in either case. Florio's mother sends him off to Montoro with his education in mind: "e' non si disdice a' giovani disiderosi di pervenire valorosi prencipi l'andare a' giovani veggendo i costumi delle varie nazioni del mondo" [*Filocolo* II.12: there is nothing to keep young men desirous of becoming mighty princes from going to see the manners of the different nations of the world]. Similarly, Girolamo's mother sends him off to Paris so that he can learn the ways of the nobleman: "'noi ci contenteremmo molto che tu andassi a stare a Parigi alquanto, dove gran parte della tua ricchezza vedrai come si traffica, senza che tu diventerai molto migliore e più costumato e più da bene là che qui non faresti, veggendo quei signori e quei baroni e quei gentili uomini che vi sono assai'" [§11: "We would therefore be very happy if you were to go and stay for a while in Paris, where you will not only see how a sizable part of your business is managed, but you will also, by mixing with all those lords and barons and nobles who abound in that part of the world, become a much better man, and acquire greater experience and refinement, than by remaining here"]. In the *Filocolo,* Boccaccio had already commented harshly on the uselessness of separating lovers, for "Niuna cosa è più disiderata che quella che è impossibile, o molto malagevole, ad avere. Per qualche altra cagione diventò il gelso vermiglio se non per l'ardente fiamma costretta, la quale prese più forza ne' due amanti costretti a non vedersi? ... O re, tu credi apparecchiare fredde acque all'ardente fuoco, e tu v'aggiungi legne" [Nothing is more desired than what is impossible, or very difficult, to obtain. Why else did the mulberry turn red, if not through the burning flame constrained in it, which took greater force in two lovers who could not meet? ... O king, you think you are bringing cold water to the fire, and you are adding logs].

Likewise, the novella of Girolamo and Salvestra opens with Neifile's continuation of the theme of foolishness masked under the pretence of wisdom in the very definition she offers of love as a force resistant to all counsel:

> Alcuni, al mio giudicio, valorose donne, sono li quali più che l'altre genti si credon sapere e sanno meno; e per questo non solamente a' consigli degli uomini ma ancora contra la natura delle cose presumono d'opporre il senno loro; della quale presunzione già grandissimi mali sono avvenuti e alcun bene non se ne vide giammai. E per ciò che tra l'altre naturali cose quella che riceve consiglio o operazione in contrario è amore, la cui natura

è tale che più tosto per se medisimo consumar si può che per avvedimento alcuno torre via ... (§§3–4)

[Excellent ladies, to my way of thinking there are those who imagine that they know more than others when in fact they know less, and hence they presume to set up this wisdom of theirs against not only the counsels of their fellow men, but also the laws of nature. No good has ever come of their presumption, and from time to time it has done an enormous amount of harm. Now, there is nothing in the whole of nature that is less susceptible to advice or interference than Love, whose qualities are such that it is far more likely to burn itself out of its own free will than be quenched by deliberate pressure.]

Faced with love as an ungovernable force or an irrational drive, "un'inrazionabile volontà" (*Filocolo* IV.46), the story immediately presents readers with two seemingly irreconcilable positions: the mother's faulty logic and love's rejection of such logic. By the definition given, there is nothing less susceptible to advice or interference than love, yet Girolamo's mother, in her presumption of wisdom, "non sostenea la cosa in che studiava mostrare il senno suo" [§4: by flaunting her cleverness in a matter that was beyond her competence], brings about her son's untimely death. There are two conflicting systems of values at play. The narrator informs us that this mother skilfully and loyally managed her boy's interests in conjunction with his guardians. The word "lealmente" is particularly indicative not only of her ability as administrator of her deceased husband's wealth, but of a whole set of values which the rich Florentine merchants embody. It is the loyalty to the enclosed world of the *popolo grasso*, and the ambition to climb further on the social ladder into aristocracy. Because of such ambitions she readily dismisses the object of her son's love as not suitable in a world where "suitability" is defined by wealth and social status rather than by strength of character. In Day Five of the *Decameron*, this idea is reinforced especially in the second, fourth, and seventh stories, where social status is the only reason for obtaining parental consent to wed. In the seventh story, Messer Amerigo orders the murder of his pregnant daughter and her lover, the house servant Teodoro. Amerigo's subsequent change of mind happens only when he learns that Teodoro is the true heir to a wealthy family, kidnapped as a child by pirates. In contrast, Ghismonda's lover, Guiscardo, who is of lower birth but of noble heart, is ferociously murdered by her father. All these stories play on the same theme of love among social unequals. While doing so, they pinpoint the injustice of this common social practice. Boccaccio's polemics address the evaluation of social worth based on the inherited status of wealth, which is only due to fortune and has nothing to do with true nobility. In Boccaccio's view, there is worth, which is earned, and wealth, which is inherited: nobility pertains to the former, not to empty titles or riches. The hypocrisy inherent in the system is revealed when Girolamo's mother denies the tailor's daughter, Salvestra, the hope (for a better marriage) that she herself is seeking for her son. Her peremptory refusal sets in motion the chain of events that lead to her son's death. At work here is the dramatic tension between love representing the unbridled forces of nature and parental authority representing the normative and constrictive laws of society. The tragedy of this story rests on this unbridgeable hiatus: love's ungovernability and the mother's absolute faith in the wisdom of those societal norms that allow her to believe she can establish control of her son's life. In her view, love is denied existence in itself; it can only exist in the recognized and organized form of dutiful marriage, which the difference in social class, de facto, prevents.

This story's ethical framework operates within a quartet of stories in which the focus is placed on the cruelty of family members in dealing with love: the cruel father of Ghismonda (IV.1); the merciless brothers of Elisabetta da Messina (IV.5), the uncompassionate and inflexible mother of Girolamo (IV.8); and the murderously jealous husband Guglielmo di Rossiglione (IV.9).

As Michael Sherberg has acutely noted, three symmetrically arranged stories investigate repressive male authority: the cruel father, the cruel husband, and the cruel brothers.[7] The attention to the excessive rigidity of next of kin's authority on matters of love is the *meta-topos* of this Fourth Day, in which the story of Girolamo and Salvestra plays a central role. But unique to the story of Girolamo and Salvestra is the authoritative female character as the head of the patriarchal family, which allows Boccaccio to place the blame not only on males' repressive authority but also on the repressive use of authority in general as an uncompassionate and totalitarian tool.

Bereft of her husband, Girolamo's mother seems to have taken her authoritarian role to harsh extremes. Valter Puccetti elaborates on this paternal void. The absence of the father causes Girolamo to be imprisoned in a net of suffocating bourgeois rationality: *la ragion di mercatura*, which the mother carries out so well.[8] Girolamo has no siblings and he must project his bloodline and family affairs into the ideal fulfilment

7 Sherberg, *Governance*, 119.
8 Puccetti, "Girolamo, Salvestra," 89.

of his mother's ambitions. The sacrifice required of him is expressed in the lapidary and sarcastic sentence of wishing to change a plum into a pomegranate: "come colei che si credeva per la gran ricchezza fare del pruno un melrancio" (§7). Again the reader senses the author's irony in the futile attempt of the mother to ennoble the son. In order to be accepted and loved by his mother, Girolamo must abandon who he is and become what his mother wants him to be, forfeiting the love that is the source of his well-being. However, this metamorphosis between trees does not just exemplify a change of nobility.[9] The plum is a common tree while the pomegranate is considered nobler. In its symbolism, the metamorphosis also contains a foreshadowing of death present in both Ovid and Dante. In the story of Pyramus and Thisbe (*Metamorphoses* 10.735–9), the mulberry becomes red with the blood gushing from Pyramus, just as when Adonis, the child born of Myrrah, lies dying, his blood gives birth to a pomegranate-like flower. But it is a flower destined to a brief life, the author informs us.

Dante in *Inferno* 13 also offers us a glimpse into the plum tree in the forest of suicides: "Qui le strascineremo, e per la mesta / selva saranno i nostri corpi appesi, / ciascuno al prun de l'ombra sua molesta" [vv. 106–8: We'll drag / our bodies here; they'll hang in this sad wood, / each on the stump of its vindictive shade (trans. Mandelbaum)]. There is a double reading in such trees: wealth cannot make anyone nobler, and forcing such a change of nature can bring forth death.

Until Girolamo agrees to his mother's plans, any interaction between mother and son is confined to a series of punishments and abusive words. She places her son under the guidance of tutors, and when they fail to persuade Girolamo to leave the city, she steps in with all her rage and starts to verbally abuse him: "la quale fieramente adirata del suo innamoramento, gli disse una gran villania" [§13: She was livid with anger, and gave him a fierce scolding]. Her predominant motivation is for her own happiness: "non sarò mai poscia lieta" [§8: I shall never be happy again]. She requires Girolamo to sacrifice his happiness in Florence while denying him his identity.

When all threats are revealed to be useless, she then manages to fool him with sweet words. She also makes him the promise that his sojourn in Paris will be brief – "d'oggi in doman ne verrai" – which she then proceeds to break: "vi fu due anni tenuto" [§14: he was detained by a series of delaying tactics for two whole years]. Her authority is built on the deconstructing forces of both verbal abuse and coercion, and

9 Branca explains that it was a common proverb of the fourteenth century, which meant to make something or someone nobler; see *Decameron*, ed. Branca, 556.

it develops further as a violence of separation by forcing Girolamo's physical displacement from Florence to Paris.

Nothing is said of his sojourn in Paris, other than that upon his return he is more deeply in love than before. His mother's plan seems to have succeeded at a formal level, because now Salvestra is married to a tent maker. The authority of the law is in place to prevent any further development of their love. And precisely at this point, in this intimate epic of Girolamo's emotional world being crumpled by societal rules in the name of "reason," the reader also perceives the tragic flaws of the situation. The lovelorn Girolamo becomes a tragic victim of the cultural misunderstanding that love is a disease that can be cured. For Girolamo there is no further cure.

His death happens in the enclosed space of Salvestra's bedroom. The memories of love he tries to awaken in her do not bear fruit. From Salvestra's standpoint, love is or appears to be dead, annihilated by the duties imposed onto her by marriage: "'Deh, per Dio, Girolamo vattene: egli e' passato quel tempo che alla nostra fanciullezza non si disdisse l'essere innamorati. Io sono, come tu vedi, maritata; per la qual cosa più non sta bene a me d'attendere a altro uomo che al mio marito'" [§19: "Oh, merciful heavens, do go away Girolamo. We are no longer children, and the time has passed for proclaiming our love from the house-tops. As you can see, I am married, and therefore it is no longer proper for me to care for any other man but my husband"]. One should note that Salvestra uses the word "attendere," not "amare." This "attendere" betrays at once her acceptance of marital conventions and also the absence of that love which Girolamo comes to reclaim.

In particular, Salvestra's wedding chamber is marked and enclosed further by the curtains hanging all around the walls, representing her husband's social status.[10] However, those curtains hide Girolamo also at a symbolic level: they prevent Salvestra from seeing him as the same young lover she once enjoyed. They remind Salvestra of her own status and of the rules, which now imprison her. She is frozen within them, and her "durezza" finds an echo in Girolamo's deadly "freddezza." It is yet another symbolic correspondence: her "durezza" has the aspect of one who is now insensitive to the fire of love and therefore of life, as Girolamo understands it: "Coricossi adunque il giovane allato a lei senza toccarla: e raccolti in un pensiero il lungo amor portatole e la presente durezza di lei e la perduta speranza, diliberò di più non vivere" [§23: So the young man lay down at her side without attempting to touch her, and, concentrating his thoughts on his long love for her, on

10 Puccetti, "Girolami, Salvestra," 93.

her present coldness towards him and on the dashing of his hopes, he resolved not to go on living].

Valter Puccetti affirms that this coldness of Salvestra's is to be attributed to the suspension of the flow of time. Girolamo lives suspended in Paris while Salvestra lives her time in Florence entirely and therefore is transformed by it.[11] However, considering that the same time gap happens in the *Filocolo* with the opposite outcome, one may argue that Salvestra's coldness is produced rather by her rejection of awareness: she either does not recognize him or pretends not to. But since a few lines later, by her own admission, she does in fact remember her past love quite well, one can safely affirm that ignoring Girolamo is part of her defence mechanism. Her coldness becomes the protective barrier of a fate (being married) that, in her integrity as wife, she perceives as sealed.

Upon discovering the dead Girolamo next to her, she turns to her husband for guidance. He treats Girolamo as a corpse to be rid of quickly, failing in his simplicity to acknowledge that even death does not break love's legacy. The husband, in all his practical wisdom, with the disposal of Girolamo's corpse also dismisses his wife's emotional world. More interested in hiding the truth than in investigating it, he proceeds by asking his wife to put on a cloak and go to the wake to hear if there were any rumours of their involvement with the death. Consequently, his actions are dictated not out of compassion for either his wife or the broken-hearted Girolamo, but to make sure that no one was aware of Salvestra and her husband's involvement in the matter. His sole preoccupation with the façade of respectability defines him within the society he represents: that of the *popolo minuto*. It also creates a superficial communication between him and his wife, where death and love remain confined in the practical act of ridding themselves of a dead body. The common thread that binds Girolamo and Salvestra is precisely their isolation, which leads to failed communication with their next of kin and with the people around them. There is no kind friend or relative to ease the pain.

For Salvestra this isolation is made even more evident by the cloak she is ordered to wear, which conceals her identity. Puccetti acutely notices that the light veil in the Ovidian tale that covered Thisbe's head has in Boccaccio's story become a heavy cape, which wraps the whole of Salvestra's figure. In addition, unlike her visit to the neighbour's house of the previous night, accompanied by the husband, Salvestra now goes alone to church.

11 Ibid.

Away from the home that defines her as a possession of her husband, hidden under the cape that protects her identity, Salvestra's love comes rushing back to her. The narrator comments on this apparently inexplicable surge of love: "Maravigliosa cosa è a pensare quanto sieno difficili a investigare le forze d'amore!" [§32: What a wonderful thing Love is, and how difficult it is to fathom its deep and powerful currents!]. It is interesting that her epiphany occurs when Salvestra is not recognizable by others. The cape that separates her from the outer world also gives her a more intimate protected space in which she comes to face herself, free of her societal belonging. At that moment she regains the authenticity of her feelings, but, alas, it is too late.

There is a correspondence in opposition even in the lovers' moment of death. Although Salvestra dies by his side, Girolamo had died quietly, while she lets out an "altissimo strido" [§32: piercing scream]. His death is a moment of intense dignity, in which he meets and accepts her rejection with a calm resolve to die. By contrast, Salvestra dies out loud. Her scream is not present in Ovid's tale. Puccetti notices that it is a "dilagato assenso alla morte" and it contrasts with the hostile scream that Girolamo utters in her wedding chamber.[12] If Girolamo's ultimate affirmation of the self, once words fail him, is fulfilled by his pre-death silence, Salvestra's own affirmation rests in that scream which cuts through the mourning women's cries. In that anonymous (for the audience gathered at church) scream we gather Salvestra's reinstatement of love forever lost. Her scream has the same resonance as Girolamo's silence, rebellion against a fate they did not choose.

In a later work, *De mulieribus claris*, Boccaccio will turn once more to the fable of Pyramus and Thisbe to reflect on parental cruelty, asserting that their fate was not the fault of loving each other but of their wretched parents.[13] His effort to describe an ideal society regulated

12 Ibid., 102.

13 Boccaccio, *De mulieribus claris*, XIII.12: "Chi non proverà pietà per la sorte dei due giovanetti? Chi non verserà almeno una lacrimetta per così tragico destino? Chi la negasse, avrebbe il cuore di pietra. I giovanetti, è vero, si amarono: ma non per questo meritarono morte cruenta. L'amore è un peccato dell'età giovanile, ma non detestabile, almeno per coloro che sono liberi da altri vincoli; e il loro avrebbe potuto sboccare nel matrimonio. Il vero peccato fu quello del perfido destino e forse dei loro disgraziati genitori. È vero che bisogna frenare gli impulsi dei giovinetti, ma gradatamente, per non spingerli disperati al precipizio, proprio mentre si cerca di resistere con improvvisi ostacoli al loro amore. La passione dei sensi è per se stessa smodata ed è un malanno e quasi peste comune a tutti i giovani. Ma bisogna proprio in essi saperla tollerare con pazienza. La natura stessa vuole che, fin che siamo giovani, sentiamo spontaneo lo stimolo a procreare; in modo che la stirpe umana non si estingua, se i congiungimenti carnali siano differiti al tempo della

by compassion and reason in the *Decameron* surprisingly finds an echo even in the changed perspective of the *De mulieribus*. There he may condemn love as a sin, yet not a despicable one among the young. And yet he still puts the blame both on fate and on the parents. Possibly, at the very bottom of these polemics lies the author's own wound caused by the love of his youth, a love that may have been for a lady of much higher status with whom an unauthorized wedding would have meant certain death. The idea that love can cross social barriers promotes the rejection of repressive authority and becomes one of the *Decameron*'s pedagogical goals. From the prologue of Day Four, displaying the failure of Filippo Balducci's hermit-like education of his son, to the series of enraged family members who cannot grasp the magnitude of the *amore per diletto*, Boccaccio aims to create a system of exempla in which the unintelligible force of love can be made less damaging and better accepted. Nowhere in the *Decameron*, neither by penance, fasting, abstention, societal impositions, rationality, nor honour codes, it is possible to extinguish the flames of love. If a new remedy is to be effective, it will be that of compassion and patience rather than that of restriction. In a more reasonable world, for example, in contrast to the cruelty of a father like Tancredi or Girolamo's mother we can find a corresponding happier and more sensible solution devised by a more tolerant father, Lizio di Valbona (V.4). Ser Lizio, who finds his daughter in bed with her lover, opts to wed her to him rather than taking revenge on them, although it must be noted that his daughter's lover comes from an equal social status. Similarly King Agilulfo, upon finding out that one of his grooms has made love to his wife, spares the young man's life, impressed by his cleverness, and thus simply concludes that whoever did it had better not do it again (II.2).

The tragic love stories of Day Four, particularly those in which family members react with cruelty to the pangs of love, respond to the necessity

---

vecchiaia" [Who will not pity the two young people? Who does not shed at least a single tear for their tragic end? Such a person must be made of stone. They had loved each other from the time they were children: yet not for this did they deserve a bloody death. To love while in the flower of youth is a fault, but it is not a frightful crime for unmarried persons since they can proceed to matrimony. The worst sin was Fortune's, and perhaps their wretched parents were guilty as well. Certainly the impulses of the young should be curbed, but this should be done gradually lest we drive them to ruin in their despair by setting up sudden obstacles in their path. Passionate desire is ungovernable; it is the plague and the disgrace of youth, yet we should tolerate it with patience. Nature intends us, while young and fit, to feel spontaneously the procreative urge; the human race would die out if intercourse were delayed until old age (*Famous Women*, trans. Brown)].

for the *Decameron* to be an example to its readers: mothers, fathers, husband, wives, and lovers. The Boccaccian moralist of later years, who recognizes that love's passion is an evil pest, still turns to compassion and patience rather than cruelty to tame such disease, exactly as he suggested in the *Decameron*. Thus the story of Girolamo and Salvestra not only rightly occupies a pivotal place within the *Decameron* but also serves as a bridge on the subject of love's effects and nefarious consequences between Boccaccio's earlier and later works.

How the *vida* of Guilhem de Cabestanh "quasi tutta si disfece" (IV.9)

JULIE SINGER

Quegli che queste cose cosí non essere state dicono, avrei molto caro che essi recassero gli originali: li quali se a quel che io scrivo discordanti fossero, giusta direi la loro riprensione e d'amendar me stesso m'ingegnerei; ma infino che altro che parole non apparisce, io gli lascerò con la loro oppinione, seguitando la mia, di loro dicendo quello che essi di me dicono. (IV.Intro. §39)

[I would be greatly obliged to the people who claim that these accounts are inaccurate if they would produce the original versions, and if these turn out to be different from my own, I will grant their reproach to be just, and endeavour to mend my ways. But so long as they have nothing but words to offer, I shall leave them to their opinions, stick to my own, and say the same things about them as they are saying about me.]

Filostrato's tale, the culmination of the *aspra giornata*, tells of the knight Guiglielmo Guardastagno, murdered by his lover's jealous husband, Guiglielmo Rossiglione. Rossiglione excises Guardastagno's heart from his body and serves it to his unfaithful wife for dinner; upon learning what she has eaten, the lady throws herself from a tower, and after Rossiglione flees, Guardastagno and his lover are interred together. The novella famously takes up the "eaten heart" motif as elaborated in the *vida* (biography) of Guilhem de Cabestanh and in the Old French *Lai de Guirun*, *Lai d'Ignauré*, and *Castelain de Coucy* – and, indeed, *Decameron* IV.9 has most frequently been read in light of that textual tradition.[1] Analyses of the novella have thus

1 See Paris, "Le roman du Chatelain"; Matzke, "Legend"; Hauvette, "La 39e nouvelle"; and Rossi, "Il cuore" and "Suggestion métaphorique." Syntheses of scholarship on the eaten heart include Buschinger, "Le Herzmaere de Konrad von Würzburg" and Di Maio, *Le cœur mangé*.

focused primarily on the figure of Guiglielmo and the trope of the (male) lover's heart.[2] However, I propose to read the novella by thinking through the *woman's* consuming body. Such a reading will show that this story situated between Occitania and Italy, between verse and prose, and between oral and written traditions is not just a variation on the eaten heart motif, but an illustration and a performance of the consumption, digestion, and reconstitution of texts. The specific modifications made to the *vida* of Guilhem de Cabestanh – the novella's putative source – are telling. When the troubadour *vida* becomes a savoury *vivandetta* (delicacy), the Occitan text is cannibalized in a way that denies food's (*vivanda*'s) etymological life-giving qualities, instead undoing the *vida* and erecting a tomb over the broken body. Read in the broader context of Day Four, and especially of Boccaccio's introductory self-defence, the Guardastagno novella is revelatory of a broader Boccaccian theorization of reading, adaptation, composition, and literary influence.

The plot of *Decameron* IV.9, like that of its sources and analogues, cleverly represents the consequences of the literalization and embodiment of cultural commonplaces and courtly language.[3] Unlike other related texts, however – such as the *Castelain de Coucy*, with its play on the courtly bromide according to which lovers exchange hearts – the novella pays no attention to the female lover's heart at all. This is not to say that in the Boccaccian text the woman's body is not important: on the contrary, the novella hinges on the woman's consuming (and tasting, and enjoying, and eventually falling apart) body. Absent any reference to the lady's heart, the story's narrator focuses instead on her head, her mouth, her stomach, and, ultimately, the shattering of her body and her decomposition within the tomb.

The lady's physiological processes play a key role in the novella's plot, and therefore in its theorization of literary adaptation and appropriation. Not only does desire for the same woman's body give rise to the (ultimately homicidal) tension between the two Guiglielmos, but Rossiglione's revenge is designed to play out within his wife's body. His unusual attention to culinary detail is designed to appeal to his

---

2 See, for example, Branca, "Ostensione del cuore e 'amore e morte,'" an analysis primarily concerning the tale of Ghismonda; Mazzotta, *World at Play*, 131–58; and Doueihi, "Cor ne edito" and *Perverse History*.

3 On the literalization of metaphor in "eaten heart" stories, see especially Jeay, "Consuming Passions" and Grange, "Guilhem de Cabestanh's Eaten Heart"; on the "eaten heart" as a vulgarization of courtly ideals, see Rossi, "Il cuore," 33.

concupiscent wife's appetite, ensuring her unwittingly perverse enjoyment of the dish.

> Il Rossiglione, smontato, si fece chiamare il cuoco e gli disse: "Prenderai quel cuor di cinghiare e fa che tu ne facci una vivandetta la migliore e la più dilettevole a mangiar che tu sai; e quando a tavola sarò, me la manda in una scodella d'argento." Il cuoco, presolo e postavi tutta l'arte e tutta la sollecitudine sua, minuzzatolo e messevi di buone spezie assai, ne fece uno manicaretto troppo buono. (IV.9.16)

> [when he had dismounted, he summoned the cook and said to him: "You are to take this boar's heart and see to it that you prepare the finest and most succulent dish you can devise. When I am seated at table, send it to me in a silver tureen." The cook took the heart away, minced it and added a goodly quantity of fine spices, employing all his skill and loving care and turning it into a dish that was too exquisite for words.]

The husband's instructions and the cook's final product both emphasize that the proof of the dish is in the eating: Rossiglione insists that the fare be "dilettevole a *mangiar*," designing the menu with his wife's gustatory pleasure in mind; the cook, with "arte" and "sollecitudine," minces and seasons the heart, adding spices in order to satisfy the diner ("assai," from the Latin *ad satis*), turning the heart into a "manicaretto" (from *manicare*, to eat). Indeed, the language used to characterize this unusual preparation is deceptively charming.[4] There is an abundance of diminutives, from the "pennoncello" in which Rossiglione wraps the heart to the "vivandetta," the "scodella," and the "manicaretto" he requests: minced words that evoke a dainty delicacy.[5] Likewise, the passage's recurrent language of superlative or even excessive goodness – "migliore," "buone spezie assai," "troppo buono" – indicates that Rossiglione is setting a trap for his wife's senses, as revenge is a dish best served scrumptious. He praises the cuisine ("lodogliele molto" [§17: He remarked on how delicious it looked]),

---

4 As Barbara Santich points out, the refinement of the flesh's preparation serves to "disguise, neutralise and naturalise the cannibalism" ("Revenge, Cannibalism and Self-Denial," 93). On the text's attention to culinary detail, see Sanguineti White, *La scena conviviale*, 59.

5 For Cottino-Jones, the elegance of the culinary preparation "dramatizes again Rossiglione's break with the code of chivalric comportment" ("The Mode and Structure of Tragedy," 66).

emphasizing the meal's flavour while ensuring that only his wife will experience it. Everything is set up to engage her sense of taste and thus ensure that she swallows the deception.

Once the lady has eaten, Rossiglione converts his vengeance from dinner to discourse, from physical pleasure to mental torture.[6] As he did when he lured Guardastagno into the woods and when he arranged for the deliciousness of the dish, Rossiglione begins by laying an inviting trap: "Come il cavaliere ebbe veduto che la donna tutto l'ebbe mangiato, disse: 'Donna, chente v'è paruta questa vivanda?'" [§18: On observing that the lady had finished it down to the last morsel, the knight said: "What did you think of that, Madam?"]. The question is innocent enough, but he only asks it after he has seen that his wife has already cleaned her plate – that is, he asks a question to which he already knows the answer, for the sole purpose of leading his wife into the revelation of her already-inflicted punishment. The lady's good-faith affirmation of her gustatory enjoyment ("'Monsignore, in buona fé ella m'è piaciuta molto'" [§19: "In good faith, my lord, I liked it very much"] invites him to continue. Again Rossiglione defers the disclosure of his terrible secret, this time dropping an insinuating remark that his wife cannot leave unanswered: "'Se m'aiti Idio,' disse il cavaliere 'io il vi credo, né me ne maraviglio se morto v'è piaciuto ciò che vivo più che altra cosa vi piacque'" [§20: "So help me God," exclaimed the knight, "I do believe you did. But I am not surprised to find that you liked it dead, because when it was alive you liked it better than anything else in the whole world"]. The statement is cryptic enough to pique curiosity, and unsettling in its frank reminder that the meat his wife has just eaten is nothing more than a carcass; its parallel structure ("morto" – "v'è piaciuto" – "vivo" – "vi piacque"), with the change in verb tenses perversely associating deadness with the present perfect and aliveness with the preterite, foregrounds Guardastagno's fate without yet stating it explicitly. Rossiglione has already transformed Guardastagno from a person to a foodstuff ("chente v'è paruta questa *vivanda*?") and now just a thing ("più che altra *cosa*"). The lady pauses ("alquanto stette" [§21: was silent for a while]) before asking outright what her husband has made her eat. Again, both the lady's question

6 I use the language of conversion deliberately, as, indeed, processes of conversion and digestion impel the novella's entire narrative trajectory: from the conversion of Rossiglione's love for Guardastagno into hate ("il grande amore che al Guardastagno portava in mortale odio convertì," §8) to the transformation of Guardastagno's heart into a culinary delicacy, and finally, the lady's consumption of the heart and the ultimate dissolution of her body.

("'che *cosa* è questa che voi m'avete fatta mangiare?'" [§21: "What is this that you have caused me to eat?"]) and her husband's reply underscore the thingness of Guardastagno's heart.

> Il cavalier rispose: "Quello che voi avete mangiato è stato veramente il cuore di messer Guiglielmo Guardastagno, il qual voi come disleal femina tanto amavate; e sappiate di certo che egli è stato desso, per ciò che io con queste mani gliele strappai, poco avanti che io tornassi, del petto." (§22)
>
> ["That which you have eaten," replied the knight, "was in fact the heart of Guillaume de Cabestanh, with whom you, faithless woman that you are, were so infatuated. And you may rest assured that it was truly his, because I tore it from his breast myself, with these very hands, a little before I returned home."]

Rossiglione maintains a firm distinction between Guardastagno and his heart, emphasizing that his wife has eaten the latter ("'egli è stato desso'"). He even re-enacts the violent dismemberment by inserting himself, in a subordinate clause, between Guardastagno's heart and his chest: "'gliele strappai, *poco avanti che io tornassi*, del petto.'"

Only now might the lady understand Rossiglione's reply to the first question she posed, *before* dinner, a reply that we can now see as an allusion to her consumption of Guardastagno's body. The lady asked why Guardastagno had not come to dinner as expected, to which Rossiglione responded, "'Donna, io ho avuto da lui che egli non ci può essere di qui domane'" [§15: "Madam, I have received word from him that he cannot be here until tomorrow"]. What Rossiglione has "received from him" ("avuto da lui") is his heart, and the cryptic description of Guardastagno as gone today, here tomorrow is a cruel scatological joke. With this seemingly innocuous answer, Rossiglione already recognizes and anticipates that the success of his ploy will be written in his wife's body: he seeks to manipulate not just her taste and enjoyment, but her digestive process, exploiting the innermost workings of her body to get her lover out of her system.[7] But while the quip presumes normal bodily function on the woman's part (she will consume her lover's heart today and excrete it tomorrow), the lady responds with bodily disturbance: "un poco turbatetta rimase" [§15: feeling somewhat perturbed]. This disturbance of the head shows the inadequacy of Rossiglione's

7 This is not the first remark to be proven true in retrospect, albeit in unexpected manner: see also Guardastagno's promise, the day before his murder, that "senza fallo il dì seguente andrebbe a cenar con lui [Rossiglione]" (§9).

"excremental mode of reading"[8] and presages the ultimate disturbance of digestion – as indeed, overall, the story simultaneously emphasizes and stymies the lady's digestion of her lover's heart.

Rossiglione's scheme is predicated on his wife's consumption and digestion of her lover's heart; however, throughout the novella, and especially at the end of the lady's life, contemporaneous understandings of and cultural expectations about digestion are repeatedly overturned. In the later Middle Ages and into the early modern period, digestion is typically conceived as a form of "cooking" within the body.[9] Rossiglione's particular emphasis on the culinary preparation of the heart mirrors the further "cooking" that can be expected to take place in his wife's body once she has consumed it. Yet Guardastagno's heart remains undigested, as the lady kills herself before her body has had time to "cook" and assimilate what she has just eaten. She thereby disrupts her own digestion and thwarts her husband's revenge plot by precluding the final stage, disgust/excretion, the one to which her husband earlier alluded. With his private scatological joke, and with his triumphant revelation of the composition of his wife's dinner, Rossiglione clearly seeks to engender disgust, playing into pre-modern sensibilities of digestion as "that magical yet mundane moment when dead animal and vegetable matter is ingested to sustain life, when something alien is brought into the self and something alien is excreted by the self, when, as Edward Reynolds suggests [in *Treatise of the Passions and Faculties of the Soule of Man*, London, 1640], the object of appetite is rendered the source of repugnance."[10]

Yet this does not come to pass. The lady persists in expressing admiration for the nobility of the heart she has consumed, and her disgust is reserved for her husband's treachery.

> Voi faceste quello che disleale e malvagio cavalier dee fare; ché se io, non isforzandomi egli, l'avea del mio amor fatto signore e voi in questo oltraggiato, non egli ma io ne doveva la pena portare. Ma unque a Dio non piaccia che sopra a così nobil vivanda, come è stata quella del cuore d'un così valoroso e così cortese cavaliere come messer Guiglielmo Guardastagno fu, mai altra vivanda vada! (§23)

> [This can only have been the work of an evil and treacherous knight, for if, of my own free will, I abused you by making him the master of my

8 Stone, *Death of the Troubadour*, 103.

9 Durling, "Deceit and Digestion," 68; Pouchelle, "Une parole médicale," 185.

10 Schoenfeldt, "Fables of the Belly," 245.

love, it was not he but I that should have paid the penalty for it. But God forbid that any other food should pass my lips now that I have partaken of such excellent fare as the heart of so gallant and courteous a knight as Guillaume de Cabestanh.]

With her repeated use of the word "vivanda" the lady holds her own in the *giostra intellettuale,*[11] picking up her husband's language and throwing it back in his face; while Rossiglione clearly relished the irony of killing "ciò che vivo piú che altra cosa [le] piacque" and turning the *vivo* into a *vivanda,* his wife shows him that she, too, can turn life into death. Her act of suicide interrupts and thereby denies the very physiology of digestion (as, literally, the nourishment by which food is converted to flesh),[12] demonstrating instead that Guardastagno's heart has nourished her own courage and love.[13] The lover's body is ingested but not excreted; with her suicidal act she finds a way to expose the secret inside her body, while keeping her own hands clean.[14] Indeed, the only disgust that Rossiglione engenders is directed towards himself: he has acted as a "disleale e malvagio cavalier"; seeing his wife's dead body "parvegli aver mal fatto" [§24: made him repent the wickedness of his deed].

Digestion is a key image for *Decameron* IV.9, it being not just the premeditated mechanism of Rossiglione's revenge on his wife but also, in fourteenth-century medical and medicalizing discourse, "an image for the dissolution of the body in death."[15] Indeed, Boccaccio emphasizes just such dissolution when he evokes – in a departure from his Occitan source material – the shattered state of the lady's body: "E levata in piè, per una finestra, la quale dietro a lei era, indietro senza altra diliberazione si lasciò cadere. La finestra era molto alta da terra, per che, come la donna cadde, non solamente morì ma quasi tutta si disfece" [§24: And rising to her feet, she retreated a few steps to an open window, through which without a second thought she allowed herself

11 Russo, *Letture critiche,* 173.

12 The precise mechanisms of this process of conversion remain unknown, and contested, in the fourteenth century; see Wood, "What Price the Horror Vacui?"

13 In this she echoes Ghismonda and Lisabetta: Ghismonda, whose courageous speech is similarly inspired; Lisabetta, whose tears combine with her lover's head to nourish the basil. On the themes of hunger, consumption, nourishment, digestion, fragmenting of the body, interment and disinterment, and transformation running through Day Four, see Barberi Squarotti, "Amore e morte."

14 This stands in contrast to Chaucer's Prioress's and Nun's Priest's Tales, in which the bodies of murder victims are hidden in excrement and "the exposure of the violent actions necessitates the seeker to wade through mire, possibly sullying himself": see Morrison, *Excrement,* 1.

15 Pouchelle, *The Body and Surgery,* 182.

to fall. The window was situated high above the ground, so that the lady was not only killed by her fall but almost completely disfigured]. Her self-destructive act fragments her body even as it halts the further breakdown of her lover's minced, cooked, chewed, and swallowed heart. Digestion, in its etymological sense, is still taking place: as Robert Durling points out, "Latin *digero* meant properly to force apart, to separate."[16] Here, instead of food being broken down and nutrients distributed throughout the consumer's body, it is the consumer's entire body that is broken down (with the lover's heart, incompletely processed, still inside it). The lovers are brought together, and made alike, through their joint dissolution: the lady's ingestion of Guardastagno's heart "embodies their spiritual fusion and as a symbolic act works paradoxically through the body to deny the limits of the body."[17] The notion that the two lovers have become one is reinforced by the complementarity in the descriptions of their deaths. Guardastagno dies suddenly, has no time to speak, and just falls and expires ("Il Guardastagno, senza potere alcuna difesa fare o pur dire una parola, passato di quella lancia *cadde* e poco appresso *morì*" [§12: Cabestanh was powerless to defend himself, or even to utter a word, and on being run through by the lance he fell to the ground. A moment later he was dead]; the lady gives a noble speech, then "*cadde*, non solamente *morì* ma quasi tutta si disfece." The lady's words belatedly supply the defence that Guardastagno was never able to mount; and once physically reunited with her lover, she dashes her body to pieces along with the chewed-up heart within, mutilating both Guardastagno *and* herself even more thoroughly than her husband had mutilated Guardastagno in cutting out his heart.[18]

By breaking apart her own body along with the part of Guardastagno's body that she has consumed, the lady effectively defeats her husband at his own game. She renders her and her lover's reunion permanent; she manages to achieve the ideal of a shared death with a man who predeceased her by several hours.[19] Whereas Rossiglione takes flight, his wife is accorded a religious burial in her castle's chapel – despite having committed suicide.[20] Indeed, her sepulture paves the

16 Durling, "Deceit and Digestion," 61.

17 Gaunt, *Love and Death*, 98.

18 The incorporation of Guardastagno's heart into his lover's body is reminiscent of Old Provençal wordplay on heart (*cor*) and body (*cors*): see Tavera, "Ancien provençal 'cor(s) et 'cor(p)s.'"

19 On the ideal of shared death, see Gaunt, *Love and Death*, especially 75.

20 Daniel Rolfs expresses surprise at this ("Dante, Petrarch, Boccaccio," 219), but Alexander Murray notes that burial of suicides in consecrated ground appears to have happened with some frequency despite being technically outlawed (*Suicide*, 2:464).

way for reconciliation and remembrance, as this novella, like many others in Day Four, ends with the interment of the lovers in a double tomb.[21] If the novella's climactic dialogue between the lady and her husband centres on the question of *what* we put in our bodies, its elegiac conclusion shows *where* we put the bodies.

> La mattina seguente fu saputo per tutta la contrata come questa cosa era stata: per che da quegli del castello di messer Guiglielmo Guardastagno e da quegli ancora del castello della donna, con grandissimo dolore e pianto, furono i due corpi ricolti e nella chiesa del castello medesimo della donna in una medesima sepoltura fur posti, e sopr'essa scritti versi significanti chi fosser quegli che dentro sepolti v'erano, e il modo e la cagione della lor morte. (§25)

> [By next morning the circumstances of the affair had become common knowledge throughout the whole of the district, and people were sent out from the castles of the lady's family and of Guillaume de Cabestanh to gather up the two bodies, which were later placed in a single tomb in the chapel of the lady's own castle amid widespread grief and mourning. And the tombstone bore an inscription, in verse, to indicate who was buried there and the manner and the cause of their deaths.]

The peculiar disposition of the lovers' remains renders their monument rather different from the other tombs of Day Four, and from the historical tombs being produced in Boccaccio's Italy.[22] While the latter tend to consist of horizontal elements stacked vertically – a sarcophagus, often decorated with heraldic devices, surmounted by horizontal effigies and canopies or other decorative elements – Guardastagno's lover refuses to put anything else atop his body ("'Ma unque a Dio non piaccia che *sopra* a così nobil vivanda ... mai altra vivanda vada,'" §23). Instead, the Boccaccian tomb is organized as a *mise en abyme*. The lady, having eaten her lover's heart, becomes, quite literally, a sarcophagus.[23] Her cadaver is presumably laid in a "real" sarcophagus alongside the remainder of Guardastagno's body; the repetition of the language of sameness

21 On burials and especially double burials in Day Four *novelle*, see Francillon, "Quelques observations," 27; and Fedi, "Il 'regno' di Filostrato," 53; on annihilation and remembrance, see Sanguineti White, *La scena conviviale*, 74.

22 See Herklotz, *"Sepulcra" et "monumenta,"* and Panofsky, *Tomb Sculpture*.

23 *Sarcophagus* is derived from the Greek for *flesh-eating*. Incidentally, Boccaccio is the first author (or among the first) to introduce the term *sarcofago* in written Italian: he uses it in his commentary on Canto IX in the *Esposizioni sopra la Commedia*. See "Sarcofago" in *TLIO*.

("nella chiesa del castello *medesimo* della donna in una *medesima* sepoltura fur posti," §25) emphasizes the lovers' identity, suggesting that this tomb contains not two proximate bodies, but one composite one. The syntax of the tomb description reinforces the *mise en abyme*, as the bodies are placed *in* a tomb *in* a chapel *in* a castle *of* a lady ("*nella* chiesa *del* castello medesimo *della* donna *in* una medesima sepoltura"). Finally, the sarcophagus, surmounted by a verse epitaph telling the lovers' story, is embedded within a memorializing prose narrative (the novella itself) that recounts the same story. The text is then to be devoured by Boccaccio's (female) readers, who consume the "eaten heart" narrative and become its outermost tomb.[24] Each of these nested sarcophagi "swallows" the last, digesting its contents, enabling conversion into text that can be consumed and communicated in multiple forms: as an epitaph, as a popular oral legend, as an Italian novella.

The images of digestion and undoing ("quasi tutta si disfece") are likewise helpful for thinking in a broader sense about Boccaccio's process of literary adaptation.[25] The established metaphor of reading as eating, as Victoria Kirkham explains, "reflects the notion that knowledge is something to be consumed; that we ingest what others have said or written in order to digest it and from that put forth enunciations of our own."[26] Building on this longstanding tradition, Petrarch writes of his own digestion and absorption of the classics:

> mane comedi quod sero digererem, hausi puer quod senior ruminarem. Hec se michi tam familiariter ingessere et non modo memorie sed medullis affixa sunt unumque cum ingenio facta sunt meo, ut etsi per omnem vitam amplius non legantur, ipsa quidem hereant, actis in intima animi parte radicibus.[27]

> [I ate in the morning what I would digest in the evening, I swallowed as a boy what I would ruminate upon as an older man. I have thoroughly

24 This interpretation is informed by Roberta Krueger's reading of the *Castelain de Coucy*, wherein she argues most persuasively that the romance's inscribed female reader is made to devour the text in a re-enactment of its plot and in fulfilment of the author's desire (*Women Readers*, 182–215). See also Solterer, "Dismembering, Remembering," 121.

25 "The term *digestion* itself is one of the interfaces between ideas of bodily and mental process ... Any multiple can be categorized and arranged: digested" (Durling, "Deceit and Digestion," 61).

26 Kirkham, *Dante the Book Glutton*, 6. There is good reason to think that this trope was well known to Boccaccio; Kirkham traces it in Cicero's *De finibus*, in the Bible (Ezekiel and John – Revelation), Macrobius's *Saturnalia*, Augustine's *Confessions*, Peter Comestor, and the *Convivio*. On alimentary metaphors, see Curtius, *European Literature*, 134–6.

27 Petrarch, *Familiari*, 4:106.

absorbed these writings, implanting them not only in my memory but in my marrow, and they have so become one with my mind that were I never to read them for the remainder of my life, they would cling to me, having taken root in the innermost recesses of my mind. (trans. Bernardo)]

He develops this metaphor, as it so happens, in *Familiares* 22.2, "the famous letter on imitation written to Boccaccio in 1359."[28] Here, in his meditation on the use of literary sources, Petrarch is not introducing a new idea to his friend: *Decameron* IV.9, in framing a recognizably adapted "eaten heart" story with overt allusions to "Provençal" source material, has already anticipated Petrarch's digestive "absorption" and invited the reader to ruminate on the consumption and (re)production of texts as a digestive process.[29]

The shattering of the lady's body is, at the plot level, a catalyst for textual creation. The action gives rise to oral accounts of indeterminate authorship ("La mattina seguente fu saputo," §25), which are then converted into verse that is inscribed on a commemorative monument. Thus the same story has already inspired multiple narratives: the morning-after gossip, the epitaph, as well as the possibly separate oral tradition to which Filostrato alludes at the very beginning of his narration ("Dovete adunque sapere che, secondo che raccontano i provenzali, in Provenza furon già due nobili cavalieri" [§4: You must know, then, that according to the Provençals, there once lived in Provence two noble knights"]) – and, of course, the novella itself (which is purportedly a transcription of Filostrato's oral account). The novella's overt signalling of its own corpus of intertexts heightens the same association between "dismemberment, incorporation, and commemoration" that Simon Gaunt has discussed in other eaten heart narratives.[30] Like her body, the lady's story has split into multiple narrative fragments, which can be reconstituted and reshaped by each reteller of the tale.

In this spirit, the novella is framed, at beginning and end, by references to its source material; these references, like the novella itself, deform the sources – but only slightly – both hiding and revealing their continued presence in the new work. This phenomenon of "hiding in

28 Cachey, "The Place of the *Itinerarium*," 237. The digestive metaphor also appears in Seneca (Durling, "Deceit and Digestion," 62), Quintilian, and later Poliziano and others (Della Neva, *Ciceronian Controversies*, 234n13). Apian and digestive analogies are also discussed in Greene (*Light in Troy*, 98–9).

29 My reading of this novella thus lends further weight to Jonathan Usher's portrayal of Boccaccio as "a serious theorist of reading" ("Boccaccio on Readers and Reading," 63).

30 Gaunt, *Love and Death*, 96–7.

plain sight" manifests itself clearly in the novella's final sentence: in the epitaph explaining "chi fosser quegli che dentro sepolti v'erano, e il modo e la *cagione* della lor morte" we may see allusion to Boccaccio's Occitan sources, the *vidas* (i.e., the biographies, which tell *chi fosser* the troubadours) and the *razos* (which give the reason, the *razo* – or, in its Italian cognate, the *cagione* – that is, the backstory for the troubadours' compositions).[31] The plot itself, along with the closing characterization of the narrative as a textual explanation of a *cagione*, ties this novella to the troubadour corpus that clearly informed it – and yet, Boccaccio modifies his source material in significant and highly visible ways. These conspicuous changes expose the seams between the textual traditions Boccaccio is incorporating and the new narrative he produces from them.

The direct sources of *Decameron* IV.9, the *vidas* and *razos*, are themselves a genre emblematic of transcultural adaptation, fragmentation, and recomposition.[32] Though they tell of Occitan troubadours and their songs, these narratives first appear in thirteenth-century Italian manuscripts. The composition and/or compilation of many of these texts is generally attributed to Uc de Saint Circ, a Quercy-born and Montpellier-educated poet who created his troubadour anthologies in the Veneto, writing in Italian-inflected Occitan under the patronage of Alberico and Ezzelino da Romano.[33] As Simon Gaunt writes, "the *vidas* and *razos* were probably composed at or shortly after the turn of the twelfth and thirteenth centuries to introduce Italian readers and listeners to troubadour poetry at a stage in the transmission of these texts when they had become largely unhooked from performance (at least in Italy), and firmly anchored in a written tradition";[34] they arise at a moment of transformation, as a largely oral (and Occitan) art form becomes a largely written (Italian) one. The *vidas* and especially the *razos* are composite texts that pull apart the troubadours' lyrics, either adapting them wholesale into a biographical prose narrative (as is typical of the

31 Gregory Stone has pointed out the link between Boccaccio's *cagione* and the troubadour *razo* (*Death of the Troubadour*, 104). One should note, however, that the tale of Lisabetta (IV.5), which is not adapted from a *razo*, also presents "la cagione per che fosse stata fatta" a popular song (IV.6.2).

32 It may be overly simplistic to write of this novella's "direct sources." Although, as Luciano Rossi justly points out, this is one of the few moments where Bocacccio seems to follow faithfully a written source ("Il cuore," 120), we cannot follow Neuschäfer ("Die 'Herzmäre'") in taking Boccaccio's declaration of a Provençal source at face value.

33 The best study of the *razos* is Burgwinkle, *Love for Sale*; see also Meneghetti, "'Enamoratz' e 'Fenhedors.'"

34 Gaunt, *Love and Death*, 76.

vidas) or citing them, piecemeal, within a prose narrative that purports to explain the circumstances under which they were composed (in the *razos*). In other words, they are "producers of discourse"[35] made out of discrete lyric texts that were compiled, consumed, and digested in order to be incorporated in a narrative form; as such they constitute a "textual community" and they "stimulate renewed poetic life" for their subject.[36] The *vidas* and *razos* of Guilhem de Cabestanh survive in multiple forms, with four versions appearing in nine manuscripts: versions A and B are categorized as *vidas*, versions C and D as *razos*.[37] The first three versions essentially tell the same story, while version D, famously translated by Stendhal and included in his essay *De l'amour*, introduces extensive dialogue and subplots. Boccaccio is thought to have used a version B manuscript as his primary source for *Decameron* IV.9.[38] Still, his novella diverges from all known versions of the *vida* and *razo* in significant ways.

Boccaccio's most immediately evident modifications of the *vida* and *razo* are changes to the three characters' names and identities. In the Occitan biographies, the husband is called Raimon de Castel Rossillon, the murdered lover is Guilhem de Cabestanh, and the lady is Soremonda. While Boccaccio's names have been referred to as "systematic Italianizations" of the originals,[39] their import goes far beyond a linguistic adaptation. Boccaccio changes the husband's name to Guiglielmo, which, in conjunction with the erasure of the lady's name, engages a much-discussed "play of doubles."[40] More to our point, however, the "Italianized" names fundamentally alter the lovers' embodiment, echoing their "undoing" and the de-composition and re-composition of their tale. When Guilhem de Cabestanh (whose loconym derives from "*caput*, head or extremity, and *stagnum*, pond, according to Compan)[41] becomes Guiglielmo Guardastagno, his name quite literally loses its head – a loss to which Boccaccio draws the reader's attention, for, as Stone observes

35 Burgwinkle, *Love for Sale*, 14.

36 See Grange, "Guilhem de Cabestanh's Eaten Heart," 104.

37 I follow Boutière and Schutz's designations of the versions in *Biographies des Troubadours*. The manuscripts are described in Avalle, *I manoscritti*.

38 Tavera, "Ancien provençal 'cor(s) et 'cor(p)s,'" 177.

39 Adroher, *Les troubadours roussillonnais*, 82.

40 Mazzotta, *World at Play*, 152.

41 Compan, "L'inspiration amoureuse chez Guilhem de Cabestanh," 133n3. Luciano Rossi offers an alternate derivation of *Cabestanh* as "inteso come 'testa di stagno' 'testa bianca,' e non come 'alla fine d'uno stagno,' come forse, più correttamente, potrebbe essere spiegato" ("Il cuore," 57–8). Rossi posits that if this reading is correct, Guilhem de Cabestanh may be identified with the poet called "Tremoleta" in the Monge de Montaudon's satirical song *Pois Peire d'Alvernha a chantat*.

(though he draws a different conclusion from it), "the name by which Boccaccio replaces *Cabestaing* tells us to look: *Guarda-*."[42] The manipulation of the lover's name also becomes an onomastic signal of his own destruction: Cabestanh-turned-Guardastagno is taken by surprise because he travels unarmed, "sì come colui che di niente da lui si *guardava*" [§11: he never suspected for a moment that he was running into danger]. The erasure of the lady's identity is noteworthy, too, as the name *Soremonda* highlights its bearer's golden or auburn hair.[43] In suppressing her name, Boccaccio removes a part of her body, too, and disentangles her worth from a prominent biological marker of beauty.

The author-reader is both a dismemberer and a regenerator – but also, crucially, a preserver of his Occitan intertext and the courtly tradition in which it is inscribed.[44] It would indeed be an oversimplification to see Boccaccio's "Italianizations" and erasures of the characters' names as a complete overwriting of the source text. The relatively large number of Italian manuscripts containing the *vida* of Guilhem de Cabestanh, as well as the allusion to Guilhem in Petrarch's *Trionfi* (*Triumphus cupidinis* IV.53–4), indicates that the story was well known; many readers of Boccaccio's novella could still have detected the protagonists' original identities in palimpsest.[45] The same is true for Guardastagno's/Cabestanh's identity *as poet*. Boccaccio famously strips his protagonist of this status, refashioning the troubadour into a *cavaliere*.[46] Given the "open secret" of the protagonist's identity, however, we can interpret Boccaccio's narrative as an overlay, not a rewrite, of the *vidas* and *razos*. Still, the change bears serious implications for the question of textual form. Boccaccio's Occitan sources belong to a genre that is, by definition, the biography *of a troubadour* and the explication *of a lyric poem*. The novella, instead, tells of a non-poet and alludes to two absent, hypothetical texts (the "Provençal" story and the verse epitaph) that it does not directly cite. While the Boccaccian novella does mimic the *razos* in

---

42 Stone, *Death of the Troubadour*, 107.

43 Adroher, *Les troubadours roussillonnais*, 86n157.

44 Stone argues that in changing or suppressing the principals' names and in doubling up the two Guiglielmos' use of the same heraldic device, "Boccaccio has re-versified the *vida*, has fashioned a world whose system of nomenclature is extremely limited or underdeveloped – nothing other than the discursive world of courtly lyric" (*Death of the Troubadour*, 106).

45 This circumstance neatly echoes the novella's framing within Day Four, as that day's theme and its closing *ballata* are inspired by Filostrato's unrequited love for a lady whose identity, though unspoken, appears to be an open secret. On the *ballata* see Rossi, "Il cuore," 125–6.

46 See Stone, *Death of the Troubadour*, 104; Jeay, "Consuming Passions," 82.

offering "the fiction or simulacrum of the source/'source' as part of the artifice and craft of the text,"[47] Boccaccio recounts without explicating, offering a *cagione* while distancing the story from its still-visible roots as a *vida* and a *razo*. The elimination of the embedded verses undoes the "strategy of embodiment" that underlies *razos* and other similarly organized texts: for if "lyrics are 'fleshed out' by the surrounding narrative, much as a heart is by the body around it," as Helen Solterer writes in reference to the *Castelain de Coucy*,[48] Boccaccio's elision of Guilhem de Cabestanh's verse makes him complicit in Rossiglione's disembowelment of the poet. Moreover, Boccaccio's adaptation rewrites the implicit pathways of textual transmission that underpin the logic of the *razo*. In the *razo*, as Gregory Stone notes, "the narrated material pretends to precede the sung material";[49] this fiction inverts the historical circumstances of the texts' composition, as the *vidas* and *razos* were produced after their lyrical pretext. Boccaccio shatters this model, emphasizing textual simultaneity in lieu of precedence, creating a branching *stemma* rather than a linear chain of textual transmission. Filostrato's declared source is not a lyric, but an oral tradition, one that coexists with the *Decameron* rather than simply preceding it (it is a story "che raccontano i provenzali," not one that they *raccontarono*). The only poem mentioned in the novella, the tomb inscription, is inspired by the same events that Filostrato recounts, but it does not seem to inform the novella directly. Is the verse epitaph an intertextual source or is it a dead end?

This denial of the epitaph's textual influence disrupts the story's conditioning of its own reception. In the *vida* and *razo* of Guilhem de Cabestanh, the epitaph is designed for a built-in audience and a collective social purpose: the King of Aragon "fetz desseignar desobre·l monumen cum ill eron estat mort; et ordenet per tot lo comtat de Rossillon que tuich li cavallier e las dompnas lor vengesson far anoal chascun an" [had written above the monument how they had died; and ordered throughout the county of Roussillon that all of the knights and ladies come there on an annual pilgrimage].[50] In Boccaccio's story, though the epitaph serves an obvious commemorative purpose, no audience is obligated to read it – and in fact, since the novella does not directly cite the epitaph, Boccaccio's readers *cannot* read it. In other ways, too, the *Decameron* novella is truncated in a manner that deprives its intradiegetic and extradiegetic audiences of some of the satisfaction that

47 Selig, "Form and Form," 6.

48 Solterer, "Dismembering, Remembering," 105.

49 Stone, *Death of the Troubadour*, 60.

50 Version B, in Boutière and Schutz, *Biographies des Troubadours*, 532–3.

comes at the end of the Occitan sources. Filostrato declares at the outset that his novella is calculated to provoke a compassionate response among his listeners ("vi converrà non meno di compassione avere che alla passata" [§3: must inevitably arouse as much pity among you as the previous one]). In contrast to the many Day Four tales that are framed with allusions to the listeners' pity for the tragic protagonists, though, the *brigata* does not react to the ninth story at all.[51] The transition from this tale to Dioneo's is particularly abrupt, denying the *brigata* an opportunity to react. The rupture is only deepened by the violence and the suddenness of the ninth story's ending – a violence that stems, in part, from changes that Boccaccio introduces. Relative to his Occitan sources, Boccaccio minimizes the violence of the lady's jump from the tower even as he heightens the gruesomeness of its aftermath. But he cuts out a major plot element, too, removing the royal justice by which Raimon de Castel Rossillon is metaphorically undone. Thus Boccaccio reconfigures the narrative equilibrium, hastening the resolution, redefining who is undone and who remains whole.

In the *vidas* and *razos*, Soremonda is driven to suicide as an act of self-defence. As version B reads, "E qand el [Raimon] auzic so, el cors ab s'espaza e volc li dar sus en la testa; et ella cors ad un balcon e laisset se cazar jos, et enaissi moric" [And when he heard this, he ran at her with his sword and wanted to strike her in the head; and she ran to a balcony and let herself fall down, and so she died].[52] Raimon, sword drawn, threatens his wife with dismemberment; she acts out of desperation and without any apparent premeditation. In *Decameron* IV.9, though, the lady's act is a conscious choice, "a mindful and violent act."[53] Although she stands up and allows herself to fall out of the window behind her "senza altra diliberazione," without a second thought, she has already paused to think, delivering her final speech "dopo alquanto" [§23: after a while]. Her action, though swift, gives every indication of having been planned in the painful pause between her husband's revelation and her noble reply. She is not driven to her death at the point of a sword.

The lady's suicidal fall calls to mind another Boccaccian lady, one whose never-committed suicide is explicitly premeditated but never enacted. In the sixth chapter of the *Elegia di Madonna Fiammetta*, the title character resolves that death is the surest way to reunite with her

51 Fedi groups this novella among the "novelle tragiche per eccellenza" (with IV.1 and IV.5), which lack elaborate opening frames ("Il 'regno' di Filostrato," 50).

52 Boutière and Schutz, *Biographies des Troubadours*, 532. In these particulars there is relatively little variation among the versions. For exhaustive comparison of the manuscripts, see Rossi, "Il cuore."

53 Getto, *Vita di forme*, 121.

former lover ("con lui mi ricongiugnerò," 149) and that this recoupling can best be achieved through self-fragmentation.

> Io dell'alte parti della mia casa gittandomi, il corpo, rotto in cento parti, per tutte e cento renderà la infelice anima maculata e rotta alli tristi iddii, né fia chi quinci pensi crudeltà o furore in me stato di morte, anzi a furtunoso caso imputandolo, spandendo pietose lagrime per me, la fortuna maladiranno. (149)
>
> [If I throw myself from the highest part of my house, my body, shattering into hundreds of pieces, will release my unhappy, stained, and broken soul through each piece to the fiendish gods; thus, no one will be able to think that I was so cruel or insane to seek death, but by attributing my death to an unfortunate accident one will curse Fortune and shed tears of pity for me! (trans. Causa-Steindler and Mauch)]

Fiammetta decides to throw herself from an upper story of her home precisely because nobody will know for sure whether her death is a suicide or accident ("questo solo modo mi piacque di seguitare per infallibile morte e vòta d'ogni infamia" [150: it pleased me to choose this kind of sure death free from all infamy (trans. Causa-Steindler and Mauch)]); she envisages a foolproof mode of death that will allow her, from beyond the grave, to condition other people's response to her demise. Rossiglione's wife seemingly makes a similar calculation (she fragments herself in order to preserve her reunion with her lover) and obtains the result Fiammetta fantasizes about (other people crying for her, remembering her). These strong echoes of the *Elegia di Madonna Fiammetta* substantiate the claim that the shattering of the lady's body is a Boccaccian intervention in the legend.

This is not to say that Boccaccio invents the lady's "undoing" out of whole cloth, though. Most surviving iterations of Guilhem de Cabestanh's *vida* simply report Soremonda's death without saying she was dashed to pieces. Two manuscripts, however – H, made near Padua in the late thirteenth century, and P, made in Gubbio in 1310 – specify that the lady "esmodega se·l col" [broke her neck].[54] The unusual "esmodega" is significant in that it is an Italianism in the Occitan *vida*, a linguistic marker of the text's composition in the Treviso-Belluno region.[55] Therefore the moment when the woman's body breaks is

54 MS H, 538. On manuscript H, see Careri, *Il canzoniere provenzale H*.

55 Folena, *Culture e lingue*, 103. See the thorough discussion of "esmodega" in Pellegrini, "Di un venetismo alpino."

also a moment when the illusion of Occitan-ness breaks, revealing the cultural and linguistic transfer already underway. As for Boccaccio's "disfece," it does have a cognate in the *vidas* and *razos* – wherein it is Raimon who is undone.

> E venc s'en a Perpignan, en Rossillon, e fetz venir Raimon de Castel Rossillon denan si; e, qand fo vengutz, si·l fetz prendre e tolc li totz sos chastels e·ls fetz *desfar*; e tolc li tot qant avia, e lui en menet en preison. E pois fetz penre Guillem de Cabestaing e la dompna, e fetz los portar a Perpignan e metre en un monumen denan l'uis de la gleisa; e fetz desseignar desobre·l monumen cum ill eron estat mort ; et ordenet per tot lo comtat de Rossillon que tuich li cavallier e las dompnas lor vengesson far anoal chascun an. E Raimons de Castel Rossillon moric en la preison del rei.[56]

> [And he [the King of Aragon] came to Perpignan, in Roussillon, and had Raimon de Castel Rossillon come before him; and when he had come, he had him arrested and took away all of his castles and had them confiscated; and took away everything he had, and imprisoned him. And then he had Guilhem de Cabestanh and the lady retrieved and brought to Perpignan and put in a tomb before the church door; and he had written above the monument how they had died; and ordered throughout the county of Roussillon that all of the knights and ladies come there on an annual pilgrimage. And Raimon de Castel Rossillon died in the king's prison.]

In the conclusions of versions B, C, and D, the King of Aragon learns of Raimon's crimes; dispossesses him of all of his lands, which he redistributes to the victims' families; and has a double tomb built for Guilhem and Soremonda. When the king seizes Raimon's property, "Raimon becom[es] to the king what Guillem was to Raimon, a disposable asset and an object of consumption."[57] What's more, in all of the manuscripts that include this part of the story, the word used for Raimon's dispossession is *desfar*. Boccaccio's characterization of the lady's body that "quasi tutta si disfece" transfers the story's lexical "undoing" from husband to wife, from material wealth to bodily integrity, from seigneurial to poetic justice. Boccaccio completes this transfer by translating the lovers' remains from a church door in Perpignan (where they are buried in the Occitan texts) to the interior of the lady's castle. As Fidel Fajardo-Acosta has pointed out, the church doorway is a liminal space, and the word used to describe it, *uis*, derives from the

56 Version B, Boutière and Schutz, *Biographies des Troubadours*, 532–3; emphasis added.
57 Fajardo-Acosta, "The Heart of Guillem de Cabestaing," 85.

Latin *os* (mouth) such that "the lovers' burial quite literally dramatizes their ingestion and devouring."[58] Boccaccio, in clutching the lovers from the maw of the church in Perpignan and moving them inside the castle, changes the story's moral and physical geography. He also, subtly, redistributes Rossiglione's goods just as the King of Aragon had redistributed Raimon's: for the lovers are buried, not in Rossiglione's castle, but "nella chiesa del castello medesimo *della donna*."

The move from Perpignan to the lady's castle is part of a broader set of spatial displacements that Boccaccio enacts in order to highlight, and rewrite, the tale's routes of cultural transfer. The Occitan versions are quite insistent on the identity of the king who metes out justice ("lo reis d'Aragon"), on the geographic location of Cabestanh ("que confina ab Cataloigna et ab Narbones"), and on the location of the tomb; manuscript P especially belabours the latter point, the *razo* following up its earlier explanation that the tomb was erected "denan l'uis de la gleisa a Perpignac" [before the door of the church in Perpignan] with the seemingly tacked-on final sentence "E·l borc en lo cal foron seppellitz G[uillelm] e la dopna a nom Perpignac" [And the town in which Guilhem and the lady were buried is called Perpignan].[59] Perpignan, like the rest of Roussillon, is situated (in Guilhem de Cabestanh's time and again in Boccaccio's) in Catalonia, within the Aragonese sphere of influence.[60] Guilhem de Cabestanh was one of the many troubadours active at the court of Alfonso II of Aragon.[61] But Boccaccio, of course, situates the story "in Provenza," has Rossiglione flee the "conte di Proenza," and identifies his source as a legend "che raccontano i provenzali." Instead of moving from Catalonia to Tuscany via an Occitan-Venetian textual tradition, the story now cuts a new path across the Mediterranean, coming directly to Tuscany from Provence – a territory more closely tied, through its Angevin rulers, to the kingdoms of France and Naples.[62] Rossiglione, we may remember, ensnares Guardastagno with the

58 Ibid., 100.

59 Boutière and Schutz, *Biographies des Troubadours*, 549.

60 See Pascot, *Le Roussillon*, 90–119.

61 Cabestanh and other troubadours "traveled busily from Alfonso II's court in Aragón and Cataluña to Castilla, and back to the Plantagenet domains, making the allies aware of their ties and reinforcing their common front against the ambitious French kings in the north" (Sánchez Jiménez, "Catalan and Occitan Troubadours," 115). See also Cots, "Notas Históricas sobre el trovador Guillem de Cabestany."

62 This fits in with Kirkham and Menocal's argument (in "Reflections on the 'Arabic' World") that the *Decameron*'s ninth stories belong to an "Arabic" Mediterranean world, a sphere in which they include nearby Narbonne. On the geopolitical situation of Provence and its ties to France and to Naples, see Baratier, *Histoire de la Provence*, especially chapters 6 and 7.

fraudulent promise of a trip to a tournament in France ("sopravenne che un gran torneamento si bandì in Francia; il che il Rossiglione incontanente significò al Guardastagno e mandogli a dire che, se a lui piacesse, da lui venisse e insieme diliberrebbono se andar vi volessono e come" [§9: Roussillon happened to hear of a great tournament that was to be held in France. He promptly sent word of it to Cabestanh and asked him whether he would care to call upon him, so that they could talk it over together and decide whether or not to go and how they were to get there]).[63] Boccaccio, too, invents a false lure of (quasi-) Frenchness as he effaces the story's more complicated geographical and cultural itinerary. Moreover, even while situating the story in Provence, he erases the *vida*'s geographic identifiers (Castel Rossillon, Cabestanh, Perpignan) and replaces them with Italianized names, names that have already made the cultural leap. These are changes that highlight the work of the author; "così la Giornata volge al termine nel segno della massima letterarietà possibile."[64]

As a reclamation of "literariness" and of the role of the author, the ninth story elaborates on the vision of authorship put forth at the beginning of Day Four. In the day's Introduction, Boccaccio's authorial voice intervenes, interrupting the storytelling to answer five charges: that the author is overly fond of ladies, that he is too old to be writing of such matters, that he would do better to spend his time with the Muses than with flesh and blood women, that he ought to give more consideration to the practical question of his own sustenance, and that his tales diverge too much from the events that inspired them. Boccaccio answers these charges by appealing to biological imperatives (appetites for sex and food) and literary precedent. Filostrato's tale uses the same instruments, biology and intertextuality, synthesizing the Introduction's images and showing how the theory of reading and (re)writing that they elaborate might be put into practice. As such, our tale completes Boccaccio's first fictional counterattack on his critics, the "partial novella" of Filippo Balducci – and in feeding a lady her lover's heart, IV.9 perversely fulfils the partial novella's promise of giving female objects of desire something to *beccare*.[65] It is telling that in the ninth

63 This cooked-up enticement is unique to Boccaccio's retelling of the story, dependent as it is on what Luciano Rossi has pointed out as one of Boccaccio's main additions to the tradition: the two men's shared passion for the joust ("Il cuore," 122).

64 Fedi, "Il 'regno' di Filostrato," 53.

65 Mazzotta also connects the Ghismonda and Guardastagno stories to the Introduction and its partial novella, observing that "Since suicide is itself a form of violence, it actually puts Ghismunda [and, I add, Rossiglione and his wife] in the same realm

story the "consuming woman" is no longer incidental, but central: Boccaccio has refocused his efforts, from a defence against (presumably male) critics to a reading lesson for the "carissime donne" who are to devour his body of work.

Presenting the fragmentation and reconstitution of bodies as a vehicle for literary adaptation and cultural transfer, the ninth novella redirects and responds to the hypothetical charges levelled against Boccaccio at the beginning of the day: attacks that are themselves couched in overtly corporeal terms. The author's bodily integrity is threatened by those who misread his work – in the Day Four Introduction he declares himself "tutto da' morsi della 'nvidia esser lacerato" [IV.Intro. §4: nearly torn to pieces by envy] and "sospinto, molestato e infino nel vivo trafitto" [IV.Intro. §8: buffeted, battered, and pierced to the very quick]; the critics "riprenderannomi, morderannomi, lacererannomi" (IV.Intro. §32: "abused ... mauled and mangled] – just as the lovers in IV.9 are lacerated and bitten, and their story is taken up ("ripresa") and adapted by a new author. But the novella complicates Boccaccio's defences even as it puts them in action.

The arguments Boccaccio presents in the day's Introduction, especially his refutations of the first three critiques, suggest a "pragmatic" or "realist" enjoyment of the body. To the accusation that he is overly fond of ladies, Boccaccio retorts that his body was made for love ("io, il corpo del quale il cielo produsse tutto atto a amarvi" [IV.Intro. §32: Heaven has given me a body with which to love you]). He counters complaints that his material is age-inappropriate, initially, with a dirty joke couched in a vegetable metaphor: "E quegli che contro alla mia età parlando vanno, mostra mal che conoscano che, perché il porro abbia il capo bianco, che la coda sia verde" [IV.Intro. §33: As for those who keep harping on about my age, they are clearly unaware of the fact that although the leek's head is white, it has a green tail]. He thus reduces the leek's anthropomorphized form (or his own dehumanized one) to a head and a penis, sketching a humorous nexus of sex and food and a body in pieces that will see its tragic counterpart in the tales of Ghismonda, Lisabetta, and Guiglielmo Guardastagno.[66]

---

where are the critics who in their rabid fury dismember the body of Boccaccio's text, Filippo Balducci who educates his son against the laws of nature, and Tancredi who mutilates Guiscardo's heart" (*World at Play*, 149).

66 If Luciano Rossi is correct about the name Cabestanh referring to the troubadour's prematurely white hair, then Boccaccio's remark about the leek has even more resonance with the ninth story.

And thirdly, to the accusation that he is not sufficiently guided by the Muses, Boccaccio responds with a literalizing justification for seeking the company of women: as physical proximity to the mythic Muses is impossible ("né noi possiam dimorare con le Muse né esse con essonoi" [IV.Intro §35: one cannot actually live with the Muses, any more than they can live with us], it is logical to accept real ladies, who resemble them, as a substitute ("esse hanno nel primo aspetto simiglianza di quelle, sì che, quando per altro non mi piacessero, per quello mi dovrebber piacere" [IV.Intro. §35: they resemble them at first sight, and hence it is natural, if only for this reason, that I should be fond of them]). Boccaccio interweaves these pragmatic, materialist arguments with appeals to literary precedent: already, in his answer to the second criticism, for instance, he follows up his leek joke by declaring that if writing for ladies was good enough for Cavalcanti, Dante, and Cino da Pistoia in their old age, it is good enough for him: "lasciando il motteggiar da l'un de' lati, rispondo che io mai a me vergogna non reputerò infino nello stremo della mia vita di dover compiacere a quelle cose alle quali Guido Cavalcanti e Dante Alighieri già vecchi e messer Cino da Pistoia vecchissimo onor si tennero, e fu lor caro il piacer loro" [IV.Intro. §33: But joking apart, all I would say to them is that even if I live to be a hundred, I shall never feel any compunction in striving to please the ones who were so greatly honoured, and whose beauty was so much admired, by Guido Cavalcanti and Dante Alighieri in their old age, and by Cino da Pistoia in his dotage]. Likewise, when his imagined critics ask him with false pity where his next meal will come from, Boccaccio conflates literary and nutritional sustenance: as for bread, he writes, "già più ne trovarono tralle loro favole i poeti, che molti ricchi tra' lor tesori" [IV.Intro. §38: the poets have always found more to sustain them in their songs, than many a rich man has found in his treasures]. And lastly, when the author's adversaries charge him with having distorted the truth, he challenges them to track down his sources and to carry out a comparative close reading.

> Quegli che queste cose così non essere state dicono, avrei molto caro che essi recassero gli originali: li quali se a quel che io scrivo discordanti fossero, giusta direi la loro riprensione e d'amendar me stesso m'ingegnerei; ma infino che altro che parole non apparisce, io gli lascerò con la loro oppinione, seguitando la mia, di loro dicendo quello che essi di me dicono. (IV.Intro. §39)
>
> [I would be greatly obliged to the people who claim that these accounts are inaccurate if they would produce the original versions, and if these

> turn out to be different from my own, I will grant their reproach to be just, and endeavour to mend my ways. But so long as they have nothing but words to offer, I shall leave them to their opinions, stick to my own, and say the same things about them as they are saying about me.]

Philology is Boccaccio's ultimate defence. Or, in the case of a tale like IV.9 that has so blatantly altered the textual and physical bodies of its source, the *difficulty* of philology is the ultimate defence. For a body pulverized and dispersed, like that of Guardastagno's lady, can no longer be "altro che parole." So the author will proceed,

> dando le spalle a questo vento e lasciandol soffiar: per ciò che io non veggo che di me altro possa avvenire che quello che della minuta polvere avviene, la quale, spirante turbo, o egli di terra non la muove, o se la muove la porta in alto e spesse volte sopra le teste degli uomini, sopra le corone dei re e degl'imperadori, e talvolta sopra gli alti palagi e sopra le eccelse torri la lascia; delle quali se ella cade, più giù andar non può che il luogo onde levata fu. (IV.Intro. §40)

> [turning my back on these winds and letting them blow as hard as they like. For whatever happens, my fate can be no worse than that of the fine-grained dust, which, when a gale blows, either stays on the ground or is carried aloft, in which case it is frequently deposited upon the heads of men, upon the crowns of kings and emperors, and even upon high palaces and lofty towers, whence, if it should fall, it cannot sink lower than the place from which it was raised.]

This vindication of authorial freedom, which marks the transition from Boccaccio's self-defence to the resumption of the *brigata*'s storytelling, announces the ninth novella in a manner that is striking and, in retrospect, difficult to miss. Already in the opening sentence of his Introduction, Boccaccio has characterized the targets of envy as "l'alte torri" [IV.Intro. §2: lofty towers]; now he presents himself, pulverized, as capable of rising to the heights of the tallest towers – and of falling down again, disaggregated but none the worse for wear. Thus Boccaccio doubles the lady, who will herself rise in a tower only to fall and shatter, dust to dust. This parallel reveals the power of literature to open the body and take its secrets as fodder for fiction.[67] Yet

67 On the revelation of secrets as crucial to creation of narrative from lyric, with specific reference to eaten heart narratives, see Huot, "Troubadour Lyric," 277.

it also underscores an unbridgeable distance between the author and his subject. Unlike the author, the textual body is fundamentally and irrevocably altered through this digestive process: the decomposed and recomposed narrative, transferred from Catalonia to Tuscany via a fictive detour through Provence, can never return to "il luogo onde levata fu."

Happy Endings (IV.10)

FABIAN ALFIE

During Day One of the *Decameron*, Dioneo received dispensation to tell his tales after everyone else, and he was exempted from the themes imposed on the other nine narrators. Therefore, the tenth story is not bound by Filostrato's theme for Day Four, love stories with unhappy endings. Nonetheless, as the title of this study suggests, Dioneo's tale is not at all divorced from the day's subject matter. On the contrary, his narrative acts as a commentary, in part, on the sad love stories the others have recounted; it constitutes, in short, the happy ending to the day. At the same time, it is itself another example of a love story, this time with a happy ending. Yet the title of this study implies more than that. In common speech, "happy ending" also has a sexual meaning, and as with many of Dioneo's stories, that connotation is not unintended. As is well known, Dioneo has a unique repertory that distinguishes him from the other tellers; his tales tend to be quite bawdy.[1] The last story of Day Four is no exception. Sex is an important element of the story because it sets the narrative in motion, and it constitutes the happy ending to the tale (in more ways than one). Thus, as will be illustrated in this study, the novella both *is* and *has* several happy endings.

First, an overview of the narrative is necessary. Dioneo relates the misadventures of the unnamed young wife of an elderly doctor, Mazzeo della Montagna. Mazzeo believes that intercourse is harmful, so he reduces his infrequent sexual contact with her, and she becomes so sexually frustrated that she takes a lover, Ruggieri d'Aieroli. One day, Mazzeo prepares an opiate suspension for an amputation but is called away unexpectedly. In Mazzeo's absence, his wife brings Ruggieri into the house. At precisely the wrong time, other family members drop by, distracting her from Ruggieri. While he waits for her by himself

1 See Ahern, "Dioneo's Repertory."

he drinks the opiate suspension. When she returns to him, she cannot wake him and concludes that he is dead. She calls out to her servant for help, and the servant explains that she saw a large chest outside the carpenter's house. The servant recommends putting Ruggieri's body in the chest; other people will think that criminals murdered him, so no one will suspect the wife of having an adulterous affair. After the servant puts him in the chest, a family of usurers steals it. Several hours later, the effects of the suspension wear off and Ruggieri awakens, but as he climbs out of the chest it topples over. The moneylenders' family thinks he is a thief; they call for help, Ruggieri is arrested for burglary, and he is dragged before the magistrate. Under torture, he confesses to robbing the usurers.

The next morning, Mazzeo returns home and he discovers that the opiate suspension has disappeared. When he asks his wife about it, she realizes that Ruggieri has drunk it. At the same time the servant learns about Ruggieri's impending execution. She tells Mazzeo's wife about his situation, and together they develop a plan. The servant begs Mazzeo to allow her to intervene on Ruggieri's behalf, telling Mazzeo that she brought Ruggieri into the house in his absence, but narrating the rest of the night's events exactly as they occurred. Fearing that an innocent man could be put to death, he allows her to go before the magistrate to secure Ruggieri's release. There, the servant tells the same story, identifying herself as Ruggieri's lover. The magistrate becomes convinced of Ruggieri's innocence and eventually frees him, but he fines the moneylenders for taking the chest. From this point on, Dioneo concludes, Ruggieri and Mazzeo's wife can enjoy each other sexually. The ability to continue their affair, therefore, is the happy ending for all their pains, but it is not the only happy ending for the tenth story of Day Four.

As Dioneo begins his narration, he refers to the theme that Filostrato imposed on the *brigata*, love stories with tragic endings. Dioneo explains that the unhappy tales of love have lowered his spirits, saying: "Le miserie degl'infelici amori raccontate, non che a voi, donne, ma a me hanno già *contristati gli occhi e 'l petto*" [IV.10.3: These sorrowful accounts of ill-starred loves have brought so much affliction to my eyes and heart (to say nothing of yours, dear ladies) (emphasis added)]. Claiming that the narratives have distressed his eyes and heart, Dioneo cites directly from the first canto of *Purgatorio*. In that passage, Dante refers to the similar emotional effects of hell, from which he has just exited: "l'aura morta / che m'avea *contristati gli occhi e 'l petto*" [vv. 17–18: the air of death / that had afflicted both my sight and breast (trans. Mandelbaum; emphasis added)]. Dioneo's allusion to *Purgatorio* establishes a parallel between the day's sad stories and hell, of course, but it also anticipates Day Five, which is dedicated to love stories with happy endings, "forse buono indizio dando a ciò che nella seguente giornata si dee raccontare" [§3: which will possibly offer some sort of guide to the subject we ought to discuss on the morrow]. So the story both draws Day Four to an end and serves as an introduction to Day Five with its theme of love stories with happy endings. Dioneo's reference to *Purgatorio* also introduces the author's critical self-awareness into his text. By recalling *Purgatorio,* Dioneo draws a connection between the other tales of Day Four and *Inferno* in its structural function as the unhappy start to the *Commedia.* With Dioneo's story, Day Four does not end unhappily. Dioneo positions his narrative, in other words, as the happy ending to the otherwise despondent day. With his comic story he transforms the day of tragic tales into a comedy itself.

Dioneo does not only allegorize the sadness of the previous narratives as infernal, but he also provides a critical definition of the story under examination as a comedy. In the *Epistle to Cangrande della Scala,* for example, Dante explicates the title of his work, *Commedia,* by means of a structural commonplace: comedies begin horribly, in chaos and discord, but end happily (X, 29).[2] Since the *Commedia* opens with the depiction of hell but finishes in heaven, the epistle explains, it too follows the pattern of comedies (X, 31). This is not to say that Boccaccio necessarily composed the narrative with Dante's *Epistle to Cangrande* in mind. The depiction of comedies as possessing a bad-to-good structure was ubiquitous in the literary theory of the Middle Ages. There also exist some valid reasons to doubt Dante's authorship of the epistle. Yet Boccaccio also cited the letter elsewhere in the *Decameron.*[3] Nevertheless, what is important in this discussion is the commonplace definition of comedy, reiterated in the *Epistle to Cangrande,* as a genre with happy endings. At the end of the narrative, when the servant reveals Ruggieri's innocence, the magistrate laughs heartily at the turn of events, and he asks those present to retell the story several times: "Lo stradicò, queste cose udendo e gran piacer pigliandone, e alla fante e a Ruggieri e al legnaiuolo e a' prestatori più volte ridir la fece" [§52: The judge was greatly entertained by what he had heard, and made Ruggieri and the maid and the carpenter and the money-lenders repeat their stories several times over]. By concluding in such a manner, the tale too adheres to the structural commonplace of comedies, as it begins in misery but ends with mirth and laughter. Furthermore, comedy was not merely a stylistic designation in the Middle Ages, as laughter was sometimes the

2 References to the *Epistle to Cangrande* are from Dante Alighieri, *Epistola a Cangrande.*

3 Hollander, *Boccaccio's Dante,* 25.

expected response to comic literature, including jocose poetry such as Rustico Filippi's sonnets.[4]

Further clarification of the medieval genre of comedy is warranted. During the Middle Ages, the definition of comedy was counterpoised to tragedy in terms of the two genres' ethical objectives; tragedy was the art of praising the virtuous, while comedy was the art of blaming the sinful.[5] At the outset of the European Averroistic movement, Hermann the German provided an expansive definition of comedy that encompassed the moral function – blaming – classically served by satire.[6] At the same time, the medieval discussions of satire employed much the same vocabulary: the purpose of satire was to reprehend vice.[7] Averroes specified that the target of comedy was not every kind of base behaviour, only the ridiculous; it needed to treat contemptible but not painful vices.[8] Laughter, therefore, fulfilled the ethical aims of comedy. It was, at times, the method by which the derision of vice was fulfilled.

From the outset, therefore, Dioneo establishes the expectation that the tale will be a comedy, as defined by medieval critical theory. And in fact, Boccaccio employs numerous comedic topoi throughout the story. Mazzeo della Montagna is an old man married to a young and beautiful wife, a trope of comic tales.[9] In keeping with the comic stereotype, Mazzeo has intercourse with her infrequently. Mazzeo, while educated, is a medical doctor, and some elements of medieval culture considered medicine as a type of physical labour inferior to intellectual pursuits.[10] In the Trecento, many humanists followed Petrarch's lead and derided physicians for their intellectual failings,[11] and as Douglas Biow notes, Boccaccio presented doctors ambivalently in his *Decameron*.[12] The humanistic derision of physicians had to do, in part, with the fact that medicine is mute; while humanists interpreted words and rhetoric, doctors interpreted silent objects, such as medicine, the body, and its by-products.[13] Certainly, Boccaccio presents Mazzeo as

4 See Alfie, "Yes ... but Was It Funny?"

5 Allen, *Ethical Poetic*, 19–20.

6 Allen, "Hermann the German's Averroistic Aristotle," 68.

7 Miller, "John Gower," 80–1. See also Reynolds, "*Orazio satiro*," 132.

8 See Heffernan, *Comedy in Chaucer and Boccaccio*.

9 Bloch, *Medieval Misogyny*, 168–71.

10 Petrarch, *Invectiva contra medicum*, 125–6. As corroboration, see Adriano de' Rossi's invective against a doctor, the sonnet "S'accordar non sapete medicina." For further background in the topos of slander against medical doctors, although focused on fifteenth-century poetry, see Lanza, "Aspetti e figure," 275.

11 Siraisi, *Medieval and Early Renaissance Medicine*, 46.

12 Biow, *Doctors, Ambassadors, Secretaries*, 64.

13 Struever, "Petrarch's *Invective contra medicum*," 662.

generally absent and silent in this story, speaking only when the situation requires it. When he does speak, Mazzeo's words are not always wise; in explaining Mazzeo's decision to reduce his sexual contact with his wife, for instance, Boccaccio describes his statements as mere idle speech: "così costui a costei mostrava che il giacere con una donna una volta si penava a ristorar non so quanti dì, *e simili ciance*; di che ella viveva pessimamente contenta" [§5: he pointed out to the girl that you needed heaven knows how many days to recover after making love to a woman, and spouted a lot of *similar nonsense*, all of which made her wretchedly unhappy (emphasis added)]. Mazzeo bases his sexual restraint, which drives his wife into Ruggieri's bed, on medical reasons, implying that Boccaccio, too, structured this novella around the negative stereotype of doctors.

Conversely, little is known about Mazzeo's wife, not even her name; the narrator must instead refer to her as "lady" ("donna"),[14] emphasizing her noble status. Thus, the marriage may be composed of members of two distinct social classes, with the wife possibly outranking the husband. Ruggieri, moreover, while of noble birth, leads an evil life, to the extent that none of his relatives recognizes him any longer; he bears the bad reputation of a thief. Comedies speak of vile and rustic individuals, and when they discuss people of high station like Ruggieri and Mazzeo's wife, they treat them as private persons and not as exemplars of their positions.[15] The tale does indeed depict blameworthy characters with ridiculous, but not grave, faults.

Equally importantly, Boccaccio introduces several citations of comic poetry to the narrative. Scholars have long acknowledged that this tale contains a reference to Dante's *tenzone* with Forese Donati.[16] Near the beginning of the story, the narrator describes the wife's sexual desperation. Mazzeo gives his young wife *almost* everything she could possibly want: "di nobili vestimenti e ricchi e d'altre gioie e tutto ciò che a una donna può piacere meglio che altra della città teneva fornita; vero è che ella il più del tempo stava *infreddata, sì come colei che nel letto era male dal maestro tenuta coperta*" [§4: lavishly supplied ... with expensive and elegant dresses, jewellery, and all the other things a woman covets; but the fact is that for most of the time she felt *chilly, because the surgeon failed to keep her properly covered over in bed* (emphasis added)].

14 For example, the narrator calls the wife "la donna" in the following paragraphs: 7, 8, 12, 14, 16, 17, 18, 20, 32, 33, 35, 39, 41, and 53.

15 Schiaffini, *Lettura del "De Vulgari Eloquentia,"* 284–5.

16 Michele Barbi mentions the intertextuality between the *tenzone* and the tales IV.10 and VII.8 of the *Decameron* in "Tenzone con Forese Donati," in *Opere*, 2:281, 285–92.

In his first sonnet addressed to Forese Donati, "Chi udisse tossir la mal fatata," Dante explained that Forese's hapless wife, Nella, felt *chilly* even in August:

Di mezzo agosto la truovi *infreddata;*
or sappi che de' far d'ogn'altro mese!
E no.lle val perché dorma calzata,
merzé del copertoio c'ha cortonese. (vv. 5–8; emphasis added)

[In mid-August you'll find her chilly,
Imagine how she must fare other months.
And it is no use for to sleep clothed
Thanks to her coverlet from Cortona. (my translation)][17]

According to the *Opera del Vocabolario Italiano*, a database of over 1,800 vernacular texts, the only precedent to Boccaccio's tale is Dante's sonnet.[18] Like Dante before him, Boccaccio speaks of the woman's coldness ("infreddata"), and the fault for it lies with her coverings ("coperta," "copertoio"). Yet that may not be the only allusion to Dante's *tenzone* with Forese Donati in the story. Later, after Ruggieri has been arrested, the narrator describes how the news has spread through Salerno: "La novella fu la mattina per tutto Salerno che Ruggieri era stato *preso a imbolare* in casa de' prestatori" [§30: During the course of the morning, the news that Ruggieri had been *caught red-handed burgling* the money-lenders' house spread like wildfire through the whole of Salerno (emphasis added)]. The phrase "preso a imbolare" echoes a verse from another sonnet of the *tenzone* between Dante and Forese Donati. In "Bicci novel, figliuol di non so cui," Dante described Forese's father, Simone, as being fearful that his son would be caught red-handed: "E tal giace per lui nel letto tristo, / per tema non sia *preso a lo 'mbolare*, / che gli apartien quanto Giusep a Cristo" [vv. 9–11: And that one lies in his bed, sad about him, / Fearing that he'll be caught while robbing – / He belongs to him like Christ did to Joseph (my translation; emphasis added)]. The *Opera del Vocabolario Italiano* lists only the sonnet and the novella as examples of the phrase "preso a imbolare" ("preso a lo 'mbolare").[19] Dante used Forese's thievery to cast the nobility of the Donati into doubt. Boccaccio

17 The sonnets of the *tenzone* between Dante and Forese are cited from Dante Alighieri, *Rime, Testi*, vol. 3.

18 See the *Opera del Vocabolario Italiano* under *infreddata*. See also the related entries of *infreddato, infreddati,* and *infreddate*.

19 See the entry in the *Opera del Vocabolario Italiano* under *imbolare*.

uses the same expression to underscore how the high-born Ruggieri, who lived a dissolute life, was immediately believed to be engaged in criminal behaviour. Years after the *Decameron*, Boccaccio would also cite the eleventh verse of the same sonnet in his misogynistic work *Corbaccio*, so clearly he knew the poem.[20] But references to Dante's sonnets are not the only example of comic poetry in the novella.

When the servant begs Mazzeo to intervene on Ruggieri's behalf, she claims to have brought him into the house to have sex with him. Mazzeo answers that she does not deserve further punishment, claiming: "'Tu te n'hai data la perdonanza tu stessa, per ciò che, dove credesti questa notte un giovane avere che molto bene il *pillicion* ti scotesse, avesti un dormiglione'" [§46: "You have been hoist with your own petard," he replied. "For you thought you had a young man who would shake your *skin-coat* well and truly last night, instead of which you had a slug-abed'" (emphasis added)]. According to Branca, Boccaccio uses the expression "scotere il pillicion" in two other instances in the *Decameron* (VIII.7.103 and X.10.69). The narrative under discussion represents the first use of the expression within the collection of short stories. According to the *Dizionario storico del lessico erotico italiano*, Boccaccio's *Decameron* does not contain the first recorded use of the word *pillicione* in a sexual manner.[21] The term *pillicione* also appeared in Rustico Filippi's sonnet "Io fo ben boto a Dio: se Ghigo fosse":

per *pillicion* di quella c'ha le fosse,
non si riscalderia, tant'è gelato.
Non vedi che di mezzo luglio tosse
e 'l guarnel tien di sotto foderato? (vv. 2–5; emphasis added)[22]

[Even with the *pelt* of the pitted woman,
He wouldn't be so heated, so cold is he.
Don't you see that he coughs in mid-July,
And he keeps his mantle stuffed in his lapel? (my translation)]

Undoubtedly, Rustico influenced not only Boccaccio but also Dante in the *tenzone* with Forese Donati. Dante borrowed from Rustico's poem when he described Nella as coughing in August. The presence of the

20 Boccaccio writes: "Ma non sarà senza vendetta l'offesa: per ciò che, se nel mondo, nel quale io dimoro, non si mente, che nol credo né mi pare, egli ha della moglie un tal figliuolo, e per suo il nutrica e allieva, *che gli appartiene meno che non fe' Gioseppo a Cristo ...* " (*Corbaccio*, l. 319; emphasis added).

21 Boggione and Casalegno, *Dizionario storico*, 393–4, par. 3.1.4.

22 Rustico Filippi's sonnet is cited from Marrani, "I sonetti di Rustico Filippi."

term "pillicion" in the story suggests that Boccaccio knew of the intertextuality between Dante's *tenzone* with Forese and Rustico's sonnet.[23]

The recollection of Rustico's poem may indicate more than a chain of influence stretching back to the thirteenth century. Instead, Boccaccio is deliberately evoking the poetics for which Rustico was famous. During the Middle Ages, Rustico's poetry was characterized as the castigation of female sexuality.[24] For Rustico the trope of misogyny served the greater purpose of affecting a socio-political satire, because women's misbehaviours reflected the decadence of their class, clans, or families. In the *tenzone* with Forese Donati, Dante co-opted to an extent Rustico's literary intentions. His barbs against Forese's wife, Nella, are really a way to criticize the Donati family. Given that Boccaccio's story deals with both the actual adultery of Mazzeo's wife and the fictional adultery of her servant, the introduction of the literary aims of Rustico Filippi does not seem entirely out of place. But Boccaccio does not wholly share Rustico's misogynistic ideology. Mazzeo's wife never receives any comeuppance for her infidelity, and the narrator generally smiles upon her illicit activities. Throughout the tale the only woman to be chastised, albeit mildly, is the servant, who in fact is innocent of any sexual misconduct up until that point. Instead, the adulterous wife gets off scot free, and the cuckolded husband remains none the wiser.

At the same time, Boccaccio's novella conveys the social satire implicit in Rustico's poetics. Dante shared Rustico's aims as well. Throughout the Duecento the concept of nobility was hotly debated,[25] and some people, like Dante in the fourth book of the *Convivio*, defined nobility strictly as inner virtue.[26] Dante seems to express a similar view about nobility in his *tenzone* with Forese Donati. In "Bicci novel, figliuol di non so cui," Dante's point was to emphasize the corruption of the entire Donati clan, as well as the urban high nobility to which they belonged. In Boccaccio's tale, the wife, a noblewoman, engages in adultery with a fellow aristocrat. Her lover, however, is hardly a paragon of the nobility: "Era costui chiamato Ruggieri d'Aieroli, di nazione nobile ma di cattiva vita e di biasimevole stato, in tanto che parente nè amico lasciato s'avea che ben gli volesse o che il volesse vedere; e per tutto Salerno

---

23 See Chapter 5 of Alfie, *Dante's "Tenzone,"* 100–21.

24 Around 1317 a critical statement about Rustico appeared in the commentary to Francesco da Barberino's *Documenti d'amore*. It characterized Rustico as a misogynistic writer: "Quid enim Rusticus barbutus et alij quidam, laudis ex vituperiis per eos impintis contra dominas reportarunt[:] vedeant quot et qui eorum super hiis scripta honorant" (Francesco da Barberino, *I documenti d'amore*, 90–1).

25 Jones, *The Italian City-State*, 224.

26 Simonelli, "Il tema della nobiltà in Andrea Cappellano e in Dante," 56.

di ladronecci e d'altre vilissime cattività era infamato" [§7: His name was Ruggieri d'Aieroli, and he was of noble birth. But he led such a disreputable life, and mixed with so many undesirable characters, that he had alienated all his friends and relatives, none of whom wished him any good or wanted anything to do with him. He was notorious throughout Salerno for his acts of larceny and for other highly unsavoury activities].

Like the age he lived in, Boccaccio generally adhered to the idea of the superiority of the nobility.[27] The ideal of his time was chivalric and noble, while the society itself was not.[28] But Boccaccio's satire could cut against all strata of society. In this narrative he underscores the corruption of the nobility. The high-born Ruggieri is a far cry from the definition of nobility offered by Ghismunda in the first story of Day Four: "La vertù primeramente noi, che tutti nascemmo e nasciamo uguali, ne distinse; e quegli che di lei maggior parte avevano e adoperavano nobili furon detti, e il rimanente rimase non nobile" [IV.1.40: We were all born equal, and still are, but merit first set us apart, and those who had more of it, and used it the most, acquired the name of nobles to distinguish them from the rest]. Not that the non-nobility fare any better in Dioneo's story. Mazzeo all but ensures his wife's infidelity by not satisfying her in bed. As a doctor, he should know better: the anatomical science of the Middle Ages taught that a woman's uterus, if denied sex, would become medically troublesome.[29] Thus through Mazzeo Boccaccio seems to underscore the insipidness of the medical profession. Through his use of citations, Boccaccio highlights the socio-political aims of the reprehension of women.

Yet Dioneo's tale is not a social satire per se. Instead, its barbs against the aristocracy accentuate the basic point of the tale. Like the other *novelle* of Day Four, the tenth is a type of love story. Traditionally speaking, love was a subject matter associated with medieval nobility. Andreas Capellanus, for instance, asserted that the peasantry did not feel passion, but only copulated like animals;[30] only the upper classes truly loved. The tales of Day Four repeatedly evoke the romance and *lai* traditions of the age, which presented a similar ideology about love.[31] Indeed, several of the sad stories are redactions of the *Chatelain of Coucy*, *Lai Guiron*, the *Roma de Chatelain de Covey*, a Minnesang,

27 Potter, *Five Frames*, 11–15.

28 Petronio, "La posizione del *Decameron*," 481–5.

29 Cadden, *Meanings of Sex Difference*, 15. See also Brundage, "Carnal Delight," 376.

30 Capellanus, *Art of Courtly Love*, 149–50.

31 Picone, "'L'amoroso sangue,'" 118.

and a ballad, among other texts.[32] Throughout Day Four when women fall in love with low-born individuals, they often acknowledge the men's virtuous inner nobility. For example, in the first story of the day Ghismunda defends Guiscardo to her father: "Raguarda tra tutti i tuoi nobili uomini e essamina la lor vita, i lor costumi, e le loro maniere, e d'altra parte quelle di Guiscardo raguarda: se tu vorrai senza animosità giudicare, tu dirai lui nobilissimo e questi tuoi nobili tutti esser villani" [IV.1.41: Consider each of your nobles in turn, compare their lives, their customs and manner with those of Guiscardo, and if you judge the matter impartially, you will conclude that he alone is a patrician whilst all these nobles of yours are plebeians]. Ghismunda echoes the opinion expressed by Dante in the *Convivio* when she defends the poor but virtuous Guiscardo. The narrator, Fiammetta, seems to share Ghismunda's opinion. Even though Guiscardo is low-born, she states, he possesses the inner nobility that makes him worthy to be loved: "un giovane valletto del padre, il cui nome era Guiscardo, uom di nazione assai umile ma per vertù e per costume nobili" [IV.1.6: a young valet of her father's called Guiscardo, who was a man of exceedingly humble birth but noble in character and bearing]. In the sixth tale, Gabriotto is similarly low-born, but in possession of inner nobility. In presenting the comical story of Ruggieri and Mazzeo's wife, Dioneo's story capitalizes on the memory of the other sad love stories of the day, and the literary traditions from which they are derived.

To be blunt, the tenth story is a parody of the other tales of Day Four. For example, when Mazzeo's wife finds Ruggieri passed out, she concludes that he died suddenly:

> per che ella, che medica non era come che medico fosse il marito, senza alcun fallo lui credette esser morto ... e non osando far romore, tacitamente sopra lui cominciò a piagnere e a dolersi di così fatta disaventura. (§16)
>
> [And hence, being no physician herself even though she was married to one, she was convinced that he must be dead ... Not daring to make any noise, she began to weep in silence over his body and lament her ghastly misfortune.]

Unexpected deaths, like Ruggieri's purported demise, take place repeatedly throughout the day's sad love stories. Andreuola dreams of the

32 The examples are drawn from Lee, *The "Decameron."* In Day Four, the *Chatelain de Coucy* is the source for Story 1 (116), and the other texts mentioned are the sources for Story 8 (140–4).

death of Gabriotto; he too has a similar dream; and after they talk about their dreams he dies suddenly in her arms (IV.6). Girolamo returns from Paris to find his beloved, Salvestra, married; he sneaks into her house, climbs next to her in bed, and dies (IV.8). Poison reminiscent of Mazzeo's opiate suspension also figures in several tales. Tancredi, the Prince of Salerno, has his daughter's lover killed, and then serves her his heart in a gold chalice; she pours poison over it, drinks it, and kills herself (IV.1). Pasquino dies when he rubs a sage leaf against his teeth; Simona, under accusation of murder, imitates his action and also dies; later it is discovered that a large venomous toad made a nest under the sage plant and infused it with its poison (IV.7). The difference between the other stories and Dioneo's tale is that the readers know a vital piece of information that Mazzeo's wife lacks: Ruggieri is not dead. The imbalance between what the readers know about the situation and what Mazzeo's wife believes generates much of the humour of the narrative.[33] Instead of commiserating with her grief, the readers maintain an emotional distance.

The similarities between the tenth story and eight of the other tales in Day Four[34] go beyond Ruggieri's death. Like the protagonists of the other sad love stories, when the servant claims to be Ruggieri's lover, she too is put to the test. In the seventh novella, Simona must prove that she did not poison Pasquino with the sage plant, and she dies in the process. In the sixth tale, the magistrate examines Andreuola's guilt: "[Il podestà] volle usar la forza: ma l'Andreuola, da sdegno accesa e divenuta fortissimo virilmente si difese, lui con villane parole e altiere ributtando indietro" [IV.6.35: [The magistrate] attempted to take her by force. But Andreuola, seething with indignation and summoning every ounce of her strength, defended herself vigorously and hurled him aside with a torrent of haughty abuse]. Historical factors are implicit in Boccaccio's description of Andreuola's magistrate because, during the fourteenth century, the accused were tortured as part of the juridical process.[35] Like Andreuola, Mazzeo's wife's servant undergoes a trial:

> Il quale [lo stradicò], prima che ascoltar la volesse, per ciò che fresco e gagliarda era, volle una volta attaccar l'uncino alla cristianella di Dio, e

---

33 In this regard, the novella exemplifies John Morreall's theory of humour as the result of a pleasant conceptual shift from one perspective to another (*Taking Laughter Seriously*, 38–42).

34 The second story of the day, about Frate Alberto who disguises himself as the Angel Gabriel to have sex with Lisetta, is another comic story almost in violation of Filostrato's rule.

35 Peters, *Torture*, 46.

> ella, per essere meglio udita, non ne fu punto schifa; e dal macinio levatasi disse: "Messere, voi avete qui Ruggieri d'Aieroli preso per ladro, e non è così il vero." (IV.10.48)
>
> [The judge saw that she was a tasty-looking dish, and thought he would have just one little nibble before listening to what she had to say. Knowing that she would obtain a better hearing, the girl did not object in the slightest, and when the snack was finished she picked herself up and said: "Sir, you are holding Ruggieri d'Aieroli here on a charge of theft, but you have arrested the wrong man."]

Boccaccio again reflects the juridical practices of the age, whereby witnesses were put to torture to ensure that they were telling the truth.[36] Thus, the magistrate first subjects the servant to the hook ("l'uncino"); only afterwards can she rise up from the ordeal ("macinio") and defend Ruggieri. But in the tenth tale, Dioneo's references to torture are not literal. After the story ends, Boccaccio recounts the listeners' laughter: "Se le prime novelle li petti delle vaghe donne avevano contristati, questa ultima di Dioneo le fece ben tanto ridere, *e spezialmente quando disse lo stradicò aver l'uncino attaccato*" [IV.Concl. §1: If the earlier stories had saddened the fair ladies' hearts, this last one of Dioneo's caused so much merriment, especially the bit about the judge and his little nibble (emphasis added)]. In the light of this later statement, it is clear that the magistrate's "hook" is actually a metaphor for his penis; the "ordeal" was intercourse. In this way, the narrator transforms an excruciating experience – testifying on someone's behalf – into a sexual one. It is yet another happy ending, at least for the magistrate but possibly also for the servant ("non ne fu punto schifa").

The impetus for the action of the tenth tale also recalls the tragic ending in another novella. As mentioned above, Dioneo describes how Mazzeo's lack of sexual contact left his wife with perpetual coldness ("infreddata"). In the process, Dioneo calls to mind the character Girolamo of the eighth story. Abandoned by Salvestra, he climbs into bed with her after he became cold while waiting: "ché era agghiacciato aspettandola" [IV.8.22: his limbs had turned numb with cold whilst he was waiting for her]. Girolamo's situation is not entirely dissimilar to that of Mazzeo's wife – nor, for that matter, to that of Forese Donati's wife, Nella. Salvestra then awakens to find him icy – and dead – beside her: "e toccandolo il trovò come ghiaccio freddo" [IV.8.25: he was cold as ice to the touch]. By changing the adjective from "agghiacciato" to

36 Fiorelli, *La tortura giudiziaria*, 258.

"infreddata" in the tenth story, Boccaccio supplants the sad outcome of the eighth story with Dante's comic *tenzone* with Forese Donati. The memory of the comic text, Dante's barbed poem to Forese, replaces the memory of the sad tale of Girolamo, who dies of a broken heart.

Boccaccio's language reveals the true nature of Ruggieri's love for Mazzeo's wife. That their love is born from sexual impulses is not surprising. Mazzeo's wife's decision to take a lover is much like Ghismunda's in the first story of the day. When their affair is discovered, Ghismunda explains that she, a widow, also found it difficult to resist her sexual urges: "ricordar ti dovevi e dei ... chenti e quali e con che forza vengano le leggi della giovinezza" [IV.1.33: you should have remembered, indeed you should still remember, the nature and power of the laws of youth]. This is similar to the ideological point made in the introduction to Day Four. The humorous tale of Filippo Balducci's son explains why Boccaccio, even in old age, is still in love with beautiful women; in short, through much of the *Decameron*, love grows out of the sexual impulse. Yet in the tenth tale, Dioneo's explanation for Mazzeo's wife's actions warrants close examination:

> E sì come savia e di grande animo, per potere quello da casa risparmiare, si dispose di gittarsi alla strada e voler logorare dell'altrui; e più e più giovani riguardati, alla fine uno ne le fu all'animo, nel quale ella pose tutta la sua speranza, tutto il suo animo e tutto il ben suo. (§6)
>
> [but as she was a woman of considerable spirit and intelligence, she resolved to put the family jewels in cotton wool and wear out some other man's gems. Having gone out into the streets, she cast a critical eye over a number of young bloods, eventually finding one who was exactly to her liking, and she made him the sole custodian of her hopes, heart, and happiness.]

Mazzeo's wife, unable to stand much more, decides to take matters into her own hands. Like a prostitute, she casts herself out into the streets and begins searching out men until she finds one pleasing. Moralists, such as Giles of Rome, warned that women going out in public, and out of the social control of the family, risked falling prey to indecency;[37] of course, for Dioneo's protagonist, indecency is the point. But Dioneo describes her situation as the opposite of Ghismonda's: Ghismonda first fell in love with Guiscardo, and then found herself subject to the "laws of youth," while the protagonist of IV.10 seeks out someone in

37 Casagrande, "The Protected Woman," 84–5.

public – anyone! – who will suit her needs, and then describes her attraction in terms of romantic love ("nel quale ella pose tutta la sua speranza, tutto il suo animo e tutto il ben suo"). Furthermore, Dioneo's expression "to put the family jewels in cotton wool and wear out some other man's gems" ("per potere quello da casa risparmiare ... voler logorare dell'altrui") associates her sexual activity with goods, calling to mind the mercantile world of commerce. Dioneo's language is a far cry from the ideal of medieval aristocracy, which viewed trade as beneath it. In the final tale of Day Four, Boccaccio deftly generates humour from commonplace terminology, expressions, and opinions about love.

According to Pier Massimo Forni, one of Boccaccio's artistic processes is "actualization," in that the writer takes a metaphorical turn of phrase and treats it as literal, transforming an abstract expression into concrete events.[38] Perhaps the best example of "actualization" occurs when Ruggieri rouses from his opiate-induced stupor. At that moment he speaks in the manner of a traditional lover: "'Che è questo? dove sono io? dormo io? o son desto?'" [§24: "What's all this? Where am I? Am I asleep, or awake?"]. Love poets frequently pose similar questions as a means to describe their ecstasy at being with, or simply contemplating, their beloved. Petrarch famously made similar remarks at the end of his *canzone* "Chiare fresche e dolci acque": "Qui come venn'io o quando?" [126.62: How did I come here and when? (trans. Durling)]. In Boccaccio's narrative poem *Filostrato*, as Troiolo makes love to Criseida, he asks: "Hotti in braccio, o sogno, sei tu desso?" [III.34.8: Am I holding you in my arms, or am I dreaming, are you you?]. But in Ruggieri's case, the questions are literal. He does not know where he is. He is not passionately ecstatic, merely confused from the opium and the change in his location. Dioneo transforms the questions, which are typically metaphorical, and in the process Boccaccio makes the reader see the absurdity in the stereotypical language of love poetry.

With Dioneo's story, Boccaccio, however, does not merely talk about love in humorous ways. The tale itself portrays love – or at least, the love between Mazzeo's wife and Ruggieri – in a satiric fashion. Many writers wrote about the transformative effects of love. Among troubadoric poets, for instance, the lover changed into a more perfect nobleman; among the poets of the *dolce stil nuovo*, the emotion brought about a moral and spiritual improvement.[39] Ruggieri, as has been noted, lived a dissolute life. Yet loving Mazzeo's wife does not bring about any improvement in his character. Instead she needs to actively turn

---

38 Forni, *Adventures in Speech*, 57–8.

39 Mario Marti, "Introduzione," in *Poeti del Dolce Stil Nuovo*, 16.

him from his criminality: "E poi che alquanto diletto preso ebbero, la donna gli cominciò a biasimare la sua passata vita e a pregarlo che, per amor di lei, di quelle cose si rimanesse; e a dargli materia di farlo lo incominciò a sovenire quando d'una quantità di denari e quando d'un'altra" [§8: after they had been making love together for a while she began to censure his way of life and to entreat him for her sake to reform his ways. And in order to make it worth his while to do so, she furnished him from time to time with various sums of money]. Love does not change him, not even her reprimands work, and she eventually bribes Ruggieri not to rob. But probably the most telling statement about their love is when Mazzeo's wife discovers Ruggieri's "dead" body. At first she weeps silently, but then she thinks of another problem: "Ma dopo alquanto, temendo la donna di non aggiugnere al suo danno vergogna, pensò che senza alcuno indugio da trovare era modo come lui morto si traesse di casa" [§17: After a while, however, being afraid that she might lose her reputation on top of losing her lover, the lady saw that she must immediately devise some means for getting his body out of the house]. She fears the shame of having her affair with Ruggieri exposed. Her attitude is contrasted with that of Lisabetta in the fifth story, who asks about the missing Lorenzo, and after his ghost reveals his fate to her, digs up his head and buries it in the potted basil. Perhaps the greatest contrast is with Andreuola, who, after Gabriotto's death, announces to her servant: "vorre' io che noi prendessimo modo convenevole a servare il mio onore e il segreto amore tra noi stato, e che il corpo, del quale la graziosa anima s'è partita, fosse sepellito" [IV.6.23: I want us to do all things necessary to preserve my good name, to keep our love a secret, and to ensure that his body, from which his noble spirits had departed, will receive a proper burial]. Andreuola is concerned with the proper burial of Gabriotto's body, even when it puts her at risk of the accusation of murder. But what do Mazzeo's wife and her servant do with Ruggieri's body? They stuff it in a chest and hope that the blame falls elsewhere. With his parodic overturning of amorous topoi, it is not clear if Dioneo merely calls into question the love between Ruggieri and Mazzeo's wife. Perhaps he is suggesting that whatever they feel, it is not true love. True love brings about noble transformations and a willingness to die, and they never show either. Or perhaps, he is calling into question the topoi of love themselves. Perhaps love does not really improve the lover, because it does not have that kind of power.

In conclusion, from start to finish, Dioneo's story is a parody of the sad love tales that Filostrato, the king of Day Four, imposed on the *lieta brigata*. As Roberto Fedi asserts, with this story Dioneo demonstrates the possibility of a comic alternative to such unhappy material.[40] Its key events recollect other examples from the tragic *novelle* but it recasts them in a humorous vein. It echoes other examples of comic and satiric literature of the age, thus requiring its readers to see its comicality. Its literary references also heighten its social satire, with the purpose of challenging the love literature upon which the rest of Day Four depends. It also presents love in an unflattering light and presents its lovers, nobles all, as base. At its centre is the death of a lover, which is not a death at all; Dioneo thereby takes the unhappy ending of the day's other stories and tacks onto it a happy ending. Despite their misadventures, in the end Ruggieri and Mazzeo's wife will continue their lovemaking. And by making his story humorous, Dioneo provides the happy ending to an otherwise unhappy day. He, in short, transforms Day Four into a comedy itself, and provides a bridge to Day Five, dedicated to love stories with happy endings.

40 Fedi, "Il 'regno' di Filostrato," 42.

Bibliography

Primary Sources

Andreas Capellanus. *The Art of Courtly Love*. Translated by John Jay Parry. New York: W.W. Norton, 1941.

Barberino, Francesco da. *I documenti d'amore secondo i mss. originali*. Edited by Francesco Egidi. Milan: Archè, 1982.

Bede. *De orthographia*. In *Patrologia Latina*, edited by J.-P. Migne, vol. 90, cols. 123b–30d. Paris: Garnier, 1862.

Bible. Good News Translation. American Bible Society, 1995.

Boccaccio, Giovanni. *Amorosa visione*. Edited by Vittore Branca. Vol. 3 of *Tutte le opere di Giovanni Boccaccio*, edited by Vittore Branca. Milan: Mondadori, 1974.

– *Amorosa visione*. Bilingual edition. Translated by Robert Hollander, Timothy Hampton, and Margherita Frankel. Hanover, NH: University Press of New England, 1986.

– *Boccaccio's Expositions on Dante's Comedy*. Translated by Michael Papio. Toronto: University of Toronto Press, 2009.

– *The Corbaccio, or the Labyrinth of Love*. Translated by A.K. Cassell. Binghamton, NY: Medieval and Renaissance Texts and Studies, 1993.

– *Corbaccio*. Edited by Giorgio Padoàn. Vol. 5, pt. 2 of *Tutte le opere di Giovanni Boccaccio*, edited by Vittore Branca. Milan: Mondadori, 1994.

– *Decameron*. Edited by Giuseppe Petronio. Turin: Einaudi, 1950.

– *Decameron*. Edited by Cesare Segre. Milan: Mursia, 1975.

– *Decameron*. Edited by Vittore Branca. Vol. 4 of *Tutte le opere di Giovanni Boccaccio*, edited by Vittore Branca. Milan: Mondadori, 1976.

– *Decameron*. Edited by Vittore Branca. Turin: Einaudi, 1992.

– *The Decameron*. Translated by G.H. McWilliam. London: Penguin, 1995.

– *Decameron*. Edited by Amedeo Quondam, Maurizio Fiorilla, and Giancarlo Alfano. Milan: Rizzoli, 2013.

– *Il Decameron: 49 novelle commentate da Attilio Momigliano*. Milan: Vallardi, 1936.

– *De casibus vivorum illustrium*. Edited by Vittore Branca, Armando Balduino, and Pier Giorgio Ricci. Vol. 9 of *Tutte le opere di Giovanni Boccaccio*, edited by Vittore Branca. Milan: Mondadori, 1983.
– *De mulieribus claris*. Edited by Vittorio Zaccaria. Vol. 10 of *Tutte le opere di Giovanni Boccaccio*, edited by Vittore Branca. Milan: Mondadori, 1970.
– *Elegia di Madonna Fiammetta*. Edited by Carlo Delcorno. Vol. 5, pt. 2 of *Tutte le opere di Giovanni Boccaccio*, edited by Vittore Branca. Milan: Mondadori, 1994.
– *The Elegy of Lady Fiammetta*. Translated by Mariangela Causa-Steindler and Thomas Mauch. Chicago: University of Chicago Press, 1990.
– *Esposizioni sopra la Comedia di Dante*. Edited by Giorgio Padoàn. Vol. 6 of *Tutte le opere di Giovanni Boccaccio*, edited by Vittore Branca. Milan: Mondadori, 1965.
– *Famous Women*. Translated by Virginia Brown. Cambridge, MA: Harvard University Press, 2003.
– *Filocolo*. Edited by Antonio F. Quaglio. Vol. 1 of *Tutte le opere di Giovanni Boccaccio*, edited by Vittore Branca. Milan: Mondadori, 1967.
– *Il Filocolo*. Translated by Donald Cheney, with Thomas G. Bergin. New York: Garland, 1985.
– *Filostrato*. Edited by Vittore Branca. Vol. 2 of *Tutte le opere di Giovanni Boccaccio*, edited by Vittore Branca. Milan: Mondadori, 1964.
– *Genealogie deorum gentilium*. Edited by Vittorio Zaccaria. Vols. 7–8 of *Tutte le opere di Giovanni Boccaccio*, edited by Vittore Branca. Milan: Mondadori, 1998.
– *Opere in Versi, Corbaccio, Trattatello in Laude di Dante, Prose Latine, Epistole*. Edited by Pier Giorgio Ricci. Milan: Riccardo Ricciardi, 1965.
Boncompagno da Signa. *De malo senectutis et senii: Un manuale duecentesto sulla vecchiaia*. Edited by Paolo Garbini. Florence: SISMEL-Edizioni del Galluzzo, 2004.
Boutière, Jean, and A.-H. Schutz. *Biographies des Troubadours*. Edited by J. Boutière with I.-M. Cluzel. Paris: Nizet, 1964.
Carducci, Giosuè, and Alessandro D'Ancona. *Cantilene e ballate, strambotti e madrigali nei secoli XIII e XIV*. Pisa: Nistri, 1871.
Cassian. *Instituti* and *Collationes*. Vol. 49 of *Patrologia Latina*, edited by J.-P. Migne. Paris: Garnier, 1846.
Christine de Pizan. *The Book of the City of Ladies*. Translated by Rosalind Brown-Grant. New York: Penguin, 1999.
Cicero. *On Old Age. On Friendship. On Divination*. Translated by W.A. Falconer. Cambridge, MA: Harvard University Press, 1923.
Dante Alighieri. *La Commedia secondo l'antica vulgata*. Edited by Giorgio Petrocchi. Milan: Mondadori, 1966–7.
— *Il Convivio (The Banquet)*. Translated by Richard H. Lansing. New York: Garland, 1990.
– *The Divine Comedy of Dante Alighieri*. Translated by Allen Mandelbaum. 3 vols. Toronto: Bantam Books, 1980.
– *Epistola a Cangrande*. Edited by Enzo Cecchini. Prato: Giunti, 1995.

– *Opere*. Edited by Michele Barbi. Florence: Società Dantesca Italiana, 1960.
– *Rime*. Edited by Domenico de Robertis. Vol. 3 of *Testi*, edited by Domenico de Robertis. Florence: Le Lettere, 2002.
Documents inédits sur le commerce de Marseille au Moyen Age. Edited by Louis Blanchard. 2 vols. Marseille: Barlatier-Feissat, 1884–5.
D'Orbigny, Robert. *Le conte de Floire et Blanchefleur. Nouv. éd. critique du texte manuscrit A (Paris, BNF, fr. 375)*. Edited by Jean Luc Leclance. Paris: Champion Classiques, 2003.
English Medieval Religious Lyrics. Edited by Douglas Gray. Exeter: University of Exeter Press, 1992.
Gregory, Saint. *Moralium in Job*. Vol. 75 of *Patrologia Latina*, edited by J.-P. Migne, cols. 509d–1162b. Paris: Garnier, 1862.
Horace. *Satires, Epistles and Ars Poetica*. Translated by H. Rushton Fairclough. Cambridge, MA: Harvard University Press, 1978.
Hugh of St Victor. *Expositio moralis in Abdiam*. Vol. 175 of *Patrologia Latina*, edited by J.-P. Migne, cols. 371a–406a. Paris: Garnier, 1854.
Latini, Brunetto. *The Book of the Treasure (Li livres dou tresor)*. Edited by Paul Barrette and Spurgeon Baldwin. New York: Garland, 1993.
Marie de France. *The Lais of Marie de France*. Translated by Glyn Sheridan Burgess and Keith Busby. London: Penguin, 1999.
Molière. *Le Tartuffe*. Edited by Claire Lelouch. Paris: Gallimard, 2000.
Nabokov, Vladimir. *Lolita*. New York: Putnam, 1958.
Il novellino. Edited by Alberto Conte. Rome: Salerno, 2001.
L'Ottimo Commento della Divina Commedia. Edited by F. Mazzoni. 3 vols. Bologna: Arnaldo Forni, 1995.
Ovid. *Metamorphoses*. Translated by Rolfe Humphries. Bloomington: Indiana University Press, 2018.
Passavanti, Jacopo. *Lo specchio della vera penitenzia*. Edited by Ginetta Auzzas. Florence: Accademia della Crusca, 2014.
Petrarch. *Canzoniere*. Edited by Marco Santagata. Milan: Mondadori, 2001.
– *Le Familiari*. Edited by Vittorio Rossi. 4 vols. Florence: Sansoni, 1942.
– *Invectiva contra medicum. Testo latino e volgarizzamento di ser Domenico Silvestri*. Edited by Pier Giorgio Ricci. Rome: Edizioni di Storia e Letteratura, 1950.
– *Invectives*. Edited and translated by David Marsh. Cambridge, MA: Harvard University Press, 2003.
– *Letters on Familiar Matters*. Translated by Aldo S. Bernardo. 3 vols. Baltimore: Johns Hopkins University Press, 1985.
– *Petrarch's Lyric Poems. The "Rime sparse" and Other Lyrics*. Translated and edited by Robert M. Durling. Cambridge, MA: Harvard University Press, 1976.
– *Petrarch's Remedies for Fortune Fair and Foul: A Modern English Translation of "De remediis utriusque fortune."* Translated by Conrad H. Rawski. Bloomington: Indiana University Press, 1991.
– *Rime, Trionfi e poesie latine*. Edited by Ferdinando Neri. Milan: Ricciardi, 1951.

– *Sine nomine. Lettere polemiche e politiche.* Edited by Ugo Dotti. Bari: Laterza, 1974.

Poe, Edgar Allan. *The Complete Tales and Poems.* New York: Modern Library, 1938.

Poeti del Dolce Stil Nuovo. Edited by Mario Marti. Florence: Le Monnier, 1969.

Richard of St Victor. *The Twelve Patriarchs.* Translated by Grover A. Zinn. New York: Paulist Press, 1979.

Sacchetti, Franco. *Il Trecentonovelle.* Edited by Davide Puccini. Turin: UTET, 2004.

Seneca. *De ira.* Translated by John W. Basore. Vol. 1 of *Moral Essays.* Cambridge, MA: Harvard University Press, 1998.

Shakespeare, William. *The New Oxford Shakespeare.* Edited by Gary Taylor et al. Oxford: Oxford University Press, 2017.

Thomas Aquinas, Saint. *In Aristotelis stagiritae commentaria.* Vol. 4 of *Opera omnia.* Parma: Ficcadori, 1867.

– *Commentary on Aristotle's "Nichomachean Ethics."* Translated by C.I. Litzinger. Notre Dame, IN: Dumb Ox, 1964.

– *On Evil.* Translated by Richard Regan. Oxford: Oxford University Press, 2003.

– *On Kingship.* Translated by Gerald B. Phelan, revised by I. Th. Eschmann. Toronto: Pontifical Institute of Mediaeval Studies, 1949.

– *Summa theologiae.* Blackfriars Edition. London: Eyre and Spottiswoode, 1964.

– *Summa Theologica of St. Thomas Aquinas.* Translated by Fathers of the English Dominican Province. 1920. Online ed.

Tolstoy, Leo. *Anna Karenina.* Translated by R. Pevear and L. Volokhonsky. New York: Penguin, 2002.

Secondary Sources

Adroher, Michel. *Les troubadours roussillonnais (XIIe–XIIIe siècles).* Pézilla-la-Rivière: Publications de l'Olivier, 2012.

Ahern, John. "Dioneo's Repertory: Performance and Writing in Boccaccio's *Decameron.*" In *Performing Medieval Narrative*, edited by Evelyn Birge Vitz, Nancy Freeman Regalado, and Marilyn Lawrence, 41–58. Cambridge: D.S. Brewer, 2005.

Alfie, Fabian. *Dante's "Tenzone" with Forese Donati: The Reprehension of Vice.* Toronto: University of Toronto Press, 2011.

– "Yes ... but Was It Funny? Cecco Angiolieri, Rustico Filippi, and Giovanni Boccaccio." In *Laughter in the Middle Ages and Early Modern Times: Epistemology of a Fundamental Human Behavior, Its Meaning, and Consequences*, edited by Albrecht Classen, 265–82. Berlin: De Gruyter, 2010.

Allen, Judson Boyce. "Hermann the German's Averroistic Aristotle and Medieval Poetic Theory." *Mosaic* 9 (1976): 67–81.

– *The Ethical Poetic of the Later Middle Ages: A Decorum of Convenient Distinction.* Toronto: University of Toronto Press, 1982.

Almansi, Guido. *The Writer as Liar: Narrative Technique in the "Decameron."* London: Routledge and Kegan Paul, 1975.

Andreaux. Patrizio Alberto. "Cosa resta degli angeli?: Una rilettura della novella di Fra' Alberto (*Decameron* IV, 2), tra le maschere dell'angelo e dell'uom salvatico." *Incontri* 29 (2014): 95–103.

Asaro, Brittany. "Unmasking the Truth about *Amor de Lonh*: Giovanni Boccaccio's Rebellion against Literary Conventions in *Decameron* I.5 and IV.4." *Comitatus* 44 (2013): 95–120.

Ascoli, Albert Russell. "Boccaccio's Auerbach: Holding the Mirror Up to Mimesis." In *A Local Habitation and a Name: Imagining Histories in the Italian Renaissance*, 49–79. New York: Fordham University Press, 2011.

Auerbach, Erich. *Mimesis: The Representation of Reality in Western Literature.* Translated by Willard R. Trask. Princeton: Princeton University Press, 1953.

Avalle, D'Arco Silvio. *I manoscritti della letteratura in lingua d'oc.* Edited by Lino Leonardi. Turin: Einaudi, 1993.

Barański, Zygmunt G. "Dante Alighieri: Experimentation and (Self-)Exegesis." In *The Middle Ages*, edited by Alastair Minnis and Ian Johnson, 559–82. Vol. 2 of *The Cambridge History of Literary Criticism.* Cambridge: Cambridge University Press, 2005.

Baratier, Édouard. *Histoire de la Provence.* Toulouse: Privat, 1969.

Baratto, Mario. *Realtà e stile nel "Decameron."* Rome: Riuniti, 1984.

– "Struttura narrativa e messaggio ideologico." In *Il testo moltiplicato: Lettura di una novella del "Decameron,"* edited by Mario Lavagetto, 29–47. Parma: Pratiche, 1982.

Barberi Squarotti, Giorgio. "Amore e morte (non senza qualche vicenda di commedia)." In *Prospettive sul Decameron*, 59–83. Turin: Tirrenia, 1989.

Barolini, Teodolinda. "Giovanni Boccaccio." In *European Writers: The Middle Ages and the Renaissance*, edited by W.T.H. Jackson, 509–34. New York: Charles Scribner's Sons, 1983.

– "'Le parole son femmine e i fatti sono maschi': Toward a Sexual Poetics of the *Decameron* (*Decameron* II, 10)." *Studi sul Boccaccio* 21 (1993): 175–97.

– "The Wheel of the *Decameron.*" *Romance Philology* 36 (1983): 521–38.

Barthes, Roland. *S/Z.* Translated by Richard Miller. New York: Hill & Wang, 1974.

Battaglia Ricci, Lucia. *Ragionare nel giardino: Boccaccio e i cicli pittorici del "Trionfo della Morte."* Rome: Salerno, 2000.

– *Scrivere un libro di novelle: Giovanni Boccaccio autore, lettore, editore.* Ravenna: Longo, 2013.

Belden, H.M. "Boccaccio, Hans Sachs, and the Bramble Briar." *PMLA* 33 (1918): 327–95.

Best, Myra. "*La peste e le papere*: Textual Repression in Day Four of the *Decameron.*" In *Boccaccio and Feminist Criticism*, edited by Thomas Stillinger and F. Regina Psaki, 157–68. Chapel Hill, NC: Annali d'Italianistica, 2006.

Biow, Douglas. *Doctors, Ambassadors, Secretaries: Humanism and Professions in Renaissance Italy*. Chicago: University of Chicago Press, 2002.

Bloch, R. Howard. *Medieval Misogyny and the Invention of Western Romantic Love*. Chicago: University of Chicago Press, 1991.

Boggione, Valter, and Giovanni Casalegno. *Dizionario storico del lessico erotico italiano. Metafore, eufemismi, oscenità, doppi sensi, parole dotte e parole basse in otto secoli di letteratura italiana*. Milan: Longanesi, 1996.

Bonadeo, Alfredo. "Some Aspects of Love and Nobility in the Society of the *Decameron*." *Philological Quarterly* 47 (1968): 513–25.

Bonomo, Giuseppe. *Scongiuri del popolo siciliano*. Palermo: Palumbo, 1953.

Branca, Vittore. *Boccaccio medievale e nuovi studi sul "Decameron."* Florence: Sansoni, 1996.

– *Boccaccio: The Man and His Works*. Translated by Richard Monges and Dennis J. McAuliffe. New York: New York University Press, 1976.

– "Ostensione del cuore e 'amore e morte.'" In *Forma e parola: Studi in memoria di Fredi Chiappelli*, edited by Dennis J. Dutschke, 155–72. Rome: Bulzoni, 1992.

Brundage, James A. "Carnal Delight: Canonistic Theories of Sexuality." In *Sex, Law and Marriage in the Middle Ages*. Aldershot: Variorum, 1993.

Burgwinkle, William E. *Love for Sale: Materialist Readings of the Troubadour Razo Corpus*. New York: Garland, 1997.

Buschinger, Danielle. "Le Herzmaere de Konrad von Würzburg et la légende du 'Cœur mangé.'" In *Le récit bref au Moyen Âge. Actes du colloque des 27, 28 et 29 avril 1979*, edited by Danielle Buschinger, 263–76. Amiens: Université de Picardie, Centre d'études médiévales, 1980.

Cachey, Theodore J., Jr. "The Place of the *Itinerarium*." In *Petrarch: A Critical Guide to the Complete Works*, edited by Victoria Kirkham and Armando Maggi, 229–41. Chicago: University of Chicago Press, 2009.

Cadden, Joan. *Meanings of Sex Difference in the Middle Ages: Medicine, Science, and Culture*. Cambridge: Cambridge University Press, 1993.

Camboni, Maria Clotilde. "Lisabetta and Lorenzo's Tomb (on *Decameron* IV,5)." *Italica* 94 (2017): 431–47.

Cappozzo, Valerio. *Dizionario dei sogni nel medioevo: Il "Somniale Danielis" in manoscritti letterari*. Florence: Leo S. Olschki, 2018.

Careri, Maria. *Il canzoniere provenzale H: struttura, contenuto, e fonti*. Modena: Mucchi, 1990.

Casagrande, Carla. "The Protected Woman." In *The Silences of the Middle Ages*, edited by Christiane Klapisch-Zuber, 70–104. Vol. 2 of *A History of Women in the West*, edited by Georges Duby and Michelle Perrot. Cambridge, MA: Belknap Press, 1992.

Celenza, Christopher S. "Petrarch, Latin, and Italian Renaissance Latinity." *Journal of Medieval and Early Modern Studies* 35 (2005): 509–36.

Cesari, Anna Maria. "L'Etica di Aristotele nel Codice Ambrosiano A 204 inf.: un autografo del Boccaccio." *Archivio storico lombardo* 5–6 (1968): 69–100.

Cirese, Alberto. "Lettura antropologica." In *Il testo moltiplicato: Lettura di una novella del "Decameron,"* edited by Mario Lavagetto, 103–23. Parma: Pratiche, 1982.

Classen, Albrecht. "Anger and Anger Management in the Middle Ages." *Mediævistik* 19 (2006): 21–50.

Clubb, Louise G. "Boccaccio and the Boundaries of Love." *Italica* 37 (1960): 188–96.

Compan, André. "L'inspiration amoureuse chez Guilhem de Cabestanh." *Annales de la Faculté des Lettres et Sciences humaines de Nice* 22 (1974): 133–49.

Concina, Ennio. *Fondaci: architettura, arte, e mercatura tra Levante, Venezia, e Alemagna*. Venice: Marsilio, 1997.

Constable, Olivia. *Housing the Stranger in the Mediterranean World: Lodging, Trade, and Travel in Late Antiquity and the Middle Ages*. Cambridge: Cambridge University Press, 2004.

Cots, Montserrat. "Notas Históricas sobre el trovador Guillem de Cabestany." *Bulletí de la Reial Acadèmia de Bones Lletres de Barcelona* 37 (1977–8): 23–65.

Cottino-Jones, Marga. "The Mode and Structure of Tragedy in Boccaccio's *Decameron* (IV.9)." *Italian Quarterly* 43 (1967): 63–88.

– *Order from Chaos: Social and Aesthetic Harmonies in Boccaccio's "Decameron."* Washington, DC: University Press of America, 1982.

Curtius, Ernst Robert. *European Literature and the Latin Middle Ages*. Translated by Willard R. Trask. Princeton: Princeton University Press, 1990.

D'Andrea, Antonio. "Le Rubriche del *Decameron*." *Yearbook of Italian Studies* (1973–5): 41–67.

– *Strutture inquiete: Premesse teoriche e verifiche storico-letterarie*. Florence: Leo S. Olschki, 1993.

David, M. "Boccaccio pornoscopo." In *Medioevo e rinascimento veneto con altri studi in onore di Lino Lazzarini*, edited by R. Avesani, G. Billanovich, and G. Pozzi, 215–43. Padua: Antenore, 1979.

Dean, Trevor. *Crime and Justice in Late Medieval Italy*. Cambridge: Cambridge University Press, 2007.

Degani, Chiara. "Riflessi quasi sconosciuti di *exempla* nel *Decameron*." *Studi sul Boccaccio* 14 (1983–4): 189–208.

Delcorno Branca, Daniela. *Boccaccio e le storie di Re Artù*. Bologna: Il Mulino, 1991.

Delcorno, Carlo. *Giordano da Pisa e l'antica predicazione volgare*. Florence: Leo S. Olschki, 1975.

– "Modelli agiografici e modelli narrativi: Tra Cavalca e Boccaccio." In *La novella italiana: Atti del Convegno di Caprarola, 19–24 settembre 1988*, 2 vols., 1:337–63. Rome: Salerno, 1989.

De Sanctis, Francesco. *Storia della letteratura italiana*. Edited by Niccolò Gallo. Turin: Einaudi-Gallimard, 1996.

Della Neva, JoAnn. *Ciceronian Controversies*. Cambridge, MA: Harvard University Press, 2007.

Devoto, Daniel. "Quelques notes au sujet du 'pot de basilic.'" *Revue de littérature compare* 37 (1963): 430–6.

Di Maio, Marella. *Le cœur mangé: Histoire d'un thème littéraire du Moyen Âge au XIXe siècle*. Paris: PUPS, 2005.

Di Pino, Guido. *La polemica di Boccaccio*. Florence: Vallecchi, 1953.

Doueihi, Milad. "Cor ne edito." *MLN* 108 (1993): 696–709.

– *A Perverse History of the Human Heart*. Cambridge, MA: Harvard University Press, 1997.

Durling, Robert M. "Deceit and Digestion in the Belly of Hell." In *Allegory and Representation*, edited by Stephen J. Greenblatt, 61–93. Baltimore: Johns Hopkins University Press, 1981.

Fajardo-Acosta, Fidel. "The Heart of Guillem de Cabestaing: Courtly Lovers, Cannibals, Early Modern Subjects." *Exemplaria* 17 (2005): 57–102.

Fedi, Roberto. "Il 'regno' di Filostrato. Natura e struttura della Giornata IV del *Decameron*." *MLN* 102 (1987): 39–54.

Ferme, Valerio. *Women, Enjoyment, and the Defense of Virtue in Boccaccio's "Decameron."* New York: Palgrave Macmillan, 2015.

Filosa, Elsa. "*Decameron* 7: Under the Sign of Venus." *Annali d'Italianistica* 31 (2013): 314–53.

– "Intertestualità tra *Decameron* e *De Mulieribus claris*: La tragica storia di Tisbe e Piramo." *Heliotropia* 3 (2006). Online.

Filosa, Elsa, and Luisa Flora. "Ancora su Seneca (e Giovenale) nel *Decameron*." *Giornale storico della letteratura italiana* 175 (1998): 210–19.

Fiorelli, Piero. *La tortura giudiziaria nel diritto commune*. Milan: Giuffrè, 1953–4.

Fleming, Raymond. "Happy Endings? Resisting Women and the Economy of Love in Day Five of Boccaccio's *Decameron*." *Italica* 70 (1993): 30–45.

Folena, Gianfranco. *Culture e lingue nel Veneto medievale*. Padua: Editoriale programma, 1990.

Ford, Gertrude E. "Note on a Line in Keats's 'Isabella.'" *Modern Language Review* 8 (1913): 543–4.

Forni, Pier Massimo. *Adventures in Speech: Rhetoric and Narration in Boccaccio's "Decameron."* Philadelphia: University of Pennsylvania Press, 1996.

– *Forme complesse nel "Decameron."* Florence: Leo S. Olschki, 1992.

Francillon, Armand. "Quelques observations sur la quatrième journée du *Décameron*." *Études de lettres* 2–3 (1978): 19–30.

Frye, Northrop. *Anatomy of Criticism: Four Essays*. Princeton: Princeton University Press, 1971.

Fulton, Rachel. "The Virgin in the Garden, or Why Flowers Make Better Prayers." *Spiritus* 4 (2004): 1–23.

Gagliardi, Antonio. *L'esperienza del tempo nel "Decameron."* Turin: Tirrenia, 1984.

Gaunt, Simon. *Love and Death in Medieval French and Occitan Courtly Literature: Martyrs to Love*. Oxford: Oxford University Press, 2006.

Getto, Giovanni. *Vita di forme e forme di vita nel "Decameron."* Turin: G.B. Petrini, 1972.

Giardini, Maria Pia. *Tradizioni popolari nel "Decameron."* Florence: Leo S. Olschki, 1965.

Gillespie, Vincent. "From the Twelfth Century to c. 1450." In *The Middle Ages*, edited by Alastair Minnis and Ian Johnson, 145–235. Vol. 2 of *The Cambridge History of Literary Criticism*. Cambridge: Cambridge University Press, 2005.

Gittes, Tobias Foster. *Boccaccio's Naked Muse: Eros, Culture, and the Mythopoeic Imagination*. Toronto: University of Toronto Press, 2008.

Goldin, Daniela. "Il Boccaccio e la poesia latina francese del xii secolo." *Studi sul Boccaccio* 13 (1981–2): 327–62.

Grange, Huw. "Guilhem de Cabestanh's Eaten Heart, or the Dangers of Literalizing Troubadour Song." *Tenso* 27 (2012): 92–108.

Greene, Thomas M. *The Light in Troy: Imitation and Discovery in Renaissance Poetry*. New Haven: Yale University Press, 1982.

Grote, George. *A History of Greece; from the earliest period to the close of the generation contemporary with Alexander the Great*. London: J. Murray, 1884.

Guerri, Domenico. *Il commento del Boccaccio a Dante. Limiti della sua autenticità e questioni critiche che n'emergono*. Bari: Laterza, 1926.

Hauvette, Henri. "La 39e nouvelle du Decameron et la légende du 'Cœur mangé.'" *Romania* 41 (1912): 184–205.

Heffernan, Carl Falvo. *Comedy in Chaucer and Boccaccio*. Cambridge: D.S. Brewer, 2009.

Heidegger, Martin. "Zeit und Sein." In *Zur Sache des Denkens*. Tübingen: Niemeyer, 1976.

Herklotz, Ingo. *"Sepulcra" et "monumenta" del medioevo: Studi sull'arte sepolcrale in Italia*. Rome: Rari Nantes, 1985.

Hervieux, Léopold. *Études de Cheriton et ses dérivés*. Paris: Fermin-Didot, 1896.

Hollander, Robert. *Boccaccio's Dante and the Shaping Force of Satire*. Ann Arbor: University of Michigan Press, 1997.

Holmes, Olivia. "*Decameron* 5.8: From Compassion to Compliancy." *I Tatti Studies in the Italian Renaissance* 22 (2019): 21–36.

Huot, Sylvia. "Troubadour Lyric and Old French Narrative." In *The Troubadours: An Introduction*, edited by Simon Gaunt and Sarah Kay, 263–78. Cambridge: Cambridge University Press, 1999.

James, Steven. *The Knight*. Grand Rapids, MI: Revell Publishers, 2009.

Jansen, Katherine L. *The Making of the Magdalen: Preaching and Popular Devotion in the Later Middle Ages*. Princeton: Princeton University Press, 2000.

Javitch, Daniel. "The Assimilation of Aristotle's Poetics in Sixteenth-Century Italy." In *The Renaissance*, edited by Glyn P. Norton, 53–65. Vol. 3 of *The*

Cambridge History of Literary Criticism. Cambridge: Cambridge University Press, 1991.

Jeay, Madeleine. "Consuming Passions: Variations on the Eaten Heart Theme." In *Violence against Women in Medieval Texts*, edited by Anna Roberts, 75–96. Gainesville: University Press of Florida, 1998.

Jones, Philip. *The Italian City-State: From Commune to Signoria*. Oxford: Clarendon Press, 1997.

Kenny, Anthony, and Jan Pinborg. "Medieval Philosophical Literature." In *The Cambridge History of Later Medieval Philosophy*, edited by Norman Kretzmann, Anthony Kenny, and Jan Pinborg, 11–42. Cambridge: Cambridge University Press, 1982.

Kircher, Timothy. *The Poet's Wisdom: The Humanists, the Church, and the Formation of Philosophy in the Early Renaissance*. Leiden: Brill, 2006.

Kirkham, Victoria. "An Allegorically Tempered Decameron." *Italica* 62 (1985): 1–23.

– *Dante the Book Glutton, or, Food for Thought from Italian Poets*. Binghamton, NY: Center for Medieval & Renaissance Studies, 2004.

– *Fabulous Vernacular: Boccaccio's "Filocolo" and the Art of Medieval Fiction*. Ann Arbor: University of Michigan Press, 2001.

– "Love's Labors Rewarded and Paradise Lost (*Decameron* III, 10)." *Romanic Review* 72 (1981): 79–93.

Kirkham, Victoria, and María Rosa Menocal. "Reflections on the 'Arabic' World: Boccaccio's Ninth Stories." *Stanford Italian Review* 7 (1987): 95–110.

Knuuttila, Simo. *Emotions in Ancient and Medieval Philosophy*. Oxford: Clarendon Press, 2004.

Krueger, Roberta. *Women Readers and the Ideology of Gender in Old French Verse Romance*. Cambridge: Cambridge University Press, 1993.

Landino, Cristoforo. "Prolusione petrarchescha." In *Scritti critici e teorici*, edited by R. Cardini, 2 vols., 1:43–50. Rome: Bulzoni, 1974.

Lanza, Antonio. "Aspetti e figure della poesia comico-realistica toscana del secolo XV." In *Freschi e minii del Due, Tre e Quattrocento. Saggi di letteratura italiana antica*, 253–313. Fiesole: Edizioni Cadmo 2002.

Lawn, Brian. *The Rise and Decline of the Scholastic Quaestio Disputata*. Leiden: Brill, 1993.

Lawton, Ben. "Boccaccio and Pasolini: A Contemporary Interpretation of the *Decameron*." In *The Decameron: A New Translation*, edited and translated by Mark Musa and Peter Bondanella, 306–22. New York: W.W. Norton, 1977.

Lee, A.C. *The "Decameron": Its Sources and Analogues*. New York: Haskell House, 1909.

Levenstein, Jessica. "Out of Bounds: Passion and the Plague in Boccaccio's *Decameron*." *Italica* 73 (1996): 313–35.

Levi, Primo. *Se questo è un uomo*. Turin: Einaudi, 1977.

Mabilly, Philippe. *Les Villes de Marseille au Moyen Age. Ville supérieure et Ville de la Prévôté 1257–1348.* N.p.: Astier, 1905.

MacCracken, Henry Noble. "The Source of Keats's 'Eve of St. Agnes.'" *Modern Philology* 5 (1907): 145–52.

Maiorana, M.T. "Un conte de Boccace repris par Keats et Anatole France." *Revue de Littérature comparée* 27 (1963): 50–67.

Manni, Domenico Maria. *Istoria del "Decamerone" di Giovanni Boccaccio.* Florence: Antonio Ristori, 1742.

Marafioti, Martin. "Boccaccio's Lauretta: The Brigata's Bearer of Bad News." *Italian Culture* 19 (2001): 7–18.

Marchesi, Simone. "Dire la verità dei sogni: La teoria di Panfilo in *Decameron* IV.6." *Italica* 81 (2004): 170–83.

– *Stratigrafie decameroniane*. Florence: Leo S. Olschki, 2004.

Marcus, Millicent. "The Accommodating Frate Alberto: A Gloss on *Decameron* IV, 2." *Italica* 56 (1979): 3–21.

– *An Allegory of Form: Literary Self-Consciousness in the "Decameron."* Saratoga, CA: Anma Libri, 1979.

– "Cross-Fertilizations: Folklore and Literature in *Decameron* 4,5." *Italica* 66 (1989): 383–98.

Marenbon, John. *Later Medieval Philosophy*. London: Routledge, 1987.

Marrani, Giuseppe. "I sonetti di Rustico Filippi." *Studi di filologia italiana* 57 (1999): 33–196.

Matzke, John E. "The Legend of the Eaten Heart." *Modern Language Notes* 26 (1911): 1–8.

Mazzacurati, Giancarlo. "Rappresentazione." In *Lessico critico decameroniano*, edited by Renzo Bragantini and Pier Massimo Forni, 269–99. Turin: Bollati Boringhieri, 1995.

Mazzarino, Antonio. "Il basilico di Lisabetta da Messina (Boccaccio, *Decam.* IV. 5)." *Nuovi annali della Facoltà di magistero dell'Università di Messina* 2 (1984): 445–87.

Mazzocco, Angelo. *Linguistic Theories in Dante and the Humanists: Studies of Language and Intellectual History in Late-Medieval and Early Renaissance Italy.* Leiden: Brill, 1993.

Mazzotta, Giuseppe. *The World at Play in Boccaccio's "Decameron."* Princeton: Princeton University Press, 1986.

Meneghetti, Maria Luisa. "'Enamoratz' e 'Fenhedors': struttura ideologica e modelli narrativi nelle biografie trobadoriche." *Medioevo romanzo* 6 (1979): 271–301.

Mercuri, Roberto. "Per una lettura della IV giornata del *Decameron*." In *Filologia aperta ovvero per amicizia. Scritti offerti a Fabrizio Beggiato*, edited by Sabina Marinetti, 195–210. Perugia: Editrice Pliniana, 2009.

Migiel, Marilyn. *A Rhetoric of the "Decameron."* Toronto: University of Toronto Press, 2003.

Miller, Paul. "John Gower, Satiric Poet." In *Gower's "Confessio Amantis": Responses and Reassessments*, edited by A.J. Minnis, 79–105. Cambridge: D.S. Brewer, 1983.

Momigliano, Attilio. *Storia della letteratura italiana*. Milan and Messina: Giuseppe Principato, 1937.

Moravia, Alberto. "Boccaccio." In *L'uomo come fine e altri saggi*, 135–58. Milan: Bompiani, 1964.

Morosini, Roberta. "Penelopi in viaggio 'fuori rotta' nel *Decameron* e altrove. 'Metamorfosi' e scambi nel mediterraneo medieval." *California Italian Studies* 1 (2010): 1–32. Online.

Morreall, John. *Taking Laughter Seriously*. Albany: State University of New York Press, 1983.

Morrison, Susan Signe. *Excrement in the Late Middle Ages: Sacred Filth and Chaucer's Fecopoetics*. New York: Palgrave Macmillan, 2008.

Muellner, Leonard. *The Anger of Achilles: Mênis in Greek Epic*. Ithaca: Cornell University Press, 1966.

Murray, Alexander. *Suicide in the Middle Ages*. 2 vols. Oxford: Oxford University Press, 2000.

Muscetta, Carlo. *Giovanni Boccaccio*. Bari: Laterza, 1972.

– "Giovanni Boccaccio e i novellieri." In *Il Trecento*, edited by Emilio Cecchi and Natalino Sapegno, 251–450. Vol. 2 of *Storia della Letteratura Italiana*. Milan: Garzanti, 1965.

Neuschäfer, Hans-Jörg. *Boccaccio und der Beginn der Novelle: Strukturen der Kurzerzählung auf der Schwelle zwischen Mittelalter und Neuzeit*. Munich: Wilhelm Fink, 1969.

– "Die 'Herzmäre' in der altprovenzalischen Vida und in der Novelle Boccaccios: Ein Vergleich zweier Erzählstrukturen." *Poetica* 2 (1968): 38–47.

Ó Cuilleanáin, Cormac. *Religion and the Clergy in Boccaccio's "Decameron."* Rome: Edizioni di Storia e Letteratura, 1984.

Opera del Vocabolario Italiano. http://www.lib.uchicago.edu/efts/ARTFL/projects/OVI.

Pabst, Walter. *Venus als Heilige und Furie in Boccaccios Fiammetta-Dichtung*. Krefeld: Scherpe, 1958.

Pace, Antonio. "Sage and Toad: A Boccaccian Motif (and a Misinterpretation by Musset)." *Italica* 48 (1971): 187–99.

Paden, Michael. "Elissa: La Ghibellina del *Decameron*." *Studi sul Boccaccio* 21 (1993): 139–50.

Padoàn, Giorgio. "Sulla novella veneziana del *Decameron* (IV 2)." In *Boccaccio, Venezia e il Veneto*, 17–46. Florence: Leo S. Olschki, 1979.

Panofsky, Erwin. *Tomb Sculpture: Four Lectures on Its Changing Aspects from Ancient Egypt to Bernini*. New York: H.N. Abrams, 1992.

Papio, Michael. "'Non meno di compassion piena che dilettevole': Notes on Compassion in Boccaccio." *Italian Quarterly* 143–6 (2000): 107–25.

– "On Seneca, Mussato, Trevet and the Boethian 'Tragedies' of the *De casibus*." *Heliotropia* 10 (2013): 47–63. Online.

Paris, Gaston. "Le roman du Chatelain de Coucy." *Romania* 8 (1879): 342–73.

Pascot, Jep. *Le Roussillon dans l'Histoire. Essai de synthèse régionale*. Toulouse: Privat, 1967.

Pastore Stocchi, Manlio. "Altre Annotazioni." *Studi sul Boccaccio* 7 (1973): 189–211.

Pellegrini, G.B. "Di un venetismo alpino delle 'Vidas' nel codice H." *Archivio per l'Alto Adige* 51 (1957): 253–62.

Pennisi, Francesca A. "Un-Masking Venice: Allegory and the Politics of Reading in *Decameron* IV.2." *Heliotropia* 2 (2004). Online.

Peters, Edward. *Torture*. New York: Basil Blackwell, 1986.

Petronio, Giuseppe. "La posizione del *Decameron*." In *La civiltà comunale*, edited by Mario Fubini and Ettore Bonora, 387–414. Vol. 1 of *Antologia della critica letteraria*. Bari: Laterza, 1966.

Picone, Michelangelo. "Alle fonti del *Decameron*. Il caso di frate Alberto." In *La parola ritrovata: Fonti e analisi letteraria*, edited by Costanzo Di Girolamo and Ivano Paccagnella, 99–117. Palermo: Sellerio, 1982.

– "'L'amoroso sangue': La quarta giornata." In *Lectura Boccaccii Turicensis. Introduzione al "Decameron,"* edited by Michelangelo Picone and Margherita Mesirca, 115–39. Florence: Cesati, 2004.

– "La 'ballata' di Lisabetta (*Decameron* IV, 5)." *Cuadernos de Filología Italiana*, special issue (2001): 177–91.

– *Boccaccio e la codificazione della novella: Letture del "Decameron,"* edited by Nicole Coderey, Claudia Genswein, and Rosa Pittorino. Ravenna: Longo, 2008.

Poole, Gordon. "Boccaccio's *Decameron* IV.5." *Explicator* 47.3 (1989): 3–4.

Potter, Joy Hambuechen. *Five Frames for the "Decameron": Communication and Social Systems in the Cornice*. Princeton: Princeton University Press, 1982.

Pouchelle, Marie-Christine. *The Body and Surgery in the Middle Ages*. Translated by Rosemary Morris. New Brunswick, NJ: Rutgers University Press, 1990.

– "Une parole médicale prise dans l'imaginaire: alimentation et digestion chez un maître-chirurgien du XIVe siècle." In *Pratiques et discours alimentaires à la Renaissance. Actes du colloque de Tours de mars 1979*, edited by Jean-Claude Margolin and Robert Sauzet, 179–92. Paris: Maisonneuve et Larose for the Centre d'Etudes supérieures de la Renaissance, 1982.

Psaki, F. Regina. "The One and the Many: The Tale of the *Brigata* and *Decameron* Four." *Annali d'Italianistica* 31 (2013): 217–56.

Puccetti, Valter. "Girolamo, Salvestra e l'inferno degli amori nel *Decameron*." *Studi sul Boccaccio* 20 (1991): 85–129.

Ramat, Raffaele. *Saggi sul Rinascimento*. Florence: La Nuova Italia, 1969.

Reynolds, Suzanne. "*Orazio satiro* (*Inferno* IV, 89): Dante, the Roman Satirists, and the Medieval Theory of Satire." *Italianist* 15, Supplement 2 (1995): 128–44.

Rizzo, Sylvia. *Ricerche sul latino umanesimo*. Rome: Edizioni di Storia e Letteratura, 2002.

Rolfs, Daniel. "Dante, Petrarch, Boccaccio and the Problem of Suicide." *Romanic Review* 67 (1976): 200–25.

Rosand, David. *Myths of Venice: The Figuration of a State*. Chapel Hill: University of North Carolina Press, 2001.

Rossi, Aldo. "Dante nella prospettiva del Boccaccio." *Studi danteschi* 37 (1960): 63–140.

Rossi, Luciano. "Il cuore, mistico pasto d'amore: dal *Lai Guirun* al *Decameron*." *Studi Provenzali e Francesi* 82 (1983): 28–128.

– "Suggestion métaphorique et réalité historique dans la légende du cœur mangé." *Micrologus* 11 (2003): 469–500.

Rowe, Karen E. "To Spin a Yarn: The Female Voice in Folklore and Fairy Tale." In *Fairy Tales and Society: Illusion, Allusion and Paradigm*, edited by Ruth Bottigheimer, 53–74. Philadelphia: University of Pennsylvania Press, 1986.

Ruggiero, Guido. "Getting a Head in the Renaissance: Mementos of Lost Love in Boccaccio and Beyond." *Renaissance Quarterly* 67 (2014): 1165–90.

Russo, Luigi. *Letture critiche del "Decameron."* Bari: Laterza, 1956.

Russo, Vittorio. *Con le Muse in Parnaso: Tre studi su Boccaccio*. Naples: Bibliopolis, 1983.

– "Il senso tragico del *Decameron*." *Filologia e letteratura* 11 (1965): 29–84.

Sánchez Jiménez, Antonio. "Catalan and Occitan Troubadours at the Court of Alfonso VIII." *La Corónica* 32 (2004): 101–20.

Sanguineti, Federico. "La novella delle papere nel *Decameron*." *Belfagor* 37 (1982): 137–46.

– "Quarta giornata." *Heliotropia* 4 (2007): 1–19. Online.

Sanguineti White, Laura. *La scena conviviale e la sua funzione nel mondo del Boccaccio*. Florence: Leo S. Olschki, 1983.

– *Seduzione e privazione: il cibo nel "Decameron."* Lucca: Maria Pacini Fazzi, 2016.

Santich, Barbara. "Revenge, Cannibalism and Self-Denial." *Food and History* 1 (2003): 85–94.

Scaglione, Aldo. *Nature and Love in the Middle Ages*. Berkeley: University of California Press, 1963.

Schiaffini, Aldo. *Lettura del "De Vulgari Eloquentia" di Dante*. Rome: Edizioni dell'Ateneo, 1958–9.

Schoenfeldt, Michael. "Fables of the Belly in Early Modern England." In *The Body in Parts: Fantasies of Corporeality in Early Modern Europe*, edited by David Hillman and Carla Mazzio, 243–61. New York: Routledge, 1997.

Schonbuch, Mathias. "Le personnage tragique dans le *Décaméron*. Contrepoids ou faire-valoir?" *Arzanà. Cahiers de littérature médiévale italienne* 14 (2012): 55–66.

Segre, Cesare. "I silenzi di Lisabetta, i silenzi di Boccaccio." In *Il testo moltiplicato: Lettura di una novella del "Decameron,"* edited by Mario Lavagetto, 75–85. Parma: Pratiche, 1982.

Selig, Karl-Ludwig. "Form and Form in the *Decameron* (IV/5 & IV/9)." *Teaching Language through Literature* 22 (1982): 3–9.

Serpieri, Alessandro. "L'approccio psicoanalitico: alcuni fondamenti e la scommessa di una lettura." In *Il testo moltiplicato: Lettura di una novella del "Decameron,"* edited by Mario Lavagetto, 49–73. Parma: Pratiche 1982.

Sherberg, Michael. *The Governance of Friendship: Law and Gender in the "Decameron."* Columbus: Ohio State University Press, 2012.

– "The *laudevoli consolazioni* of Boccaccio and Boethius." *Medioevo letterario d'Italia* 12 (2015): 129–38.

Simonelli, Maria. "Il tema della nobiltà in Andrea Cappellano e in Dante." *Dante Studies* 84 (1966): 51–64.

Siraisi, Nancy G. *Medieval and Early Renaissance Medicine: An Introduction to Knowledge and Practice.* Chicago: University of Chicago Press, 1990.

Smarr, Janet. *Boccaccio and Fiammetta: The Narrator as Lover.* Urbana: University of Illinois Press, 1986.

– "Other Races and Other Places in the *Decameron.*" *Studi sul Boccaccio* 27 (1999): 113–37.

Solterer, Helen. "Dismembering, Remembering the *Châtelain de Couci.*" *Romance Philology* 46 (1992): 103–24.

Squillacioti, Paolo. "Tristano risarcito e Folchetto vendicato: Tracce di tradizione cortese in *Decameron* II 3 e IV 3." *Studi sul Boccaccio* 28 (2000): 73–86.

Steinberg, Justin. "Mimesis on Trial: Legal and Literary Verisimilitude in Boccaccio's *Decameron.*" *Representations* 139 (2017): 118–45.

Stone, Gregory B. *The Death of the Troubadour: The Late Medieval Resistance to the Renaissance.* Philadelphia: University of Pennsylvania Press, 1994.

Struever, Nancy. "Petrarch's *Invective contra medicum*: An Early Confrontation of Rhetoric and Medicine." *MLN* 108 (1993): 659–79.

Tavera, Antoine. "Ancien provençal 'cor(s) et 'cor(p)s': une quasi-homonymie riche de conséquences." In *Le "Cuer" au Moyen Age: Réalité et Senefiance,* edited by Margaret Bertrand, 409–37. Aix-en-Provence: Université de Provence, 1991.

– "Quelques réflexions sur les 'vidas' des troubadours." In *Le récit bref au Moyen Âge. Actes du colloque des 27, 28 et 29 avril 1979,* edited by Danielle Buschinger, 175–90. Amiens: Université de Picardie, Centre d'études médiévales, 1980.

Terzoli, Maria. "La testa di Lorenzo: lettura di *Decameron* IV, 5." *Cuadernos de Filología Italiana,* special issue (2001): 193–211.

TLIO. Tesoro della Lingua Italiana delle Origini. OVI-CNR, 2016. Web. 24 May 2016. http://tlio.ovi.cnr.it/TLIO/.

Todorov, Tzvetan. *Grammaire du Décaméron*. The Hague: Mouton, 1969.
Torraca, Francesco. *Giovanni Boccaccio a Napoli (1326–1339)*. Naples: n.p., 1915.
Tronci, Francesco. *La novella tra letteratura, ideologica, e metaletteratura: Studi sul "Decameron."* Cagliari: Cooperativa Universitaria Editrice Cagliaritana, 2001.
Usher, Jonathan. "Boccaccio on Readers and Reading." *Heliotropia* 1 (2003): 63–85. Online.
– "Boccaccio's 'Ars Moriendi' in the Decameron." *Modern Language Review* 8 (1986): 621–32.
– "Courtly Allusions and the Unraveling of Metaphor in the Novella of Simona and Pasquino (*Decameron*, IV,7)." *Italianist* 9 (1989): 52–65.
– "Frame and Novella Gardens in the *Decameron*." *Medium Aevum* 58 (1989): 274–84.
– "Narrative and Descriptive Sequences in the Novella of Lisabetta and the Pot of Basil (*Decameron*, IV.5)." *Italian Studies* 38 (1983): 56–69.
– "Simona and Pasquino: Cur Moriatur Homo Cui Salvia Crescit in Horto?" *MLN* 106 (1991): 1–14.
Velli, Giuseppe. "Seneca nel *Decameron*." *Giornale storico della letteratura italiana* 168 (1991): 321–34.
Vincensini, Jean-Jacques. *Pensée mythique et narrations médiévales*. Paris: Champion, 1996.
Warner, Marina. *From the Beast to the Blonde: On Fairy Tales and Their Tellers*. New York: Farrar, Straus and Giroux, 1996.
Witt, Ronald. *The Two Latin Cultures and the Foundation of Renaissance Humanism in Medieval Italy*. Cambridge: Cambridge University Press, 2012.
Wood, Rega. "What Price the Horror Vacui? Interstitial Vacua and Aristotelian Science." In *La Nature et le vide dans la physique médiévale: Etudes dédiées à Edward Grant*, edited by Joël Biard and Sabine Rommevaux, 39–66. Turnhout: Brepols, 2012.
Zak, Gur. "Between Ghismonda and Massinissa: Boccaccio, Petrarch and the Uses of Tragedy." *Heliotropia* 15 (2018): 233–51. Online.
– "'Umana cosa è aver compassione': Boccaccio, Compassion, and the Ethics of Literature." *I Tatti Studies in the Italian Renaissance* 22 (2019): 5–20.

Contributors

Fabian Alfie is a professor of Italian at the University of Arizona. He received his PhD in Italian from the University of Wisconsin, Madison, in 1995. He studies the literature of the Middle Ages and Renaissance, and he has published extensively on Dante, Boccaccio, and Petrarch, as well as on the comic/satiric authors of the fourteenth century. He is the author of *Dante's "Tenzone" with Forese Donati: The Reprehension of Vice* (Toronto, 2011).

Annelise Brody is an independent scholar. She received her PhD in Italian from The Johns Hopkins University. She has published essays on Boccaccio and Petrarch.

Alison Cornish is professor of Italian at New York University, having taught in Romance Languages at the University of Michigan for twenty-three years, and before that at Yale (1991–5). She has been a fellow at the University of Michigan Institute for the Humanities and at the Harvard Center for Renaissance Studies at Villa I Tatti. The author of two monographs (*Reading Dante's Stars*, Yale, 2000 and *Vernacular Translation in Dante's Italy: Illiterate Literature*, Cambridge, 2011) she has written essays on Dante, Petrarch, Boccaccio, and the culture of translation in which they flourished. Her interests are in science and literature, readership, translation, poetics, philosophy, theology, and sound studies. Most recently she has authored a commentary on a new translation of Dante's *Paradiso* by Stanley Lombardo (Hackett, 2017). She is currently president of the Dante Society of America.

Tobias Foster Gittes specializes in Italian literature of the Middle Ages and early Renaissance. In addition to articles on Dante, Boccaccio, and Cervantes, he has published a book on Boccaccio's myth-making activity: *Boccaccio's Naked Muse: Eros, Culture, and the Mythopoeic Imagination* (Toronto, 2008).

Timothy Kircher is the H. Curt '56 and Patricia S. '57 Hege Professor of History at Guilford College. In a number of books and articles he has investigated the work of Petrarch, Boccaccio, and Leon Battista Alberti in relation to that of their contemporaries. He is a past president of the American Boccaccio Association. His current interests include humanist philosophical expression and Renaissance epistolography. He also explores the relation of the humanities to the sciences and other fields through a website at humanitieswatch.org.

Suzanne Magnanini is associate professor and president's teaching scholar in the Department of French and Italian at the University of Colorado, Boulder. Her research focuses on the early modern literary fairy tale in the context of the Italian novella tradition, especially in regard to issues of gender, genre, and monstrosity. She is the author of *Fairy-Tale Science: Monstrous Generation in the Tales of Straparola and Basile* (Toronto, 2008) and the translator and editor of Giovan Francesco Straparola's sixteenth-century tale collection *The Pleasant Nights* (ACMRS Publications, 2015). Currently, she is studying how censorship in post-Tridentine Italy shaped the Italian fairy-tale tradition.

Kristina M. Olson is an associate professor of Italian at George Mason University. She is the author of *Courtesy Lost: Dante, Boccaccio and the Literature of History* (Toronto, 2014) and several articles on Dante, Boccaccio, and Petrarch. Her current book project, *Sartorial Poetics: Clothing and Identity in Late Medieval Literature*, explores gender and ethnic identity in Italian literature from the late Duecento through the Trecento. She is the co-editor of *Boccaccio 1313–2013* (Longo Editore, 2015), and, together with Christopher Kleinhenz, of the second edition of *Approaches to Teaching Dante's Comedy* with the Modern Language Association. She currently serves as the vice president of the American Boccaccio Association (2017–20), and was previously treasurer of the Association (2014–17). She was the vice president of the Dante Society of America from 2016 to 2018.

Michael Papio is a professor of Italian Studies at the University of Massachusetts Amherst and past president of the American Boccaccio Association. His principal scholarly interests lie in the interplay among literature, philosophy, theology, and geocriticism. Papio is the editor of *Heliotropia*, a journal dedicated to the study of Giovanni Boccaccio, and has published widely. His most important volumes are *Boccaccio's Expositions on Dante's Comedy* (Toronto, 2009), *Pico della Mirandola's Oration on the Dignity of Man: A New Translation and Commentary* (with F. Borghesi and M. Riva, Cambridge, 2012), and the forthcoming critical edition (with English translation, extensive commentary, and maps) of Boccaccio's *De montibus*.

F. Regina Psaki is professor emerita of Italian at the University of Oregon. Her research embraces Italian and French literature of the Middle Ages with a focus on medieval feminist scholarship. She has published widely on Dante's *Commedia* and Boccaccio's *Decameron* and *Corbaccio*, as well as on medieval French literature, particularly chivalric romance. A current project in both French and Italian, "The Traffic in Talk about Women: Misogyny and Philogyny in the Middle Ages," looks at non-fiction writings in praise and blame of women. In her research she privileges questions of alterity and continuity between medieval and modern; textual transmission and context; translation of/and medieval material; and metadisciplinary issues in medieval literary study.

Michael Sherberg is professor of Italian at Washington University in St Louis. A past president of the American Boccaccio Association, he is the author of *The Governance of Friendship: Law and Gender in the "Decameron"* (Ohio State, 2011), and he co-edited (with Victoria Kirkham and Janet Levarie Smarr) *Boccaccio: A Critical Guide to the Complete Works* (Chicago, 2013). He is currently preparing a translation of Jacopo Passavanti's *Specchio della vera penitenzia*.

Julie Singer is associate professor of French at Washington University in St Louis. She is the author of *Blindness and Therapy in Late Medieval French and Italian Poetry* (Boydell & Brewer, 2011) and *Representing Mental Illness in Late Medieval France: Machines, Madness, Metaphor* (Boydell & Brewer, 2018). Other recent and forthcoming publications include articles on Philippe de Mézières, Jean Froissart, and Christine de Pizan. Her current research centres on medieval representations of baby talk and young children's speech.

Gur Zak is senior lecturer and chair of the Department of Comparative Literature at Hebrew University of Jerusalem. His primary research interest lies in the interrelations between literature and ethics in the later Middle Ages and the Italian Renaissance, with a particular emphasis on the works of Dante, Petrarch, and Boccaccio. His book, *Petrarch's*

Humanism and the Care of the Self, was published by Cambridge in 2010. He is currently completing a book on Boccaccio, tentatively entitled *Boccaccio and the Consolation of Literature*. His articles have appeared in journals such as *Speculum*, *MLN*, *I Tatti Studies*, and *Le tre corone*, and he has contributed chapters to *The Cambridge Companion to Petrarch*, *The Cambridge Companion to Boccaccio*, and *The Oxford Handbook of Medieval Latin Literature*. Besides his work on Italian Renaissance Literature, he is interested in the theory and practice of autobiography from antiquity to the present.

Index

www.ingramcontent.com/pod-product-compliance
Lightning Source LLC
LaVergne TN
LVHW090158080826
844660LV00013B/855/J

* 9 7 8 1 4 8 7 5 0 7 4 7 3 *